D1566448

CONTENTS

INTRODUCTION

Things You Need to Know About Your Cuisinart Bread Machine

What is the Cuisinart Bread Machine?

Human beings have been making bread manually for thousands of years, but now you can make perfect loaves with ease using a bread maker. Modern bread makers take almost all of the guesswork out of making perfect bread in your own home: they automatically regulate mixing, kneading, time and temperature — every step of the bread making process — so all you have to do is decide which ingredients you want to use.

Tips and Tricks to Using Your Cuisinart Bread Machine

1. You must read your bread machine's manual and understand how it works.
2. Do not exceed the capacity of your bread machine pan. Even one teaspoon could make a difference.
3. Check your bread machine's instructions to know the proper order.
4. Use "bread machine bread flour" for the best result. It is the same thing as bread flour.
5. Use room-temperature eggs.
6. Do not use a delayed mix cycle when using milk
7. Cut margarine or butter into small pieces before adding them into the machine.

Bread Machine Cycles/Settings

Bread machines offer many different settings for baking different varieties of bread such as gluten-free, whole wheat bread, basic white bread, sweet bread, etc. After you add ingredients to the bread machine and start the baking process, the mixture goes through many cycles before coming out as a perfectly textured bread.

Basic/White

Use this setting for all basic bread, including white bread and some other loaves of bread. The commonly used flour for this setting is white bread flour, and the average duration is 3–4 hours.

Wholegrain/Whole Wheat

Given their heavy, high-gluten texture, whole wheat and whole grain flours need longer kneading and rising times. Use this setting to prepare all types of whole grain and whole wheat bread.

Gluten-Free

This setting is suitable for preparing all types of gluten-free bread using flour other than wheat flour. A gluten-free diet is becoming a popular choice for millions of health-conscious people across the world. However, there still aren't that many commercial gluten-free bread available, and those that exist tend to be a little expensive. One great advantage of a bread machine is that you can prepare all types of gluten-free bread with your choice of ingredients to suit your taste and texture preferences as well as your budget.

Quick/Rapid

Use this setting for loaves of bread with lower rising times and overall shorter baking times. Generally speaking, this means bread with no yeast requirement, which requires less baking time than other types of bread; however, this setting is also appropriate for some bread with yeast. Time varies from 30 minutes to 2 hours.

Dough

This setting is for preparing dough without baking the bread. It's quite useful when you're planning to bake in the oven but want to skip the kneading part. One advantage of this setting is that baking in the oven lets you create loaves of bread of different shapes. After you add the required ingredients, the bread machine mixes them and kneads a flaky dough for you. Most machines knead the dough till the first rise.

Fruit/Nut

Use this setting for preparing loaves of bread with added fruits and nuts. Many machines have a fruit/nut hopper to grind the added ingredients while the kneading process is going on. The machine will either add the nuts/fruits automatically during the baking process or signal when the time is right for you to do it.

Sweet

Use this setting for types of bread with a high amount of sweet and/or fatty ingredients, as well as for loaves of bread prepared from cheese and/or eggs. Sweet bread requires less baking time and lower baking temperature to avoid an overly dark crust.

French

Use this setting for bread that needs little or no sugar. French bread needs higher temperatures and longer rising times, and they typically have hard crusts.

Jam

Some bread makers are equipped with a jam setting to make jam your own jams. What goes better with warm a slice of freshly baked bread than jam and butter? The manufacturer will usually include recipes for this setting as it is beyond the scope of this cookbook.

Timed-Bake

This setting is like a timer for your bread machine: You add all the ingredients and the machine processes them later. For example, you can add the ingredients right before leaving for work and set the timer for mid-afternoon. The machine will start baking at the set time, and you can enjoy freshly baked bread when you return home. As the ingredients will stay inside the bread pan for a while, it is not recommended to use this setting for recipes that include perishable ingredients such as milk, cream, cheese, and eggs.

How to Store Your Bread

1. Storing bread dough: Prepare your dough according to the recipe. Allow rising. Then wrap it in a plastic wrap and place it in a plastic container or bag.

- You can refrigerate bread dough for three to four days
- You can freeze bread dough for up to one month

2. Where you slice matters: If you slice your bread at one end, then you will get an open-end moisture "leaking" problem. So slice the loaf in half down the middle, cut servings from the loaves, and then press the loaves back together before storing. This will prevent leaking moisture problems.

3. Wrapping bread in foil or plastic instead of cloth keeps the soft bread longer.

4. If you want to preserve crispy crust, store large crusty loaves on the counter (unwrapped and cut-side down) at room temperature for a day or so.

5. For long-term storage (more than two days), wrap your bread in single-day portions and freeze. Thaw and reheat servings before serving.

6. Breadbox: A large breadbox will give you air circulation and balance humidity to store your bread properly. Do not wrap the bread in paper and then place it in the bread box.

7. Do not refrigerate: Do not keep your homemade bread in the refrigerator because it will stale quickly. However, you can put store-bought bread in the refrigerator.

Bread with added fat such as brioche and challah will take longer to stale. On the other hand, low-fat bread like baguettes will stale quickly.

Classic Daily Bread

1. Bread Machine Bread

Servings: 6   Cooking Time: 3 Hours And 25 Minutes

Ingredients:
- Flour – 2 cups, sifted
- Warm water – ¾ cup
- Sugar – 1 tsp.
- Active dry yeast – 1.25 tsp.
- Salt – 1 tsp.
- Oil – 1 tsp.

Directions:
Add ingredients according to bread machine recommendation.   Select the Basic setting and press Start.   Remove the loaf once it is baked.   Cool and slice.

Nutrition Info:(Per Serving): Calories: 163; Total Fat: 1 g; Saturated Fat: 0 g; Carbohydrates: 32 g; Cholesterol: 15 mg; Fiber: 1 g; Calcium: 18 mg; Sodium: 390 mg; Protein: 4 g

2. Whole Wheat Corn Bread

Servings: 1 Loaf

Ingredients:
- 16 slice bread (2 pounds)
- 1⅓ cups lukewarm water
- 2 tablespoons light brown sugar
- 1 large egg, beaten
- 2 tablespoons unsalted butter, melted
- 1½ teaspoons table salt
- ¾ cup whole wheat flour
- ¾ cup cornmeal
- 2¾ cups white bread flour
- 2½ teaspoons bread machine yeast
- 12 slice bread (1½ pounds)
- 1 cup lukewarm water
- 1½ tablespoons light brown sugar
- 1 medium egg, beaten
- 1½ tablespoons unsalted butter, melted
- 1½ teaspoons table salt
- ½ cup whole wheat flour
- ½ cup cornmeal
- 2 cups white bread flour
- 1½ teaspoons bread machine yeast

Directions:
Choose the size of loaf you would like to make and measure your ingredients.   Add the ingredients to the bread pan in the order listed above.   Place the pan in the bread machine and close the lid.   Turn on the bread maker. Select the White/Basic setting, then the loaf size, and finally the crust color. Start the cycle. When the cycle is finished and the bread is baked, carefully remove the pan from the machine. Use a potholder as the handle will be very hot. Let rest for a few minutes.   Remove the bread from the pan and allow to cool on a wire rack for at least 10 minutes before slicing.

Nutrition Info:(Per Serving):Calories 146, fat 5.7 g, carbs 19.3 g, sodium 124 mg, protein 4.8 g

3. Carrot Cake Bread

Servings: 12 - 16   Cooking Time: 1 Hours 20 Minutes

Ingredients:
- Non-stick cooking spray
- 1/4 cup vegetable oil
- 2 large eggs, room temperature
- 1/2 teaspoon pure vanilla extract
- 1/2 cup sugar
- 1/4 cup light brown sugar
- 1/4 cup crushed pineapple with juice (from can or fresh)
- 1 1/4 cups unbleached, all-purpose flour
- 1 teaspoon baking powder
- 1/4 teaspoon baking soda
- 1/4 teaspoon salt
- 1 teaspoon ground cloves
- 3/4 teaspoon ground cinnamon
- 1 cup freshly grated carrots
- 1/3 cup chopped pecans
- 1/3 cup golden raisins

Directions:
Coat the inside of the bread pan with non-stick cooking spray.   Add all of the ingredients, in order listed, to the bread pan.   Select Express Bake, medium crust color, and press Start. While the batter is mixing, scrape the sides of the bread pan with a rubber spatula to fully incorporate ingredients.   When baked, remove from bread pan and place on wire rack to cool completely before slicing and serving.

Nutrition Info: Calories: 151, Sodium: 69 mg, Dietary Fiber: 1.2 g, Fat: 7.2 g, Carbs: 20.1 g, Protein: 2.4 g.

4. Donuts

Servings: 24   Cooking Time: 55 Minutes

Ingredients:
- 1 1/4 cups whole milk
- 1 beaten egg
- 1/4 cup shortening
- 1/4 cup sugar
- 1 teaspoon salt
- 3 1/2 cups all-purpose flour
- 1 1/2 teaspoons dry yeast

Directions:
Measure ingredients into the bread maker, first adding wet then dry ingredients as listed above, reserving yeast. Make a well in the flour; pour the yeast into the hole. Select Dough cycle and press Start.   Roll kneaded dough out to a 1/2-inch thick rectangle and cut with a 2 1/2 inch donut cutter.   Let rise, covered, for 30 minutes or until doubled in size.   Preheat a deep fryer to 375°F.   Drop donuts into fryer and turn donuts as they rise to the surface. Fry until golden brown.   Drain on paper towels to cool. Glaze or dust with your favorite donut topping while warm and serve.

Nutrition Info: Calories: 104, Sodium: 105 mg, Dietary Fiber: 0.5 g, Fat: 3 g, Carbs: 16.7 g, Protein: 2.7 g.

5.   Wheat Bran Bread

Servings: 1 Loaf
Ingredients:
- 16 slice bread (2 pounds)
- 1½ cups lukewarm milk
- 3 tablespoons unsalted butter, melted
- ¼ cup sugar
- 2 teaspoons table salt
- ½ cup wheat bran
- 3½ cups white bread flour
- 2 teaspoons bread machine yeast
- 12 slice bread (1½ pounds)
- 1⅛ cups lukewarm milk
- 2¼ tablespoons unsalted butter, melted
- 3 tablespoons sugar
- 1½ teaspoons table salt
- ⅓ cup wheat bran
- 2⅔ cups white bread flour
- 1½ teaspoons bread machine yeast

Directions:
Choose the size of loaf you would like to make and measure your ingredients.   Add the ingredients to the bread pan in the order listed above.   Place the pan in the bread machine and close the lid.   Turn on the bread maker. Select the White/Basic setting, then the loaf size, and finally the crust color. Start the cycle. When the cycle is finished and the bread is baked, carefully remove the pan from the machine. Use a potholder as the handle will be very hot. Let rest for a few minutes.   Remove the bread from the pan and allow to cool on a wire rack for at least 10 minutes before slicing.
Nutrition Info:(Per Serving):Calories 147, fat 2.8 g, carbs 24.6 g, sodium 312 mg, protein 3.8 g

6.   Honey Wheat Bread

Servings: 1 Loaf
Ingredients:
- 16 slice bread (2 pounds)
- 1⅔ cups boiling water
- ¼ cup + 4 teaspoons cracked wheat
- ¼ cup + 4 teaspoons unsalted butter, melted
- ¼ cup honey
- 2 teaspoons table salt
- 1⅓ cups whole-wheat flour
- 2⅔ cups white bread flour
- 2½ teaspoons bread machine yeast
- 12 slice bread (1½ pounds)
- 1¼ cups boiling water
- ¼ cup cracked wheat
- ¼ cup unsalted butter, melted
- 3 tablespoons honey
- 1½ teaspoons table salt
- 1 cup whole-wheat flour
- 2 cups white bread flour
- 2 teaspoons bread machine yeast

Directions:

Choose the size of loaf you would like to make and measure your ingredients.   Add the boiling water and cracked wheat to the bread pan; set aside for 25–30 minutes for the wheat to soften.   Add the other ingredients to the bread pan in the order listed above. Place the pan in the bread machine and close the lid. Turn on the bread maker. Select the White/Basic setting, then the loaf size, and finally the crust color. Start the cycle.   When the cycle is finished and the bread is baked, carefully remove the pan from the machine. Use a potholder as the handle will be very hot. Let rest for a few minutes.   Remove the bread from the pan and allow to cool on a wire rack for at least 10 minutes before slicing.
Nutrition Info:(Per Serving):Calories 168, fat 4.3 g, carbs 31.3 g, sodium 296 mg, protein 4.1 g

7.   Multi-seed Bread

Servings: 8   Cooking Time: 3 Hours And 25 Minutes
Ingredients:
- Tepid water – 1 cup
- Salt – 1 tsp.
- Olive oil – 2 tbsp.
- Whole wheat bread flour – 1 cup
- White bread flour – 2 cups
- Dried yeast – 1 ½ tsp.
- Mixed seeds – 1/3 cup sesame, pumpkin, sunflower, poppy

Directions:
Add the ingredients according to bread machine recommendation.   Select White bread/Basic cycle and press Start.   Remove the bread when done.   Cool, slice, and serve.
Nutrition Info:(Per Serving): Calories: 196.7; Total Fat: 4 g; Saturated Fat: 0.6 g; Carbohydrates: 35 g; Cholesterol: 0 mg; Fiber: 2.8 g; Calcium: 20 mg; Sodium: 293.1 mg; Protein: 5.6 g

8.   Quinoa Oatmeal Bread

Servings: 6   Cooking Time: 3 Hours And 48 Minutes
Ingredients:
- Quinoa flakes – ½ cup
- Buttermilk – 1 cup
- Salt – 1 tsp.
- Sugar – 1 tbsp.
- Honey – 1 tbsp.
- Unsalted butter – 4 tbsp.
- Quick-cooking oats – ½ cup
- Whole wheat flour – ½ cup
- Bread flour – 1 ½ cups
- Yeast – 1 ½ tsp.

Directions:
Add everything according to the bread machine instructions.   Select Whole Grain and bake. Remove the bread when done.   Cool, slice, and serve.
Nutrition Info:(Per Serving): Calories: 295; Total Fat: 14 g; Saturated Fat: 7 g; Carbohydrates: 37 g; Cholesterol: 25 mg; Fiber: 4 g; Calcium: 119 mg; Sodium: 517 mg; Protein: 6 g

9. Classic White Sandwich Bread

Servings: 1 Loaf
Ingredients:
- 16 slice bread (2 pounds)
- 1 cup water, lukewarm between 80 and 90°F
- 2 tablespoons unsalted butter, melted
- 1 teaspoon table salt
- 1/4 cup sugar
- 2 egg whites or 1 egg, beaten
- 3 cups white bread flour
- 1 1/2 teaspoons bread machine yeast
- 12 slice bread (1 ½ pounds)
- 3/4 cup water, lukewarm between 80 and 90°F
- 1 1/2 tablespoons unsalted butter, melted
- 3/4 teaspoon table salt
- 1 ½ ounces sugar
- 2 egg whites or 1 egg, beaten
- 2 1/4 cups white bread flour
- 1 1/8 teaspoons bread machine yeast

Directions:
Choose the size of loaf you would like to make and measure your ingredients.   Add the ingredients to the bread pan in the order listed above.   Place the pan in the bread machine and close the lid.   Turn on the bread maker. Select the White/Basic setting, then the loaf size, and finally the crust color. Start the cycle. When the cycle is finished and the bread is baked, carefully remove the pan from the machine. Use a potholder as the handle will be very hot. Let rest for a few minutes.   Remove the bread from the pan and allow to cool on a wire rack for at least 10 minutes before slicing.
Nutrition Info:(Per Serving):Calories 126, fat 2.3 g, carbs 23 g, sodium 137 mg, protein 4 g

10. Pizza Dough

Servings: 12 - 14   Cooking Time: 1 Hour 30 Minutes
Ingredients:
- 1 1/4 cups water
- 3 cups bread flour
- 1 teaspoon milk powder
- 1 tablespoon sugar
- 1 teaspoon salt
- 1 tablespoon yeast

Directions:
Add ingredients to the bread maker pan in the order listed above.   Select Dough cycle and press Start. When finished, prepare dough by rolling it out in a pizza pan about to a 1-inch thickness.   Top with your favorite sauce, then cheese, then other toppings like pepperoni or veggies.   Bake at 425°F for 15 to 20 minutes or until crust is golden on the edges.   Enjoy hot!
Nutrition Info: Calories: 103, Sodium: 168 mg, Dietary Fiber: 0.9 g, Fat: 0.3 g, Carbs: 21.7 g, Protein: 3.1 g.

11. Chocolate Marble Cake

Servings: 12 - 16   Cooking Time: 3 Hours 45 Minutes
Ingredients:
- 1 1/2 cups water

- 1 1/2 teaspoons vanilla extract
- 1 1/2 teaspoons salt
- 3 1/2 cups bread flour
- 1 1/2 teaspoons instant yeast
- 1 cup semi-sweet chocolate chips

Directions:
Set the chocolate chips aside and add the other ingredients to the pan of your bread maker.   Program the machine for Sweet bread and press Start.   Check the dough after 10 to 15 minutes of kneading; you should have a smooth ball, soft but not sticky.   Add the chocolate chips about 3 minutes before the end of the second kneading cycle.   Once baked, remove with a rubber spatula and allow to cool on a rack before serving.
Nutrition Info: Calories: 172, Sodium: 218 mg, Dietary Fiber: 1.6 g, Fat: 4.3 g, Carbs: 30.1 g, Protein: 3 g.

12. Orange Rolls

Servings: 20 Rolls   Cooking Time: 3 H.
Ingredients:
- For the dough:
- ¼ cup heavy cream, warmed
- ½ cup orange juice concentrate
- 2 Tbsp sugar
- 1 tsp salt
- 1 large egg + 1 yolk
- 6 Tbsp unsalted butter, softened
- 3 cups all-purpose flour
- 2 tsp bread machine yeast
- For the filling:
- 2 Tbsp unsalted butter, softened
- ½ cup sugar + 2 Tbsp grated orange zest mixture
- For the icing:
- ¼ cup heavy cream
- ¼ cup sugar
- 2 Tbsp orange juice concentrate
- 2 Tbsp unsalted butter
- ⅛ tsp salt

Directions:
Add each ingredient for the dough to bread machine. Select the dough cycle and press start.   When it is finished, the dough should have doubled in size   Move the dough from the bread machine to a floured surface. Roll the dough into rectangle. Cover it with butter and the sugar-orange zest mixture.   Roll the dough tightly from the long side. Cut into quarters. Then cut the quarters into 5 evenly-sized rolls.   Put them onto greased pan, cover it with towel, and let them rise for 45 minutes in a warm place.   Bake at 325°F in a preheated oven for 25-30 minutes.   Add each of the icing ingredients to a saucepan. Mix and cook over a medium heat until the mixture is syrupy. Let it cool. Pour icing over warm rolls and serve.

13. Honey Sunflower Bread

Servings: 1 Loaf
Ingredients:
- 16 slice bread (2 pounds)
- 1⅓ cups lukewarm water

- 2 eggs, at room temperature
- ¼ cup unsalted butter, melted
- ¼ cup skim milk powder
- 2 tablespoons honey
- 2 teaspoons table salt
- 4 cups white bread flour
- 1 cup raw sunflower seeds
- 1¾ teaspoons bread machine yeast
- 12 slice bread (1½ pounds)
- 1 cup lukewarm water
- 1 egg, at room temperature
- 3 tablespoons unsalted butter, melted
- 3 tablespoons skim milk powder
- 1½ tablespoons honey
- 1½ teaspoons table salt
- 3 cups white bread flour
- ¾ cup raw sunflower seeds
- 1 teaspoon bread machine yeast

Directions:
Choose the size of loaf you would like to make and measure your ingredients. Add the ingredients to the bread pan in the order listed above. Place the pan in the bread machine and close the lid. Turn on the bread maker. Select the White/Basic setting, then the loaf size, and finally the crust color. Start the cycle. When the cycle is finished and the bread is baked, carefully remove the pan from the machine. Use a potholder as the handle will be very hot. Let rest for a few minutes. Remove the bread from the pan and allow to cool on a wire rack for at least 10 minutes before slicing.

Nutrition Info:(Per Serving):Calories 172, fat 4.7 g, carbs 27.8 g, sodium 324 mg, protein 4.9 g

14. Whole-wheat Bread

Servings: 8   Cooking Time: 3 Hours And 48 Minutes
Ingredients:
- Water - ¾ cup
- Melted butter - 1½ tbsp., cooled
- Honey - 1½ tbsp.
- Salt - ¾ tsp.
- Whole-wheat bread flour - 2 cups
- Bread machine or instant yeast - 1 tsp.

Directions:
Add the ingredients in the machine according to the manufacturer's instructions. Press Whole-Wheat/Whole-Grain bread, choose Light or Medium crust, and press Start. When done, remove the bread from the machine and cool. Slice and serve.

Nutrition Info:(Per Serving): Calories: 146; Total Fat: 3 g; Saturated Fat: 1 g; Carbohydrates: 27 g; Cholesterol: 8 mg; Fiber: 1 g; Calcium: 14 mg; Sodium: 210 mg; Protein: 3 g

15. Pumpernickel Bread

Servings: 1 Loaf
Ingredients:
- 16 slice bread (2 pounds)
- 1 1/3 cups water, lukewarm between 80 and 90°F
- 2 large eggs, room temperature and not cold
- ¼ cup oil

- ¼ cup honey
- 3 tablespoons dry milk powder
- ¼ cup cocoa powder
- 3 tablespoons caraway seeds
- 1 tablespoon instant coffee granules
- 2 teaspoons table salt
- 1 cup rye flour
- 1 cup whole wheat bread flour
- 2 cups white bread flour
- 2 ¼ teaspoons bread machine yeast
- 12 slice bread (1 ½ pounds)
- 3/4 cups water, lukewarm between 80 and 90°F
- 2 large eggs, room temperature and not cold
- 2 tablespoons oil
- 2 tablespoons honey
- 3 tablespoons dry milk powder
- 3 tablespoons cocoa powder
- 2 tablespoons caraway seeds
- 2 teaspoon instant coffee granules
- 1 1/2 teaspoons table salt
- 3/4 cup rye flour
- 3/4 cup whole wheat bread flour
- 1 1/2 cups white bread flour
- 1 3/4 teaspoons bread machine yeast

Directions:
Choose the size of loaf you would like to make and measure your ingredients. If you want to make a 1-pound or 2 ½-pound loaf, please adjust your ingredient quantities accordingly. You can look at the conversion table at the end of the book for easy adjustments or click here. Take the bread pan; add the ingredients in order listed above. Secure the pan into the bread machine and close the lid. Power the bread maker and select the option of the bread – White/Basic – then the size of the loaf you are making, and finally the crust color you desire. Start the machine. After the bread cycle is done and the bread is cooked, carefully remove the pan from the machine. Use a potholder as the handle will be very hot. Let rest for a few minutes. Remove the bread from the pan and allow to cool down on a wired rack for at least 10 minutes or more before slicing.

Nutrition Info:(Per Serving):Calories 134, fat 3.1 g, carbs 19 g, sodium 143 mg, protein 4.2 g

16. Caramelized Onion Focaccia Bread

Servings: 4 – 6   Cooking Time: 3 Hours
Ingredients:
- 3/4 cup water
- 2 tablespoons olive oil
- 1 tablespoon sugar
- 1 teaspoon salt
- 2 cups flour
- 1 1/2 teaspoons yeast
- 3/4 cup mozzarella cheese, shredded
- 2 tablespoons parmesan cheese, shredded
- Onion topping:
- 3 tablespoons butter
- 2 medium onions
- 2 cloves garlic, minced

Directions:

Place all ingredients, except cheese and onion topping, in your bread maker in the order listed above.   Grease a large baking sheet.   Pat dough into a 12-inch circle on the pan; cover and let rise in warm place for about 30 minutes.   Melt butter in large frying pan over medium-low heat. Cook onions and garlic in butter 15 minutes, stirring often, until onions are caramelized. Preheat an oven to 400°F.   Make deep depressions across the dough at 1-inch intervals with the handle of a wooden spoon.   Spread the onion topping over dough and sprinkle with cheeses.   Bake 15 to 20 minutes or until golden brown. Cut into wedges and serve warm.
Nutrition Info: Calories: 286, Sodium: 482 mg, Dietary Fiber: 2.2 g, Fat: 12 g, Carbs: 38.1 g, Protein: 6.8 g.

17. Honey Nut Bread

Servings: 8   Cooking Time: 3 Hours And 25 Minutes
Ingredients:
- Eggs – 2
- Cottage cheese – 2/3 cup
- Milk – ½ cup
- Butter – ¼ cup
- Honey – 2 tbsp.
- All-purpose flour – 4 cups
- Instant yeast – 1 tbsp.
- Salt – 1 tsp.
- Candied nuts – ¾ cups, chopped

Directions:
Add everything, except nuts to your bread machine according to manufacturer recommendation.   Select Basic and choose Light crust type. Press Start.   Add the nuts when the machine beeps.   Remove the bread when ready.   Cool, slice, and serve.
Nutrition Info:(Per Serving): Calories: 422; Total Fat: 13.9 g; Saturated Fat: 5.2 g; Carbohydrates: 59.8 g; Cholesterol: 59 mg; Fiber: 2.8 g; Calcium: 62 mg; Sodium: 450 mg; Protein: 13.7 g

18. Banana Chocolate Chip Bread

Servings: 14 Slices   Cooking Time: 2 H.
Ingredients:
- 2 eggs
- ⅓ cup melted butter
- ⅛ cup milk
- 2 mashed bananas
- 2 cups all-purpose bread flour
- ⅔ cup sugar
- 1¼ tsp baking powder
- ½ tsp baking soda
- ½ tsp salt
- ½ cup chopped walnuts
- ½ cup chocolate chips

Directions:
Add each ingredient to the bread machine in the order and at the temperature recommended by your bread machine manufacturer.   Close the lid, select the quick bread, low crust setting on your bread machine, and press start.   When the bread machine has finished baking, remove the bread and put it on a cooling rack.

19. Classic Wite Bread I

Servings: 1 Loaf
Ingredients:
- 16 slice bread (2 pounds)
- 1½ cups lukewarm water
- 1 tablespoon + 1 teaspoon olive oil
- 1½ teaspoons sugar
- 1 teaspoon table salt
- ¼ teaspoon baking soda
- 2½ cups all-purpose flour
- 1 cup white bread flour
- 2½ teaspoons bread machine yeast
- 12 slice bread (1½ pounds)
- 1⅛ cups lukewarm water
- ¾ tablespoon + 1 teaspoon olive oil
- 1⅛ teaspoons sugar
- ¾ teaspoon table salt
- ⅛ teaspoon baking soda
- 1½ cups all-purpose flour
- ¾ cup white bread flour
- 1½ teaspoons bread machine yeast

Directions:
Choose the size of loaf you would like to make and measure your ingredients.   Add the ingredients to the bread pan in the order listed above.   Place the pan in the bread machine and close the lid.   Turn on the bread maker. Select the White/Basic setting, then the loaf size, and finally the crust color. Start the cycle. When the cycle is finished and the bread is baked, carefully remove the pan from the machine. Use a potholder as the handle will be very hot. Let rest for a few minutes.   Remove the bread from the pan and allow to cool on a wire rack for at least 10 minutes before slicing.
Nutrition Info:(Per Serving):Calories 124, fat 4.9 g, carbs 17.2 g, sodium 178 mg, protein 2 g

20. Multigrain Loaf

Servings: 12   Cooking Time: 3 Hours And 25 Minutes
Ingredients:
- Water – 1 ¼ cup
- Butter – 2 tbsp., softened
- Bread flour – 1 1/3 cups
- Whole wheat flour – 1 1/3 cup
- Multigrain hot cereal – 1 ¼ cups, uncooked
- Brown sugar – ¼ cup
- Salt – 1 ½ tsp.
- Bread machine yeast – 2 ½ tsp.

Directions:
Place all ingredients in the bread machine according to manufacture recommendation.   Select Basic/White cycle and Medium or Light crust. Press Start.   Remove the bread when done.   Cool, slice, and serve.
Nutrition Info:(Per Serving): Calories: 170; Total Fat: 2 g; Saturated Fat: 2 g; Carbohydrates: 31 g; Cholesterol: 5 mg; Fiber: 4 g; Calcium: 0 mg; Sodium: 260 mg; Protein: 5 g

21. Lemon Cake

Servings: 12   Cooking Time: 2 Hours 50 Minutes

Ingredients:
- 3 large eggs, beaten
- 1/3 cup 2% milk
- 1/2 cup butter, melted
- 2 cups all-purpose flour
- 3 teaspoons baking powder
- 1 1/3 cup sugar
- 1 teaspoon vanilla extract
- 2 lemons, zested
- For the glaze:
- 1 cup powdered sugar
- 2 tablespoons lemon juice, freshly squeezed

Directions:
Prepare the glaze by whisking the powdered sugar and lemon juice together in a small mixing bowl and set aside. Add all of the remaining ingredients to the baking pan in the order listed. Select the Sweet bread, medium color crust, and press Start. When baked, transfer the baking pan to a cooling rack. When the cake has cooled completely, gently shake the cake out onto a serving plate. Glaze the cool cake and serve.

Nutrition Info: Calories: 290, Sodium: 77 mg, Dietary Fiber: 0.6 g, Fat: 9.3 g, Carbs: 42.9 g, Protein: 4 g.

22. Cinnamon Pecan Coffee Cake

Servings: 10 - 12   Cooking Time: 2 Hours

Ingredients:
- 1 cup butter, unsalted
- 1 cup sugar
- 2 eggs
- 1 cup sour cream
- 1 teaspoon vanilla extract
- 2 cups all-purpose flour
- 1 teaspoon baking powder
- 1 teaspoon baking soda
- 1/2 teaspoon salt
- For the topping:
- 1/2 cup brown sugar
- 1/4 cup sugar
- 1/2 teaspoon cinnamon
- 1/2 cup pecans, chopped

Directions:
Add butter, sugar, eggs, sour cream and vanilla to the bread maker baking pan, followed by the dry ingredients. Select Cake cycle and press Start. Prepare topping and set aside. When kneading cycle is done, after about 20 minutes, sprinkle 1/2 cup of topping on top of dough and continue baking. During the last hour of baking time, sprinkle the remaining 1/2 cup of topping on the cake. Bake until complete. Cool on a wire rack for 10 minutes and serve warm.

Nutrition Info: Calories: 488, Sodium: 333 mg, Dietary Fiber: 2.5 g, Fat: 32.8 g, Carbs: 46.4 g, Protein: 5.7 g.

23. Baguette Style French Bread

Servings: 2 Loaves

Ingredients:
- 2 baguettes of 1-pound each
- 1 ⅔ cups water, lukewarm between 80 and 90⁰F

- 1 teaspoon table salt
- 4 ⅔ cups white bread flour
- 2 ⅔ teaspoons bread machine yeast or rapid rise yeast
- 2 baguettes of ¾-pound each
- 1 ¼ cups water, lukewarm between 80 and 90⁰F
- ¾ teaspoon table salt
- 3 ½ cups white bread flour
- 2 teaspoons bread machine yeast or rapid rise yeast
- Other Ingredients:
- Cornmeal
- Olive oil
- 1 egg white
- 1 tablespoon water

Directions:
Choose the size of crusty bread you would like to make and measure your ingredients. Add the ingredients for the bread machine to the bread pan in the order listed above. Place the pan in the bread machine and close the lid. Turn on the bread maker. Select the dough/manual setting. When the dough cycle is completed, remove the pan and lay the dough on a floured working surface. Knead the dough a few times and add flour if needed so the dough is not too sticky to handle. Cut the dough in half and form a ball with each half. Grease a baking sheet with olive oil. Dust lightly with cornmeal. Preheat the oven to 375⁰ and place the oven rack in the middle position. With a rolling pin dusted with flour, roll one of the dough balls into a 12-inch by 9 -inch rectangle for the 2 pounds bread size or a 10-inch by 8-inch rectangle for the 1 ½ pound bread size. Starting on the longer side, roll the dough tightly. Pinch the ends and the seam with your fingers to seal. Roll the dough in a back in forth movement to make it into a nice French baguette shape. Repeat the process with the second dough ball. Place loaves of bread onto the baking sheet with the seams down and brush with some olive oil with enough space in between them to rise. Dust top of both loaves with a little bit of cornmeal. Cover with a clean kitchen towel and place in a warm area with any air draught. Let rise for 10 to 15 minutes, or until loaves doubled in size. Mix the egg white and 1 tablespoon of water and lightly brush over both loaves of bread. Place in the oven and bake for 20 minutes. Remove from oven and brush with remaining egg wash on top of both loaves of bread. Place back into the oven taking care of turning around the baking sheet. Bake for another 5 to 10 minutes or until the baguettes are golden brown. Let rest on a wired rack for 5-10 minutes before serving.

Nutrition Info: (Per Serving): Calories 87, fat 0.8 g, carbs 16.5 g, sodium 192 mg, protein 3.4 g

24. French Bread

Servings: 8   Cooking Time: 3 Hours And 35 Minutes

Ingredients:
- Water - ⅔ cup
- Olive oil - 2 tsp.
- Sugar - 1 tbsp.
- Salt - ⅔ tsp.
- White bread flour - 2 cups

- Bread machine or instant yeast - 1 tsp.

Directions:
Place everything in the bread machine according to machine recommendation.   Press French bread and Light or Medium crust. Press Start.   Remove the loaf from the machine and cool.   Slice and serve.
Nutrition Info:(Per Serving): Calories: 135; Total Fat: 2 g; Saturated Fat: 0 g; Carbohydrates: 26 g; Cholesterol: 13 mg; Fiber: 1 g; Calcium: 17 mg; Sodium: 245 mg; Protein: 3 g

25. Basic Bulgur Bread

Servings: 1 Loaf
Ingredients:
- 16 slice bread (2 pounds)
- ½ cup lukewarm water
- ½ cup bulgur wheat
- 1⅓ cups lukewarm milk
- 1⅓ tablespoons unsalted butter, melted
- 1⅓ tablespoons sugar
- 1 teaspoon table salt
- 4 cups bread flour
- 2 teaspoons bread machine yeast
- 12 slice bread (1½ pounds)
- ⅓ cup lukewarm water
- ⅓ cup bulgur wheat
- 1 cup lukewarm milk
- 1 tablespoon unsalted butter, melted
- 1 tablespoon sugar
- ¾ teaspoon table salt
- 3 cups bread flour
- 1½ teaspoons bread machine yeast

Directions:
Choose the size of loaf you would like to make and measure your ingredients.   Add the water and bulgur wheat to the bread pan and set aside for 25–30 minutes for the bulgur wheat to soften.   Add the other ingredients to the bread pan in the order listed above. Place the pan in the bread machine and close the lid. Turn on the bread maker. Select the White/Basic setting, then the loaf size, and finally the crust color. Start the cycle.   When the cycle is finished and the bread is baked, carefully remove the pan from the machine. Use a potholder as the handle will be very hot. Let rest for a few minutes.   Remove the bread from the pan and allow to cool on a wire rack for at least 10 minutes before slicing.
Nutrition Info:(Per Serving):Calories 160, fat 2.6 g, carbs 28.7 g, sodium 163 mg, protein 5 g

26. Golden Turmeric Cardamom Bread

Servings: 12   Cooking Time: 3 Hours
Ingredients:
- 1 cup lukewarm water
- 1/3 cup lukewarm milk
- 3 tablespoons butter, unsalted
- 3 3/4 cups unbleached all-purpose flour
- 3 tablespoons sugar
- 1 1/2 teaspoons salt
- 2 tablespoons ground turmeric

- 1 tablespoon ground cardamom
- 1/2 teaspoon cayenne pepper
- 1 1/2 teaspoons active dry yeast

Directions:
Add liquid ingredients to the bread pan.   Measure and add dry ingredients (except yeast) to the bread pan. Make a well in the center of the dry ingredients and add the yeast.   Snap the baking pan into the bread maker and close the lid.   Choose the Basic setting, preferred crust color and press Start.   When the loaf is done, remove the pan from the machine. After about 5 minutes, gently shake the pan to loosen the loaf and turn it out onto a rack to cool.
Nutrition Info: Calories: 183, Sodium: 316 mg, Dietary Fiber: 1.2 g, Fat: 3.3 g, Carbs: 33.3 g, Protein: 4.5 g.

27. Basic Seed Bread

Servings: 1 Loaf
Ingredients:
- 16 slice bread (2 pounds)
- 1½ cups lukewarm water
- 2 tablespoons unsalted butter, melted
- 2 tablespoons sugar
- 1½ teaspoons table salt
- 3¼ cups white bread flour
- ¾ cup ground chia seeds
- 2 tablespoons sesame seeds
- 2 teaspoons bread machine yeast
- 12 slice bread (1½ pounds)
- 1⅛ cups lukewarm water
- 1½ tablespoons unsalted butter, melted
- 1½ tablespoons sugar
- 1⅛ teaspoons table salt
- 2½ cups white bread flour
- ½ cup ground chia seeds
- 1½ tablespoons sesame seeds
- 1½ teaspoons bread machine yeast

Directions:
Choose the size of loaf you would like to make and measure your ingredients.   Add the ingredients to the bread pan in the order listed above.   Place the pan in the bread machine and close the lid.   Turn on the bread maker. Select the White/Basic setting, then the loaf size, and finally the crust color. Start the cycle. When the cycle is finished and the bread is baked, carefully remove the pan from the machine. Use a potholder as the handle will be very hot. Let rest for a few minutes.   Remove the bread from the pan and allow to cool on a wire rack for at least 10 minutes before slicing.
Nutrition Info:(Per Serving):Calories 153, fat 2.3 g, carbs 24.8 g, sodium 208 mg, protein 5.3 g

28. Honey Whole Wheat Bread

Servings: 10   Cooking Time: 1 Hour And 20 Minutes
Ingredients:
- Warm water - 1 cup
- Butter - 2 tbsp., cubed
- Salt – 1 tsp.
- Honey – 2 tbsp.

- Unbleached flour – 1 ½ cups
- Whole wheat flour – 1 ½ cups
- Bread machine yeast – 2 tsp.

Directions:

Add ingredients according to bread machine instructions. Select Rapid – Whole Wheat and Medium crust. Remove bread when done. Cool and slice.

Nutrition Info:(Per Serving): Calories: 165; Total Fat: 3 g; Saturated Fat: 2 g; Carbohydrates: 31 g; Cholesterol: 6 mg; Fiber: 3 g; Calcium: 25 mg; Sodium: 253 mg; Protein: 5 g

29. Coffee Rye Bread

Servings: 6   Cooking Time: 3 Hours And 25 Minutes

Ingredients:

- Lukewarm water – ½ cup
- Brewed coffee – ¼ cup, 80ºF
- Dark molasses – 2 tbsp.
- Brown sugar – 5 tsp.
- Unsalted butter – 4 tsp., softened
- Powdered skim milk – 1 tbsp.
- Kosher salt – 1 tsp.
- Unsweetened cocoa powder – 4 tsp.
- Dark rye flour – 2/3 cup
- Whole-wheat bread machine flour – ½ cup
- Caraway seeds – 1 tsp.
- White bread machine flour – 1 cup
- Bread machine yeast – 1 ½ tsp

Directions:

Place everything in the bread machine pan according to the bread machine recommendation. Select Basic and Light crust. Press Start. Remove the bread. Cool, slice, and serve.

Nutrition Info:(Per Serving): Calories: 222; Total Fat: 3.2 g; Saturated Fat: 1.8 g; Carbohydrates: 42.9 g; Cholesterol: 8 mg; Fiber: 4.7 g; Calcium: 40 mg; Sodium: 415 mg; Protein: 6.3 g

30. Craft Beer And Cheese Bread

Servings: 10   Cooking Time: 2 Hours 10 Minutes

Ingredients:

- 1 package active dry yeast
- 3 cups all-purpose flour
- 1 tablespoon sugar
- 1 1/2 teaspoons salt
- 1 tablespoon butter, room temperature
- 1 1/4 cups craft beer, at room temperature
- 1/2 cup cheddar cheese, shredded
- 1/2 cup Monterey Jack cheese, shredded

Directions:

Add beer to a sauce pan with cheese and heat on low until just warm; stir to blend. Transfer mixture to the bread maker pan. Measure and add dry ingredients (except yeast) to the bread pan. Make a small "hole" in the flour for the yeast. Carefully pour the yeast into the "hole." Snap the baking pan into the bread maker and close the lid. Choose the Basic setting and preferred crust color and press Start. When the loaf is done, remove the pan from the machine. After about 5 minutes, gently

shake the pan to loosen the loaf and turn it out onto a rack to cool. Serve warm.

Nutrition Info: Calories: 209, Sodium: 425 mg, Dietary Fiber: 1.2 g, Fat: 5.1 g, Carbs: 31.2 g, Protein: 7.1 g.

31. Meatloaf

Servings: 14 Slices   Cooking Time: 3 H. 20 Min.

Ingredients:

- 1 lb. ground pork
- 1 lb. ground turkey
- 2 slices of soft bread, torn
- 2 Tbsp minced onions
- 2 eggs
- ¾ cup milk
- ½ tsp salt
- ⅛ tsp black pepper
- ⅛ tsp dry mustard
- ⅛ tsp celery salt
- ⅛ tsp garlic salt
- 2 tsp Worcestershire sauce
- For the topping:
- ¾ cup ketchup
- 3 Tbsp brown sugar

Directions:

Add each ingredient except the toppings to the bread machine in the order and at the temperature recommended by your bread machine manufacturer. Close the lid, select the basic bread, medium crust setting on your bread machine and press start. Mix the topping ingredients (¾ cup ketchup with 3 Tbsp brown sugar) together. When the bread machine has finished baking, remove the bread and put it on a cooling rack. Cover the top of meatloaf with topping before serving.

32. Pizza Rolls

Servings: 15   Cooking Time: 3 Hours

Ingredients:

- 1 cup warm water
- 3 tablespoons olive oil
- 3 cups bread flour
- 3 tablespoons sugar
- 1 1/2 teaspoons salt
- 2 1/4 teaspoons instant yeast
- For the Filling:
- 1 package pepperoni, sliced
- 1 bag mozzarella cheese, shredded
- 1 cup pizza sauce
- 1 jar of mild banana pepper rings

Directions:

Add the liquid ingredients to your bread maker first, then add flour and salt. Create a small hole in the flour and add the sugar and yeast. Select the Dough cycle and press Start. Once your dough has fully risen, lay it out on a lightly floured surface, and punch it back down. Knead by hand for about 30 seconds; be sure not to overwork the dough. Pinch off a small amount of dough and flatten out into the shape of a circle and baste with one teaspoon of sauce. Layer with three slices of pepperoni, a good pinch of cheese, and a few banana pepper rings. Fold one side over to the other and pinch the seams together, creating a seal. Fold corners over and do the same; repeat until all dough is used. Place rolls on a large 9-by-13-inch baking sheet and bake at 350°F for about 25 mins or until slightly golden brown. Remove rolls and allow to cool on a cooling rack for 10 to 15 minutes before eating; serve warm.

Nutrition Info: Calories: 142, Sodium: 329 mg, Dietary Fiber: 1.1 g, Fat: 3.7 g, Carbs: 23.7 g, Protein: 3.7 g.

33. Oat Bran Molasses Bread

Servings: 8   Cooking Time: 3 Hours And 48 Minutes
Ingredients:
- Water - ½ cup
- Melted butter - 1½ tbsp., cooled
- Blackstrap molasses - 2 tbsp.
- Salt - ¼ tsp.
- Ground nutmeg - ⅛ tsp.
- Oat bran - ½ cup
- Whole-wheat bread flour - 1½ cups
- Bread machine or instant yeast - 1⅛ tsp.

Directions:
Place the ingredients in the bread machine according to instructions.   Choose Whole-Wheat/Whole-Grain bread, and Light or Medium crust. Press Start. Remove when done and cool. Slice and serve.

Nutrition Info:(Per Serving): Calories: 137; Total Fat: 3 g; Saturated Fat: 2 g; Carbohydrates: 25 g; Cholesterol: 15 mg; Fiber: 1 g; Calcium: 20 mg; Sodium: 112 mg; Protein: 3 g

34. Tomato Basil Bread

Servings: 16   Cooking Time: 4 Hours
Ingredients:
- 3/4 cup warm water
- 1/4 cup fresh basil, minced
- 1/4 cup parmesan cheese, grated
- 3 tablespoons tomato paste
- 1 tablespoon sugar
- 1 tablespoon olive oil
- 1 teaspoon salt
- 1/4 teaspoon crushed red pepper flakes
- 2 1/2 cups bread flour
- 1 package active dry yeast
- Flour, for surface

Directions:
Add ingredients, except yeast, to bread maker pan in above listed order.   Make a well in the flour; pour the yeast into the hole.   Select Dough cycle and press Start. Turn finished dough out onto a floured surface and knead until smooth and elastic, about 3 to 5 minutes. Place in a greased bowl, turning once to grease top. Cover and let rise in a warm place until doubled, about 1 hour. Punch dough down and knead for 1 minute.   Shape into a round loaf. Place on a greased baking sheet. Cover and let rise until doubled, about 1 hour.   With a sharp knife, cut a large "X" in top of loaf. Bake at 375°F for 35-

40 minutes or until golden brown.   Remove from pan and cool on a cooling rack before serving.

Nutrition Info: Calories: 91, Sodium: 172 mg, Dietary Fiber: 0.8 g, Fat: 1.5 g, Carbs: 16.5 g, Protein: 2.8 g.

35. King Cake

Servings: 12 - 16   Cooking Time: 2 Hours 55 Minutes
Ingredients:
- For the Dough:
- 1 egg, lightly beaten
- 1/4 cup filtered water
- 1/2 teaspoon salt
- 2 tablespoons unsalted butter, room temperature
- 1 cup sour cream
- 3 1/2 tablespoons sugar
- 3 1/2 cups all-purpose flour
- 2 1/2 teaspoons bread machine yeast
- For the Filling:
- 1 cup cream cheese, room temperature
- 1/2 cup confectioners' sugar
- 1/2 cup sugar
- 2 teaspoons ground cinnamon
- 5 tablespoons unsalted butter, melted
- For the Icing:
- 1/2 cup cream cheese, room temperature
- 1/4 cup unsalted butter, room temperature
- 2 1/2 cups confectioners' sugar
- 1 teaspoon pure vanilla extract
- Purple, green, and yellow cake glitter
- Flour, for surface

Directions:
Add the dough ingredients to the bread machine in the order listed.   Select Dough cycle, and press Start. Check the dough after five minutes of mixing and add 1 to 2 more tablespoons of water or flour if the dough is too dry or too wet.   In a large mixing bowl, beat the cream cheese and 1/2 cup confectioners' sugar until smooth; set aside. Mix 1/2 cup sugar, 2 teaspoons cinnamon, and 5 tablespoons melted butter until combined; set aside. Line a large baking sheet with parchment paper and set aside.   Remove the dough and roll out into a 10-by-28-inch rectangle on a floured surface. Trim the edges as needed with scissors.   Spread the cream cheese mixture on the dough to within 1 inch of the edges. Spread sugar-cinnamon mixture on the cream cheese to within 1 inch of the edges of the dough.   Starting at one of the long edges, roll the dough tightly into a log. Pinch the edges to seal the log and place the rolled dough onto the lined baking sheet, seam side down, and form the dough into a ring. Moisten the ends of the dough with a little water and pinch the two ends together to seal. Place a large greased can in the center to maintain a nice circle in the center. Cover with a towel and let rise in a warm place until doubled in size, about 30 minutes. Preheat oven to 350°F. Bake the cake until the top is golden brown, about 25 minutes.   Mix the ingredients for the icing until just smooth in a mixing bowl. Remove the cake from the oven and allow to cool for 10 minutes on a wire rack.   While the cake is still warm, spoon the icing onto the cake and sprinkle with purple, green and yellow glitter.

18

Nutrition Info:Calories: 383, Sodium: 205 mg, Dietary Fiber: 1 g, Fat: 18.9 g, Carbs: 48.5 g, Protein: 5.6 g.

36. Julekake

Servings: 14 Slices   Cooking Time: 3 H.
Ingredients:
- ⅓ cup evaporated milk
- ⅔ cup water
- 1 egg, room temperature
- 3⅓ cups bread flour
- ¼ cup sugar
- ½ tsp salt
- ½ tsp cardamom
- ½ cup softened butter, cut up
- 2¼ tsp dry active yeast
- ½ cup golden raisins
- ⅔ cup candied fruit

Directions:
Add each ingredient except the raisins to the bread machine in the order and at the temperature recommended by your bread machine manufacturer. Close the lid, select the basic bread, low crust setting on your bread machine, and press start.   Add the raisins and fruit about 5 minutes before the kneading cycle has finished.   When the bread machine has finished baking, remove the bread and put it on a cooling rack.

37. Cheesy Sausage Loaf

Servings: 12   Cooking Time: 3 Hours
Ingredients:
- 1 cup warm water
- 4 teaspoons butter, softened
- 1 1/4 teaspoons salt
- 1 teaspoon sugar
- 3 cups bread flour
- 2 1/4 teaspoons active dry yeast
- 1 pound pork sausage roll, cooked and drained
- 1 1/2 cups Italian cheese, shredded
- 1/4 teaspoon garlic powder
- Pinch of black pepper
- 1 egg, lightly beaten
- Flour, for surface

Directions:
Add the first five ingredients to the bread maker pan in order listed above.   Make a well in the flour; pour the yeast into the hole.   Select Dough cycle and press Start. Turn kneaded dough onto a lightly floured surface and roll into a 16-by-10-inch rectangle. Cover with plastic wrap and let rest for 10 minutes   Combine sausage, cheese, garlic powder and pepper in a mixing bowl. Spread sausage mixture evenly over the dough to within one 1/2 inch of edges. Start with a long side and roll up like a jelly roll, pinch seams to seal, and tuck ends under. Place the loaf seam-side down on a greased baking sheet. Cover and let rise in a warm place for 30 minutes. Preheat an oven to 350°F and bake 20 minutes.   Brush with egg and bake an additional 15 to 20 minutes until golden brown.   Remove to a cooling rack and serve warm.

Nutrition Info:Calories: 172, Sodium: 350 mg, Dietary Fiber: 1.1 g, Fat: 4.7 g, Carbs: 27.1 g, Protein: 5.1 g.

38. Fat-free Whole Wheat Bread

Servings: 12   Cooking Time: 1 Hour And 20 Minutes
Ingredients:
- Water – 1 7/8 cup
- White whole wheat flour – 4 2/3 cups
- Vital wheat gluten – 4 tbsp.
- Sugar – 2 tbsp.
- Salt – 1 ½ tsp.
- Rapid rise yeast – 2 ½ tsp.

Directions:
Add the water in the bread machine pan.   Add the remaining ingredients according to bread machine recommendation.   Choose Quick-Bake Whole Wheat cycle and press Start.   Remove the bread when complete.   Cool, slice, and serve.

Nutrition Info:(Per Serving): Calories: 134; Total Fat: 0.6 g; Saturated Fat: 0 g; Carbohydrates: 27.6 g; Cholesterol: 11 mg; Fiber: 6.5 g; Calcium: 18 mg; Sodium: 221.5 mg; Protein: 6.5 g

39. Honey Pound Cake

Servings: 12 - 16   Cooking Time: 2 Hours 50 Minutes
Ingredients:
- 1 cup butter, unsalted
- 1/4 cup honey
- 2 tablespoons whole milk
- 4 eggs, beaten
- 1 cup sugar
- 2 cups flour

Directions:
Bring the butter to room temperature and cut into 1/2-inch cubes.   Add the ingredients to the bread machine in the order listed (butter, honey, milk, eggs, sugar, flour). Press Sweet bread setting, light crust color, and press Start.   Take the cake out of the bread pan using a rubber spatula, as soon as it's finished. Cool on a rack and serve with your favorite fruit.

Nutrition Info:Calories: 117, Sodium: 183 mg, Dietary Fiber: 0.3 g, Fat: 6.9 g, Carbs: 12.3 g, Protein: 1.9 g.

40. French Crusty Loaf Bread

Servings: 1 Loaf
Ingredients:
- 16 slice bread (2 pounds)
- 2 cups + 2 tablespoons water, lukewarm between 80 and 90°F
- 4 teaspoons sugar
- 2 teaspoons table salt
- 6 1/2 cups white bread flour
- 2 teaspoons bread machine yeast
- 12 slice bread (1 ½ pounds)
- 1 1/2 cups + 1 tablespoon water, lukewarm between 80 and 90°F
- 3 teaspoons sugar
- 1 1/2 teaspoons table salt

- 4 3/4 cups white bread flour
- 1 1/2 teaspoons bread machine yeast

Directions:
Choose the size of loaf you would like to make and measure your ingredients. Add the ingredients to the bread pan in the order listed above. Place the pan in the bread machine and close the lid. Turn on the bread maker. Select the French setting, then the loaf size, and finally the crust color. Start the cycle. When the cycle is finished and the bread is baked, carefully remove the pan from the machine. Use a potholder as the handle will be very hot. Let rest for a few minutes. Remove the bread from the pan and allow to cool on a wire rack for at least 10 minutes before slicing.

Nutrition Info:(Per Serving):Calories 186, fat 1.2 g, carbs 31.4 g, sodium 126 mg, protein 5.7 g

41. Panettone

Servings: 14 Slices   Cooking Time: 3 H. 10 Min.

Ingredients:
- ¾ cup warm water
- 6 Tbsp vegetable oil
- 1½ tsp salt
- 4 Tbsp sugar
- 2 eggs
- 3 cups bread flour
- 1 (¼ ounce) package Fleishman's yeast
- ½ cup candied fruit
- ⅓ cup chopped almonds
- ½ tsp almond extract

Directions:
Add each ingredient to the bread machine in the order and at the temperature recommended by your bread machine manufacturer. Close the lid, select the sweet loaf, low crust setting on your bread machine, and press start. When the bread machine has finished baking, remove the bread and put it on a cooling rack.

42. Peanut Butter Bread

Servings: 10   Cooking Time: 3 Hours And 25 Minutes

Ingredients:
- Water – 1 cup, plus 1 tbsp.
- Peanut butter – ½ cup
- Bread flour – 3 cups
- Brown sugar – 3 tbsp.
- Salt – 1 tsp.
- Bread machine yeast – 2 tsp.

Directions:
Place every ingredient in the bread machine according to the manufacturer's recommendation. Select Basic/White or Sweet and choose Medium or Light crust. Press Start. Remove the bread when finished. Cool, slice, and serve.

Nutrition Info:(Per Serving): Calories: 136; Total Fat: 8 g; Saturated Fat: 1 g; Carbohydrates: 14 g; Cholesterol: 0 mg; Fiber: 2 g; Calcium: 32 mg; Sodium: 203 mg; Protein: 4 g

43. Insane Coffee Cake

Servings: 10 - 12   Cooking Time: 2 Hours

Ingredients:
- 7/8 cup of milk
- 1/4 cup of sugar
- 1 teaspoon salt
- 1 egg yolk
- 1 tablespoon butter
- 2 1/4 cups bread flour
- 2 teaspoons of active dry yeast
- For the topping:
- 2 tablespoons butter, melted
- 2 tablespoons brown sugar
- 1 teaspoon cinnamon

Directions:
Set the topping ingredients aside and add the rest of the ingredients to the bread pan in the order above. Set the bread machine to the Dough cycle. Butter a 9-by-9-inch glass baking dish and pour the dough into the dish. Cover with a towel and let rise for about 10 minutes. Preheat an oven to 375°F. Brush the dough with the melted butter. Mix the brown sugar and cinnamon in a bowl and sprinkle on top of the coffee cake. Let the topped dough rise, uncovered, for another 30 minutes. Place in oven and bake for 30 to 35 minutes or until a wooden toothpick inserted into the center comes out clean and dry. When baked, let the coffee cake rest for 10 minutes. Carefully remove the coffee cake from the dish with a rubber spatula, slice and serve.

Nutrition Info: Calories: 148, Sodium: 211 mg, Dietary Fiber: 0.9 g, Fat: 3.9 g, Carbs: 24.9 g, Protein: 3.5 g.

44. Onion Bread

Servings: 12   Cooking Time: 3 Hours And 25 Minutes

Ingredients:
- Water – 1 ½ cup
- Butter – 2 tbsp. plus 2 tsp.
- Salt – 1 tsp.
- Sugar – 1 tbsp. plus 1 ½ tsp.
- Bread flour – 4 cups
- Nonfat dry milk – 2 tbsp. plus 2 tsp.
- Active dry yeast – 2 tsp.
- Dry onion soup mix – 4 tbsp.

Directions:
Place ingredients in the bread pan in the order listed, except the soup. Select Basic cycle. Add the onion soup mix at the fruit and nut signal. When done, remove and cool. Slice and serve.

Nutrition Info:(Per Serving): Calories: 130; Total Fat: 3 g; Saturated Fat: 2 g; Carbohydrates: 16 g; Cholesterol: 8 mg; Fiber: 1 g; Calcium: 77 mg; Sodium: 843 mg; Protein: 8 g

45. Wine And Cheese Bread

Servings: 12   Cooking Time: 3 Hours

Ingredients:
- 3/4 cup white wine

- 1/2 cup white cheddar or gruyere cheese, shredded
- 1 1/2 tablespoons butter
- 1/2 teaspoon salt
- 3/4 teaspoon sugar
- 2 1/4 cups bread flour
- 1 1/2 teaspoons active dry yeast

Directions:
Add liquid ingredients to the bread maker pan. Add dry ingredients, except yeast, to the bread pan. Use your fingers to form a well-like hole in the flour where you will pour the yeast; yeast must never come into contact with a liquid when you are adding the ingredients. Carefully pour the yeast into the well. Select Basic bread setting, light crust color, and press Start. Allow to cool on a wire rack before serving.

Nutrition Info: Calories: 132, Sodium: 138 mg, Dietary Fiber: 0.7 g, Fat: 3.3 g, Carbs: 18.8 g, Protein: 3.8 g.

46. Sausage Herb And Onion Bread

Servings: 14 Slices   Cooking Time: 3 H. 10 Min.
Ingredients:
- 3/4 tsp basil leaves
- 1½ Tbsp sugar
- 3/8 cup wheat bran
- 1 medium onion, minced
- 2¼ tsp yeast
- 3/4 tsp rosemary leaves
- ½ Tbsp salt
- 1½ Tbsp parmesan, grated
- 3 cups bread flour
- 3/4 tsp oregano leaves
- 3/4 tsp thyme leaves
- 1⅛ cups water
- 3/4 cup Italian sausage

Directions:
Remove casing from sausage. Crumble the meat into a medium nonstick skillet. Cook on medium heat, stirring and breaking up sausage until it begins to render its juices. Add onion and cook for 2-3 minuts until it softens and the sausage is no longer pink. Remove from heat and let it cool. Add each ingredient to the bread machine in the order and at the temperature recommended by your bread machine manufacturer. Close the lid, select the basic bread, medium crust setting on your bread machine, and press start. When the bread machine has finished baking, remove the bread and put it on a cooling rack.

47. Oat Quinoa Bread

Servings: 1 Loaf
Ingredients:
- 16 slice bread (2 pounds)
- 1⅓ cups lukewarm milk
- 3/4 cup cooked quinoa, cooled
- 5 tablespoons unsalted butter, melted
- 4 teaspoons sugar
- 1⅓ teaspoons table salt
- 2 cups white bread flour

- 5 tablespoons quick oats
- 1 cup whole-wheat flour
- 2 teaspoons bread machine yeast
- 12 slice bread (1½ pounds)
- 1 cup lukewarm milk
- ⅔ cup cooked quinoa, cooled
- ¼ cup unsalted butter, melted
- 1 tablespoon sugar
- 1 teaspoon table salt
- 1½ cups white bread flour
- ¼ cup quick oats
- 3/4 cup whole-wheat flour
- 1½ teaspoons bread machine yeast

Directions:
Choose the size of loaf you would like to make and measure your ingredients. Add the ingredients to the bread pan in the order listed above. Place the pan in the bread machine and close the lid. Turn on the bread maker. Select the White/Basic setting, then the loaf size, and finally the crust color. Start the cycle. When the cycle is finished and the bread is baked, carefully remove the pan from the machine. Use a potholder as the handle will be very hot. Let rest for a few minutes. Remove the bread from the pan and allow to cool on a wire rack for at least 10 minutes before slicing.
Nutrition Info: (Per Serving): Calories 153, fat 5.3 g, carbs 22.3 g, sodium 238 mg, protein 3.8 g

48. Banana Bread

Servings: 12   Cooking Time: 1 Hour And 20 Minutes
Ingredients:
- Eggs – 2
- Butter – 1/3 cup
- Milk – 1/8 cup
- Bananas – 2, mashed
- Bread flour – 1 1/3 cups
- Sugar – 2/3 cup
- Baking powder – 1 ¼ tsp.
- Baking soda – ½ tsp.
- Salt – ½ tsp.
- Chopped nuts – ½ cup, lightly toasted

Directions:
Add the butter, eggs, milk, and bananas to the bread pan and set aside. Combine the remaining dry ingredients in a bowl and add the bread pan. Use Quick Bread setting to bake the bread. Remove the bread when done. Slice and serve.
Nutrition Info: (Per Serving): Calories: 303; Total Fat: 17 g; Saturated Fat: 7 g; Carbohydrates: 33 g; Cholesterol: 14 mg; Fiber: 2 g; Calcium: 98 mg; Sodium: 523 mg; Protein: 7 g

49. Rosemary Focaccia Bread

Servings: 4 - 6   Cooking Time: 3 Hours
Ingredients:
- 1 cup, plus 3 tablespoons water
- 1 tablespoon extra-virgin olive oil
- 1 teaspoon salt
- 2 teaspoons fresh rosemary, chopped
- 3 cups bread flour

- 1 1/2 teaspoons instant yeast
- For the topping:
- 3 tablespoons olive oil
- Coarse salt
- Red pepper flakes

Directions:
Add water, oil, salt, rosemary, and flour to the bread maker pan. Make a well in the center of the dry ingredients and add the yeast. Select Dough cycle and press Start. Transfer finished dough to a floured surface. Cover and let rest for 5 minutes. Form dough into a smooth ball and roll into a 12-inch round. Place on a 12-inch pizza pan that has been lightly greased with olive oil. Poke dough randomly with fingertips to form dimples. Brush top with olive oil and sprinkle with salt and red pepper flakes to taste. Let rise uncovered in warm, draft-free space for about 30 minutes. Bake at 425°F for 18 to 22 minutes or until done. Serve warm.

Nutrition Info: Calories: 312, Sodium: 390 mg, Dietary Fiber: 2.1 g, Fat: 10.1 g, Carbs: 48.3 g, Protein: 6.9 g.

50. Whole Wheat Sunflower Bread

Servings: 1 Loaf

Ingredients:
- 16 slice bread (2 pounds)
- 1⅛ cups lukewarm water
- 2 tablespoons honey
- 2 tablespoons unsalted butter, melted
- 1 teaspoon table salt
- 3 cups whole-wheat flour
- 1 cup white bread flour
- 2 tablespoons sesame seeds
- ¼ cup raw sunflower seeds
- 2¼ teaspoons bread machine yeast
- 12 slice bread (1½ pounds)
- 1 cup lukewarm water
- 1½ tablespoons honey
- 1½ tablespoons unsalted butter, melted
- ¾ teaspoon table salt
- 2½ cups whole-wheat flour
- ¾ cup white bread flour
- 1 tablespoon sesame seeds
- 3 tablespoons raw sunflower seeds
- 1½ teaspoons bread machine yeast

Directions:
Choose the size of loaf you would like to make and measure your ingredients. Add the ingredients to the bread pan in the order listed above. Place the pan in the bread machine and close the lid. Turn on the bread maker. Select the Whole Wheat/Wholegrain setting, then the loaf size, and finally the crust color. Start the cycle. When the cycle is finished and the bread is baked, carefully remove the pan from the machine. Use a potholder as the handle will be very hot. Let rest for a few minutes. Remove the bread from the pan and allow to cool on a wire rack for at least 10 minutes before slicing.

Nutrition Info:(Per Serving):Calories 253, fat 3.3 g, carbs 27.4 g, sodium 154 mg, protein 4.2 g

51. Cinnamon Rolls

Servings: 12 Rolls   Cooking Time: 2 H.

Ingredients:
- For the cinnamon roll dough:
- 1 cup milk
- 1 large egg
- 4 Tbsp butter
- 3⅓ cups bread flour
- 3 Tbsp sugar
- ½ tsp salt
- 2 tsp active dry yeast
- For the filling:
- ¼ cup butter, melted
- ¼ cup sugar
- 2 tsp cinnamon
- ½ tsp nutmeg
- ⅓ cup nuts, chopped and toasted
- For the icing:
- 1 cup powdered sugar
- 1 - 2 Tbsp milk
- ½ tsp vanilla

Directions:
Add each ingredient to the bread machine in the order and at the temperature recommended by your bread machine manufacturer. Select the dough cycle and press start. When it's done, transfer the dough onto a floured surface. Knead it for 1 minute, then let it rest for the next 15 minutes. Roll out a rectangle. Spread ¼ cup of melted butter over the dough. Sprinkle the dough with cinnamon, ¼ cup sugar, nutmeg, and nuts. Roll the dough, beginning from a long side. Seal the edges and form an evenly shaped roll. Cut it into 1-inch pieces. Put them on a greased baking pan. Cover with towel and leave for 45 minutes to rise. Bake at 375°F in a preheated oven for 20-25 minutes. Remove from the oven. Cool for 10 minutes. Mix the icing ingredients in a bowl. Adjust with sugar or milk to desired thickness. Cover the rolls with icing and serve.

52. Pepperoni Bread

Servings: 10   Cooking Time: 3 Hours 10 Minutes

Ingredients:
- 1 cup plus 2 tablespoons warm water
- 1/3 cup mozzarella cheese, shredded
- 2 tablespoons sugar
- 1 1/2 teaspoons garlic salt
- 1 1/2 teaspoons dried oregano
- 3 1/4 cups bread flour
- 1 1/2 teaspoons active dry yeast
- 2/3 cup sliced pepperoni

Directions:
Add the first six ingredients in order listed above, reserving the yeast. Make a well in the flour; pour the yeast into the hole. Select Basic bread setting, medium crust color, and press Start. Check dough after 5 minutes of mixing and add 1 to 2 tablespoons of water or flour if needed. Just before the final kneading, add the pepperoni. Remove loaf when finished and allow to cool for 10 to 15 minutes on a cooling rack before serving.

Nutrition Info: Calories: 165, Sodium: 13 mg, Dietary Fiber: 1.4 g, Fat: 0.8 g, Carbs: 34.1 g, Protein: 4.9 g.

53. Oat Nut Bread

Servings: 14 Slices   Cooking Time: 3 H.
Ingredients:
- 1¼ cups water
- ½ cup quick oats
- ¼ cup brown sugar, firmly packed
- 1 Tbsp butter
- 1½ tsp salt
- 3 cups bread flour
- ¾ cup chopped walnuts
- 1 package dry bread yeast

Directions:
Add each ingredient to the bread machine in the order and at the temperature recommended by your bread machine manufacturer. Close the lid, select the rapid rise, medium crust setting on your bread machine, and press start. When the bread machine has finished baking, remove the bread and put it on a cooling rack.

54. Italian Easter Cake

Servings: 4 Slices   Cooking Time: 3 H.
Ingredients:
- 1¾ cups wheat flour
- 2½ Tbsp quick-acting dry yeast
- 8 Tbsp sugar
- ½ tsp salt
- 3 chicken eggs
- ¾ cup milk
- 3 Tbsp butter
- 1 cup raisins

Directions:
Add each ingredient except the raisins to the bread machine in the order and at the temperature recommended by your bread machine manufacturer. Close the lid, select the sweet loaf, low crust setting on your bread machine, and press start. When the dough is kneading, add the raisins. When the bread machine has finished baking, remove the bread and put it on a cooling rack.

55. Onion Loaf

Servings: 12   Cooking Time: 3 Hours 40 Minutes
Ingredients:
- 1 tablespoon butter
- 2 medium onions, sliced
- 1 cup water
- 1 tablespoon olive or vegetable oil
- 3 cups bread flour
- 2 tablespoons sugar
- 1 teaspoon salt
- 1 1/4 teaspoons bread machine or quick active dry yeast

Directions:
Preheat a large skillet to medium-low heat and add butter to melt. Add onions and cook for 10 to 15 minutes, stirring often, until onions are brown and caramelized;

remove from heat. Add remaining ingredients, except onions, to the bread maker pan in the order listed above. Select the Basic cycle, medium crust color, and press Start. Add 1/2 cup of the onions 5 to 10 minutes before the last kneading cycle ends. Remove baked bread from pan and allow to cool on a cooling rack before serving.
Nutrition Info: Calories: 149, Sodium: 203 mg, Dietary Fiber: 1.3 g, Fat: 2.5 g, Carbs: 27.7 g, Protein: 3.7 g.

56. Savory Bread Maker Rolls

Servings: 24   Cooking Time: 2 Hours 10 Mins
Ingredients:
- 1 cup warm milk, 70° to 80°F
- 1/2 cup butter, softened
- 1/4 cup sugar
- 2 eggs
- 1 1/2 teaspoons salt
- 4 cups bread flour
- 2 tablespoons herbes de Provence
- 2 1/4 teaspoons active dry yeast
- Flour, for surface

Directions:
Add all ingredients in the order listed above to the bread maker pan, reserving yeast. Make a well in the flour; add yeast to the hole. Select Dough setting; when Dough cycle is completed, turn dough out onto a lightly floured surface. Divide dough into 24 portions and shape into balls. Place rolls in a greased 13-by-9-inch baking pan. Cover and let rise in a warm place for 30-45 minutes; preheat an oven to 350°F. Bake for 13-16 minutes or until golden brown and serve warm.
Nutrition Info: Calories: 129, Sodium: 185 mg, Dietary Fiber: 0.6 g, Fat: 4.6 g, Carbs: 18.7 g, Protein: 3.1 g.

57. Apple Walnut Bread

Servings: 14 Slices   Cooking Time: 2 H. 30 Min.
Ingredients:
- ¾ cup unsweetened applesauce
- 4 cups apple juice
- 1 tsp salt
- 3 Tbsp butter
- 1 large egg
- 4 cups bread flour
- ¼ cup brown sugar, packed
- 1¼ tsp cinnamon
- ½ tsp baking soda
- 2 tsp active dry yeast
- ½ cup chopped walnuts
- ½ cup chopped dried cranberries

Directions:
Add each ingredient to the bread machine in the order and at the temperature recommended by your bread machine manufacturer. Close the lid, select the basic bread, medium crust setting on your bread machine, and

press start. When the bread machine has finished baking, remove the bread and put it on a cooling rack.

58. Garlic Cheese Pull-apart Rolls

Servings: 12 - 24   Cooking Time: 3 Hours
Ingredients:
- 1 cup water
- 3 cups bread flour
- 1 1/2 teaspoons salt
- 1-1/2 tablespoons butter
- 3 tablespoons sugar
- 2 tablespoons nonfat dry milk powder
- 2 teaspoons yeast
- For the topping:
- 1/4 cup butter, melted
- 1 garlic clove, crushed
- 2 tablespoons parmesan cheese, plus more if needed
- Flour, for surface

Directions:
Place first 6 ingredients in bread maker pan in order listed. Make a well in the flour; pour the yeast into the hole. Select Dough cycle, press Start. Turn finished dough onto a floured countertop. Gently roll and stretch dough into a 24-inch rope. Grease a 13-by-9-inch baking sheet. Divide dough into 24 pieces with a sharp knife and shape into balls; place on prepared pan. Combine butter and garlic in a small mixing bowl and pour over rolls. Sprinkle rolls evenly with parmesan cheese. Cover and let rise for 30-45 minutes until doubled. Bake at 375°F for 10 to 15 minutes or until golden brown. Remove from oven, pull apart, and serve warm.
Nutrition Info: Calories: 109, Sodium: 210 mg, Dietary Fiber: 0.6 g, Fat: 3.5 g, Carbs: 16.7 g, Protein: 2.6 g.

59. 100% Whole Wheat Bread

Servings: 1 Loaf
Ingredients:
- 16 slice bread (2 pounds)
- 1¼ cups lukewarm water
- 2 tablespoons vegetable oil or olive oil
- ¼ cup honey or maple syrup
- 1½ teaspoons table salt
- 3½ cups whole wheat flour
- ¼ cup sesame, sunflower, or flax seeds (optional)
- 1½ teaspoons bread machine yeast
- 12 slice bread (1½ pounds)
- 1 cup lukewarm water
- 1½ tablespoons vegetable oil or olive oil
- 3 tablespoons honey or maple syrup
- 1 teaspoon table salt
- 2 ⅔ cups whole wheat flour
- 3 tablespoons sesame, sunflower, or flax seeds (optional)
- 1 teaspoon bread machine yeast

Directions:

Choose the size of loaf you would like to make and measure your ingredients. Add the ingredients to the bread pan in the order listed above. Place the pan in the bread machine and close the lid. Turn on the bread maker. Select the Whole Wheat/Wholegrain setting, then the loaf size, and finally the crust color. Start the cycle. When the cycle is finished, and the bread is baked, carefully remove the pan from the machine. Use a potholder as the handle will be very hot. Let rest for a few minutes. Remove the bread from the pan and allow to cool on a wire rack for at least 10 minutes before slicing.
Nutrition Info:(Per Serving):Calories 147, fat 5.8 g, carbs 22.1 g, sodium 138 mg, protein 3.4 g

60. White Bread

Servings: 8   Cooking Time: 3 Hours And 25 Minutes
Ingredients:
- Water - ¾ cup
- Melted butter - 1 tbsp., cooled
- Sugar - 1 tbsp.
- Salt - ¾ tsp.
- Skim milk powder - 2 tbsp.
- White bread flour - 2 cups
- Bread machine or instant yeast - ¾ tsp.

Directions:
Add the ingredients according to the manufacturer's recommendation. Press Basic/White bread. Choose Light or Medium crust, then press Start. When done, remove the bucket from the machine. Cool for 5 minutes. Remove the bread from the bucket. Slice and serve.
Nutrition Info:(Per Serving): Calories: 140; Total Fat: 2 g; Saturated Fat: 1 g; Carbohydrates: 27 g; Cholesterol: 10 mg; Fiber: 1 g; Calcium: 7 mg; Sodium: 215 mg; Protein: 4 g

61. Apple Pecan Cinnamon Rolls

Servings: 12 Rolls   Cooking Time: 3 H.
Ingredients:
- 1 cup warm milk (70°F to 80°F)
- 2 large eggs
- ⅓ cup butter, melted
- ½ cup sugar
- 1 tsp salt
- 4½ cups bread flour
- 2½ tsp bread machine yeast
- For the filling:
- 3 Tbsp butter, melted
- 1 cup finely chopped peeled apples
- ¾ cup packed brown sugar
- ⅓ cup chopped pecans
- 2½ tsp ground cinnamon
- For the icing:
- 1½ cup confectioners sugar
- ⅜ cup cream cheese, softened
- ¼ cup butter, softened
- ½ tsp vanilla extract

- ⅛ tsp salt drained

Directions:

Add each ingredient for the dough to the bread machine in order stipulated by the manufacturer.   Set to dough cycle and press start.   When cycle has completed, place the dough onto a well-floured surface. Roll it into a rectangle. Brush it with butter.   Mix the brown sugar, apples, pecans, and cinnamon in a bowl. Spread over the dough evenly.   Beginning from the long side, roll the dough. Cut it into 1¾-inch slices.   Transfer them onto a greased baking dish. Cover and let rise for 30 minutes. Bake at 325°F in a preheated oven for 25-30 minutes. Meanwhile, mix all the icing ingredients in a bowl. Take out the rolls and let them cool   Cover warm rolls with the glaze and serve.

62. Texas Roadhouse Rolls

Servings: 18 Rolls   Cooking Time: 20 Min.

Ingredients:
- ¼ cup warm water (80°F - 90°F
- 1 cup warm milk (80°F -90°F)
- 1 tsp salt
- 1½ Tbsp butter + more for brushing
- 1 egg
- ¼ cup sugar
- 3½ cups unbleached bread flour
- 1 envelope dry active yeast
- For Texas roadhouse cinnamon butter:
- ½ cup sweet, creamy salted butter, softened
- ⅓ cup confectioners' sugar
- 1 tsp ground cinnamon

Directions:

Add each ingredient to the bread machine in the order and at the temperature recommended by your bread machine manufacturer.   Select the dough cycle and press start.   Once cycle is done, transfer your dough onto a lightly floured surface.   Roll out the rectangle, fold it in half. Let it rest for 15 minutes.   Cut the roll into 18 squares. Transfer them onto a baking sheet. Bake at 350°F in a preheated oven for 10-15 minutes. Remove dough from the oven and brush the top with butter.   Beat the softened butter with a mixer to make it fluffy. Gradually add the sugar and cinnamon while blending. Mix well.   Take out the rolls, let them cool for 2-3 minutes.   Spread them with cinnamon butter on the top while they are warm.

63. Garlic Pepperoni Bread

Servings: 14 Slices   Cooking Time: 3 H.

Ingredients:
- 1 cup water
- ¼ cup light olive oil
- 3 cups bread flour
- 1 Tbsp sugar
- 1 tsp salt
- ½-1 tsp garlic powder
- ½-1 Tbsp minced dried onions
- 1 tsp dried basil

- ¼ cup shredded mozzarella cheese
- ⅓ cup grated parmesan cheese
- ¼ cup pepperoni slice, chopped
- 2 tsp bread machine yeast

Directions:

Add each ingredient to the bread machine in the order and at the temperature recommended by your bread machine manufacturer.   Close the lid, select the basic bread, medium crust setting on your bread machine, and press start.   When the bread machine has finished baking, remove the bread and put it on a cooling rack.

64. Chocolate Chip Bread

Servings: 14 Slices   Cooking Time: 3 H.

Ingredients:
- ¼ cup water
- 1 cup milk
- 1 egg
- 3 cups bread flour
- 3 Tbsp brown sugar
- 2 Tbsp white sugar
- 1 tsp salt
- 1 tsp ground cinnamon
- 1½ tsp active dry yeast
- 2 Tbsp margarine, softened
- ¾ cup semisweet chocolate chips

Directions:

Add each ingredient except the chocolate chips to the bread machine in the order and at the temperature recommended by your bread machine manufacturer. Close the lid, select the sweet loaf, low crust setting on your bread machine, and press start.   Add the chocolate chips about 5 minutes before the kneading cycle has finished.   When the bread machine has finished baking, remove the bread and put it on a cooling rack.

65. Apple Raisin Nut Cake

Servings: 10   Cooking Time: 45 Minutes

Ingredients:
- 2 large eggs, lightly beaten
- 1/4 cup milk
- 1/3 cup butter, melted
- 1 1/2 cups all-purpose flour
- 3 teaspoons baking powder
- 1/4 cup sugar
- 1/4 teaspoon salt
- 1 teaspoon cinnamon
- 1 teaspoon pure vanilla extract
- Add after the kneading process:
- 1 small apple, peeled and roughly chopped
- 1/4 cup raisins
- 1/4 cup walnuts, chopped
- 1 teaspoon all-purpose flour

Directions:

Add ingredients in the order listed above.   Press Sweet cycle, light color crust, and Start.   Mix apples, raisins, walnuts, and flour together in a small mixing bowl. Add

to dough after the kneading process.   Allow to cool on a cooling rack for 15 minutes before serving.
Nutrition Info: Calories: 204, Sodium: 121 mg, Dietary Fiber: 1.5 g, Fat: 9.4 g, Carbs: 26.9 g, Protein: 4.4 g.

66. 10 Minute Rosemary Bread

Servings: 12   Cooking Time: 2 Hours
Ingredients:
- 1 cup warm water, about 105°F
- 2 tablespoons butter, softened
- 1 egg
- 3 cups all-purpose flour
- 1/4 cup whole wheat flour
- 1/3 cup sugar
- 1 teaspoon salt
- 3 teaspoons bread maker yeast
- 2 tablespoons rosemary, freshly chopped
- For the topping:
- 1 egg, room temperature
- 1 teaspoon milk, room temperature
- Garlic powder
- Sea salt

Directions:
Place all of the ingredients in the bread maker pan in the order listed above.   Select Dough cycle.   When dough is kneaded, place on parchment paper on a flat surface and roll into two loaves; set aside and allow to rise for 30 minutes.   Preheat a pizza stone in an oven on 375°F for 30 minutes.   For the topping, add the egg and milk to a small mixing bowl and whisk to create an egg wash. Baste the formed loaves and sprinkle evenly with garlic powder and sea salt.   Allow to rise for 40 minutes, lightly covered, in a warm area.   Bake for 15 to 18 minutes or until golden brown. Serve warm.
Nutrition Info: Calories: 176, Sodium: 220 mg, Dietary Fiber: 1.5 g, Fat: 3.1 g, Carbs: 32 g, Protein: 5 g.

67. Citrus And Walnut Bread

Servings: 14 Slices   Cooking Time: 3 H.
Ingredients:
- ¾ cup lemon yogurt
- ½ cup orange juice
- 5 tsp caster sugar
- 1 tsp salt
- 2.5 Tbsp butter
- 2 cups unbleached white bread flour
- 1½ tsp easy blend dried yeast
- ⅓ cup chopped walnuts
- 2 tsp grated lemon rind
- 2 tsp grated orange rind

Directions:
Add each ingredient except the walnuts and orange and lemon rind to the bread machine one by one, as per the manufacturer's instructions.   Close the lid, select the basic bread, medium crust setting on your bread machine, and press start.   Add the walnuts, and orange and lemon rind during the 2nd kneading cycle:

When the bread machine has finished baking, remove the bread and put it on a cooling rack.

68. Garlic Basil Knots

Servings: 10   Cooking Time: 1 Hour 45 Minutes
Ingredients:
- 1 cup water
- 2 tablespoons butter, softened
- 1 egg, room temperature
- 3 1/4 cups all-purpose flour
- 1/4 cup sugar
- 1 teaspoon salt
- 3 teaspoons regular active dry yeast
- For the topping:
- 2 tablespoons butter, melted
- 2 cloves garlic, minced
- 3 fresh basil leaves, chopped fine
- Flour, for surface

Directions:
Add all dough ingredients in the bread machine in the order listed.   Select the Dough cycle and press Start. Place parchment paper on a baking sheet and coat with cooking spray.   Flatten the dough onto a well-floured surface and cut into strips using a pizza cutter.   Tie each strip into a knot, making sure to keep them well-floured so they don't stick together. Place knots on the baking sheet and cover with a cloth; set in a warm place to rise for 30 minutes.   Preheat oven to 400°F and bake 9 to 12 minutes or until golden brown.   Serve warm!
Nutrition Info: Calories: 218, Sodium: 274 mg, Dietary Fiber: 1.4 g, Fat: 5.5 g, Carbs: 36.7 g, Protein: 5.3 g.

69. Buttermilk Bread

Servings: 1 Loaf
Ingredients:
- 16 slice bread (2 pounds)
- 1¼ cups lukewarm buttermilk
- 2 tablespoons unsalted butter, melted
- 2 tablespoons sugar
- 1½ teaspoons table salt
- ½ teaspoon baking powder
- 3½ cups white bread flour
- 2¼ teaspoons bread machine yeast
- 12 slice bread (1½ pounds)
- 1¼ cups lukewarm buttermilk
- 1½ tablespoons unsalted butter, melted
- 1½ tablespoons sugar
- 1⅛ teaspoons table salt
- ⅓ teaspoon baking powder
- 2⅔ cups white bread flour
- 1⅔ teaspoons bread machine yeast

Directions:
Choose the size of loaf you would like to make and measure your ingredients.   Add the ingredients to the bread pan in the order listed above.   Place the pan in the bread machine and close the lid.   Turn on the

bread maker. Select the White/Basic setting, then the loaf size, and finally the crust color. Start the cycle. When the cycle is finished and the bread is baked, carefully remove the pan from the machine. Use a potholder as the handle will be very hot. Let rest for a few minutes. Remove the bread from the pan and allow to cool on a wire rack for at least 10 minutes before slicing.
Nutrition Info:(Per Serving):Calories 132, fat 2.2 g, carbs 23.4 g, sodium 234 mg, protein 4.3 g

70. Multigrain Honey Bread

Servings: 1 Loaf
Ingredients:
- 16 slice bread (2 pounds)
- 1½ cups lukewarm water
- 2 tablespoons unsalted butter, melted
- 1 tablespoon honey
- 1 teaspoon table salt
- 1½ cups multigrain flour
- 2¾ cups white bread flour
- 2 teaspoons bread machine yeast

- 12 slice bread (1½ pounds)
- 1⅛ cups lukewarm water
- 2 tablespoons unsalted butter, melted
- 1½ tablespoons honey
- 1½ teaspoons table salt
- 1⅛ cups multigrain flour
- 2 cups white bread flour
- 1½ teaspoons bread machine yeast

Directions:
Choose the size of loaf you would like to make and measure your ingredients. Add the ingredients to the bread pan in the order listed above. Place the pan in the bread machine and close the lid. Turn on the bread maker. Select the White/Basic setting, then the loaf size, and finally the crust color. Start the cycle. When the cycle is finished and the bread is baked, carefully remove the pan from the machine. Use a potholder as the handle will be very hot. Let rest for a few minutes. Remove the bread from the pan and allow to cool on a wire rack for at least 10 minutes before slicing.
Nutrition Info:(Per Serving):Calories 144, fat 2.2 g, carbs 26.3 g, sodium 287 mg, protein 4.1 g

Basic Bread

71. Banana Lemon Loaf

Servings: 1 Loaf (16 Slices)   Cooking Time: 1 Hour And 30 Minutes

Ingredients:
- 2 cups all-purpose flour
- 1 cup bananas, very ripe and mashed
- 1 cup walnuts, chopped
- 1 cup of sugar
- One tablespoon baking powder
- One teaspoon lemon peel, grated
- ½ teaspoon salt
- Two eggs
- ½ cup of vegetable oil
- Two tablespoons lemon juice

Directions:
Put all ingredients into a pan in this order: bananas, wet ingredients, and then dry ingredients. Press the "Quick" or "Cake" setting of your bread machine. Allow the cycles to be completed. Take out the pan from the machine. The cooldown for 10 minutes before slicing the bread enjoy.

Nutrition Info: Calories: 120;Carbohydrates: 15g;Fat: 6g;Protein: 2g

72. Zero-fat Carrot And Pinapple Loaf

Servings: 1 Loaf   Cooking Time: 1 Hour And 30 Minutes

Ingredients:
- 2 ½ cups all-purpose flour
- ¾ cup of sugar
- ½ cup pineapples, crushed
- ½ cup carrots, grated
- ½ cup raisins
- Two teaspoons baking powder
- ½ teaspoon ground cinnamon
- ½ teaspoon salt
- ¼ teaspoon allspice
- ¼ teaspoon nutmeg
- ½ cup applesauce
- One tablespoon molasses

Directions:
Put first the wet ingredients into the bread pan before the dry ingredients. Press the "Quick" or "Cake" mode of your bread machine. Allow the machine to complete all cycles. Take out the pan from the machine, but wait for another 10 minutes before transferring the bread into a wire rack. Cooldown the bread before slicing.

Nutrition Info: Calories: 70;Carbohydrates: 16g;Fat: 0g;Protein: 1g

73. Anadama Bread

Servings: 2 Loaves   Cooking Time: 45 Minutes

Ingredients:
- 1/2 cup sunflower seeds
- Two teaspoons bread machine yeast
- 4 1/2 cups bread flour
- 3/4 cup yellow cornmeal
- Two tablespoons unsalted butter, cubed
- 1 1/2 teaspoon salt
- 1/4 cup dry skim milk powder
- 1/4 cup molasses
- 1 1/2 cups water, with a temperature of 80 to 90 degrees F (26 to 32 degrees C)

Directions:
Put all the pan's ingredients, except the sunflower seeds, in this order: water, molasses, milk, salt, butter, cornmeal, flour, and yeast. Put the pan in the machine and cover the lid. Put the sunflower seeds in the fruit and nut dispenser. Turn the machine on and choose the basic setting and your desired colour of the crust—press start.

Nutrition Info: Calories: 130 calories;Total Carbohydrate: 25 g ;Total Fat: 2 g ;Protein: 3 g

74. Dark Rye Bread

Servings: 1 Loaf   Cooking Time: 10 Minutes

Ingredients:
- 12 slice bread (1½ pounds)
- 1 cup water, at 80°F to 90°F
- 1½ tablespoons melted butter, cooled
- 1½ tablespoons unsalted butter, melted
- ⅓ cup molasses
- ⅓ teaspoon salt
- 1½ tablespoons unsweetened cocoa powder
- Pinch ground nutmeg
- ¾ cup rye flour
- 2 cups white bread flour
- 1⅔ teaspoons bread machine or instant yeast

Directions:
Preparing the Ingredients. Place the ingredients in your bread machine as recommended by the manufacturer. Select the Bake cycle Turn on the bread maker. Select the White / Basic setting, then select the dough size and crust color. Press start to start the cycle. When this is done, and the bread is baked, remove the pan from the machine. Let stand a few minutes. Remove the bread from the pan and leave it on a wire rack to cool for at least 10 minutes. Slice and serve.

75. Anadama White Bread

Servings: 14 Slices   Cooking Time: 3 H.

Ingredients:
- 1⅛ cups water (110°F/43°C)
- ⅓ cup molasses
- 1½ Tbsp butter at room temperature
- 1 tsp salt
- ⅓ cup yellow cornmeal
- 3½ cups bread flour
- 2½ tsp bread machine yeast

Directions:
Add each ingredient to the bread machine in the order and at the temperature recommended by your bread

machine manufacturer. Close the lid, select the basic bread, low crust setting on your bread machine, and press start. When the bread machine has finished baking, remove the bread and put it on a cooling rack.

76. Apricot Oat

Servings: 1 Loaf   Cooking Time: 25 Minutes
Ingredients:
- 4 1/4 cups bread flour
- 2/3 cup rolled oats
- One tablespoon white sugar
- Two teaspoons active dry yeast
- 1 1/2 teaspoons salt
- One teaspoon ground cinnamon
- Two tablespoons butter cut up
- 1 2/3 cups orange juice
- 1/2 cup diced dried apricots
- Two tablespoons honey, warmed

Directions:
Into the bread machine's pan, put the bread ingredients in the order suggested by the manufacturer. Then pout in dried apricots before the knead cycle completes. Immediately remove bread from a machine when it's done and then glaze with warmed honey. Let to cool thoroughly before serving.
Nutrition Info: Calories: 80 calories;Total Carbohydrate: 14.4 g ;Cholesterol: 5 mg ;Total Fat: 2.3 g ;Protein: 1.3 g ;Sodium: 306 mg

77. Vegan Cinnamon Raisin Bread

Servings: 1 Loaf   Cooking Time: 3 Hours
Ingredients:
- Two ¼ cups oat flour
- ¾ cup raisins
- ½ cup almond flour
- ¼ cup of coconut sugar
- 2 ½ teaspoons cinnamon
- One teaspoon baking powder
- ½ teaspoon baking soda
- ¼ teaspoon salt
- ¾ cup of water
- ½ cup of soy milk
- ¼ cup maple syrup
- Three tablespoons coconut oil
- One teaspoon vanilla extract

Directions:
Put all wet ingredients first into the bread pan, followed by the dry ingredients. Set the bread machine to "Quick" or "Cake" mode. Wait until the mixing and baking cycles are done. Remove the pan from the machine. Wait for another 10 minutes before transferring the bread to a wire rack. After the bread has completely cooled down, slice it and serve.
Nutrition Info: Calories: 130;Carbohydrates: 26g;Fat: 2g;Protein: 3g

78. Golden Corn Bread

Servings: 1 Loaf   Cooking Time: 10 Minutes
Ingredients:

- 12 to 16 slices bread (1½ to 2 pounds)
- 1 cup buttermilk, at 80°F to 90°F
- ¼ cup melted butter, cooled
- 2 eggs, at room temperature
- 1⅓ cups all-purpose flour
- 1 cup cornmeal
- ¼ cup sugar
- 2¼ cups whole-wheat bread flour
- 1½ teaspoons bread machine yeast

Directions:
Preparing the Ingredients. Place the buttermilk, butter, and eggs in your in your bread machine as recommended by the manufacturer. Select the Bake cycle   Program the machine for Quick/Rapid bread and press Start. While the wet ingredients are mixing, stir together the flour, cornmeal, sugar, baking powder, and salt in a small bowl.   After the first fast mixing is done and the machine signals, add the dry ingredients. When the loaf is done, remove the bucket from the machine. Let the loaf cool for 5 minutes. Gently shake the bucket to remove the loaf, and turn it out onto a rack to cool.

79. Homemade Wonderful Bread

Servings: 2 Loaves   Cooking Time: 15 Minutes
Ingredients:
- 2 1/2 teaspoons active dry yeast
- 1/4 cup warm water
- One tablespoon white sugar
- 4 cups all-purpose flour
- 1/4 cup dry potato flakes
- 1/4 cup dry milk powder
- Two teaspoons salt
- 1/4 cup white sugar
- Two tablespoons margarine
- 1 cup of warm water(45 degrees C)

Directions:
Prepare the yeast, 1/4 cup warm water and sugar to whisk and then let it sit in 15 minutes.   Take all ingredients together with yeast mixture to put in the pan of bread machine according to the manufacturer's recommended order. Choose basic and light crust settings.
Nutrition Info: Calories: 162 calories;Total Carbohydrate: 31.6 g ;Cholesterol: < 1 mg ;Total Fat: 1.8 g ;Protein: 4.5 g

80. Whole-wheat Buttermilk Bread

Servings: 1 Loaf   Cooking Time: 10 Minutes
Ingredients:
- 12 slice bread (1½ pounds)
- ¾ cup plus 3 tablespoons buttermilk, at 80°F to 90°F
- 1½ tablespoons melted butter, cooled
- 1½ tablespoons honey
- ¾ teaspoon salt
- 1⅛ cups whole-wheat flour
- 1¾ cups plus
- 1 tablespoon white bread flour
- 1⅔ teaspoons bread machine or instant yeast

Directions:
Preparing the Ingredients. Place the ingredients in your bread machine as recommended by the manufacturer. Select the Bake cycle Close the lid. Turn on the bread maker. Select the White / Basic or Whole Wheat setting, then select the dough size and crust color. Press start to start the cycle. When this is done, and the bread is baked, remove the pan from the machine. Let stand a few minutes. Remove the bread from the pan and leave it on a wire rack to cool for at least 10 minutes. Slice and serve.

81. Pretzel Rolls

Servings: 4   Cooking Time: 3 Hours 10 Minutes
Ingredients:
- 1 cup warm water
- 1 egg white, beaten
- 2 tablespoons oil
- 3 cups all-purpose flour
- 1/2 teaspoon salt
- 1 tablespoon granulated sugar
- 1 package dry yeast
- Coarse sea salt, for topping
- 1/3 cup baking soda (for boiling process, *DO NOT PUT IN THE PRETZEL DOUGH*)
- Flour, for surface

Directions:
Place the ingredients in bread machine pan in the order listed above, reserving yeast Make a well in the center of the dry ingredients and add the yeast. Select Dough cycle and press Start. Remove the dough out onto a lightly floured surface and divide dough into four parts. Roll the four parts into balls. Place on greased cookie sheet and let rise uncovered for about 20 minutes or until puffy. In a 3-quart saucepan, combine 2 quarts of water and baking soda and bring to a boil. Preheat an oven to 425°F. Lower 2 pretzels into the saucepan and simmer for 10 seconds on each side. Lift from water with a slotted spoon and return to greased cookie sheet; repeat with remaining pretzels. Let dry briefly. Brush with egg white and sprinkle with coarse salt. Bake in preheated oven for 20 minutes or until golden brown. Let cool slightly before serving.
Nutrition Info: Calories: 422, Sodium: 547 mg, Dietary Fiber: 2.9 g, Fat: 7.8 g, Carbs: 75.3 g, Protein: 11.3 g.

82. Double-chocolate Zucchini Bread

Servings: 1 Loaf   Cooking Time: 10 Minutes
Ingredients:
- 225 grams grated zucchini
- 125 grams All-Purpose Flour Blend
- 50 grams all-natural unsweetened cocoa powder (not Dutch-process)
- 1 teaspoon xanthan gum
- ¾ teaspoon baking soda
- ¼ teaspoon baking powder
- ¼ teaspoon salt
- ½ teaspoon ground espresso
- 135 grams chocolate chips or nondairy alternative

- 100 grams cane sugar or granulated sugar
- 2 large eggs
- ¼ cup avocado oil or canola oil
- 60 grams vanilla Greek yogurt or nondairy alternative
- 1 teaspoon vanilla extract

Directions:
Preparing the Ingredients. Measure and add the ingredients to the pan in the order mentioned above. Place the pan in the bread machine and close the lid. Select the Bake cycle Turn on the bread maker. Select the White / Basic setting, then select the dough size, select light or medium crust. Press start to start the cycle. When this is done, and the bread is baked, remove the pan from the machine. Let stand a few minutes. Remove the bread from the skillet and leave it on a wire rack to cool for at least 15 minutes. Store leftovers in an airtight container at room temperature for up to 5 days, or freeze to enjoy a slice whenever you desire. Let each slice thaw naturally

83. Honey Whole-wheat Bread

Servings: 1 Loaf   Cooking Time: 10 Minutes Or Less
Ingredients:
- 12 slice bread (1½ pound)
- 1⅛ cups water, at 80°F to 90°F
- 2 tablespoons honey
- 1½ tablespoons melted butter, cooled
- ¾ teaspoon salt
- 2½ cups whole-wheat flour
- ¾ cup white bread flour
- 1 1/4 teaspoons bread machine yeast
- 1½ teaspoons bread machine or instant yeast
- 1 teaspoon bread machine or instant yeast

Directions:
Preparing the Ingredients. Choose the size of bread to prepare. Measure and add the ingredients to the pan in the order as indicated in the ingredient listing. Place the pan in the bread machine and close the lid. Select the Bake cycle Turn on the bread maker. Select the White / Basic setting, then select the dough size and crust color. Press start to start the cycle. When this is done, and the bread is baked, remove the pan from the machine. Let stand a few minutes. Remove the bread from the pan and leave it on a wire rack to cool for at least 10 minutes. Slice and serve

84. Soft White Bread

Servings: 14 Slices   Cooking Time: 3 H.
Ingredients:
- 2 cups water
- 4 tsp yeast
- 6 Tbsp sugar
- ½ cup vegetable oil
- 2 tsp salt
- 3 cups strong white flour

Directions:
Add each ingredient to the bread machine in the order and at the temperature recommended by your bread machine manufacturer. Close the lid, select the basic

bread, low crust setting on your bread machine, and press start.   When the bread machine has finished baking, remove the bread and put it on a cooling rack.

85. Brioche

Servings: 12   Cooking Time: 2 Hours
Ingredients:
- 1/4 cup milk
- 2 eggs
- 4 tablespoons butter
- 1 1/2 tablespoons vanilla sugar
- 1/4 teaspoon salt
- 2 cups flour
- 1 1/2 teaspoon yeast
- 1 egg white, for finishing

Directions:
Place wet ingredients (except egg white for finishing) into your bread machine.   Add dry ingredients, except for yeast.   Make a well inside the flour and then add the yeast into the well.   Set to Dough cycle and press Start. Remove dough, place dough on floured surface and divide into 12 equal size rolls.   Pinch walnut-sized ball of dough off each roll, making a smaller ball; make indent on top of roll and wet with milk; attach small ball to top making the traditional brioche shape.   Let rise for 30 minutes until almost double in size.   Preheat oven to 375°F.   Beat egg white, brush tops of brioche rolls, and bake at 375°F for 10 to 12 minutes, or until golden on top. Cool on rach before serving.
Nutrition Info: Calories: 180, Sodium: 120 mg, Dietary Fiber: 0.7 g, Fat: 0.9 g, Carbs: 16.9 g, Protein: 2.6 g.

86. Pumpernickel Bread 3

Servings: 12   Cooking Time: 3 Hours 30 Minutes
Ingredients:
- 1 1/4 cups lukewarm water
- 1/4 cup molasses
- 2 tablespoons unsweetened cocoa powder
- 1 teaspoon sea salt
- 1 cup whole wheat flour
- 1 cup rye flour
- 2 cups unbleached all-purpose flour
- 2 1/2 tablespoons vegetable oil
- 1 1/2 tablespoons packed brown sugar
- 1 tablespoon caraway seeds
- 2 1/2 teaspoons instant yeast

Directions:
Add all of the ingredients in the order listed above, reserving yeast.   Make a well in the center of the dry ingredients and add the yeast .   Set the bread maker on Whole Wheat cycle, select crust color, and press Start. Remove and let the loaf cool for 15 minutes before slicing. Note: all ingredients should be at room temperature before baking.
Nutrition Info: Calories: 263, Sodium: 160 mg, Dietary Fiber: 4.7 g, Fat: 3.5 g, Carbs: 50.6 g, Protein: 7.1 g.

87. Luscious White Bread

Servings: 10   Cooking Time: 2 Hours
Ingredients:
- Warm milk – 1 cup.
- Eggs – 2
- Butter – 2 ½ tbsps.
- Sugar – ¼ cup.
- Salt – ¾ tsp.
- Bread flour – 3 cups.
- Yeast – 2 ½ tsps.

Directions:
Add all ingredients to the bread machine pan according to the bread machine manufacturer instructions. Select basic bread setting then select light crust and start. Once loaf is done, remove the loaf pan from the machine. Allow it to cool for 10 minutes. Slice and serve.

88. Easy Gluten-free, Dairy-free Bread

Servings: 12   Cooking Time: 15 Minutes
Ingredients:
- 1 1/2 cups warm water
- 2 teaspoons active dry yeast
- 2 teaspoons sugar
- 2 eggs, room temperature
- 1 egg white, room temperature
- 1 1/2 tablespoons apple cider vinegar
- 4 1/2 tablespoons olive oil
- 3 1/3 cups multi-purpose gluten-free flour

Directions:
Preparing the Ingredients   Add the yeast and sugar to the warm water and stir to mix in a large mixing bowl; set aside until foamy, about 8 to 10 minutes.   Whisk the 2 eggs and 1 egg white together in a separate mixing bowl and add to baking pan of bread maker.   Add apple cider vinegar and oil to baking pan.   Add foamy yeast/water mixture to baking pan.   Add the multi-purpose gluten-free flour on top.   Select the Bake cycle   Set for Gluten-Free bread setting and Start. Remove and invert pan onto a cooling rack to remove the bread from the baking pan. Allow to cool completely before slicing to serve.

89. Whole Wheat Rolls

Servings: 12   Cooking Time: 3 Hours
Ingredients:
- 1 tablespoon sugar
- 1 teaspoon salt
- 2 3/4 cups whole wheat flour
- 2 teaspoons dry active yeast
- 1/4 cup water
- 1 egg
- 7/8 cup milk
- 1/4 cup butter

Directions:
All ingredients should be brought to room temperature before baking.   Add the wet ingredients to the bread maker pan.   Measure and add the dry ingredients (except yeast) to the pan.   Make a well in the center of the dry ingredients and add the yeast.   Carefully place

the yeast in the hole.   Select the Dough cycle, then press Start.   Divide dough into 12 portions and shape them into balls.   Preheat an oven to 350°F. Place rolls on a greased baking pan.   Bake for 25 to 30 minutes, until golden brown.   Butter and serve warm.
Nutrition Info: Calories: 147, Sodium: 236 mg, Dietary Fiber: 3.5 g, Fat: 5.1 g, Carbs: 22.1 g, Protein: 5.1 g.

90. Simple White Bread

Servings: 10   Cooking Time: 2 Hours
Ingredients:
- Lukewarm water – 1 ½ cups.
- All-purpose flour – 2 ½ cups.
- Bread flour – 1 cup.
- Baking soda – ¼ tsp.
- Yeast – 2 ½ tsps.
- Olive oil --- 1 tbsp+1 tsp.
- Sugar – 1 ½ tsps.
- Salt – 1 tsp.

Directions:
Add all ingredients to the bread machine pan according to the bread machine manufacturer instructions. Select quick bread setting then select medium crust and start. Once the loaf is done, remove the loaf pan from the machine. Allow it to cool for 10 minutes. Slice and serve.

91. The Easiest Bread Maker Bread

Servings: 12   Cooking Time: 3 Hours
Ingredients:
- 1 cup lukewarm water
- 1/3 cup lukewarm milk
- 3 tablespoons butter, unsalted
- 3 3/4 cups unbleached all-purpose flour
- 3 tablespoons sugar
- 1 1/2 teaspoons salt
- 1 1/2 teaspoons active dry yeast

Directions:
Add liquid ingredients to the bread pan.   Measure and add dry ingredients (except yeast) to the bread pan. Make a well in the center of the dry ingredients and add the yeast .   Snap the baking pan into the bread maker and close the lid.   Choose the Basic setting, preferred crust color and press Start.   When the loaf is done, remove the pan from the machine. After about 5 minutes, gently shake the pan to loosen the loaf and turn it out onto a rack to cool.   Store bread, well-wrapped, on the counter up to 4 days, or freeze for up to 3 months.
Nutrition Info: Calories: 183, Sodium: 316 mg, Dietary Fiber: 1.2 g, Fat: 3.3 g, Carbs: 33.3 g, Protein: 4.5 g.

92. Golden Raisin Bread

Servings: 1 Loaf   Cooking Time: 10 Minutes
Ingredients:
- 8 slice bread (pounds)
- ¾ cup milk, at 80°F to 90°F
- 1 tablespoon melted butter, cooled
- ¼ cup molasses
- 1 tablespoon sugar
- ¾ teaspoon salt
- 2 cups white bread flour
- 1 teaspoon bread machine or instant yeast
- ½ cup golden raisins
- 12 slice bread (1½ pounds)
- 1⅛ cups milk, at 80°F to 90°F
- 1½ tablespoons melted butter, cooled

Directions:
Preparing the Ingredients.   Place the ingredients, except the raisins, in your bread machine as recommended by the manufacturer.   Select the Bake cycle   Program the machine for Basic/White or Sweet bread, select light or medium crust, and press Start. Add the raisins at the raisin/nut signal. When the loaf is done, remove the bucket from the machine.   Let the loaf cool for 5 minutes. Gently shake the bucket to remove the loaf, and turn it out onto a rack to cool.

93. Soft Egg Bread

Servings: 1 Loaf   Cooking Time: 10 Minutes
Ingredients:
- 16 slice bread (2 pounds)
- 1 cup milk, at 80°F to 90°F
- 5 tablespoons melted butter, cooled
- 3 eggs, at room temperature
- ⅓ cup sugar
- 2 teaspoons salt
- 4 cups white bread flour
- 1 cup oat bran
- 3 cups whole-wheat bread flour
- 1½ teaspoons bread machine or instant yeast

Directions:
Preparing the Ingredients.   Place the ingredients in your bread machine as recommended by the manufacturer.   Select the Bake cycle   Turn on the bread maker. Select the White / Basic setting, then select the dough size and medium crust. Press Start.   When this is done, and the bread is baked, remove the pan from the machine. Let stand a few minutes.   Remove the bread from the pan and leave it on a wire rack to cool for at least 10 minutes. Slice and serve.

94. 50/50 Bread

Servings: 12 Slices   Cooking Time: 15 Minutes
Ingredients:
- 1 Pound loaf
- ½ cup Lukewarm water
- ½ tbsp Honey
- 1 tbsp Unsalted butter, diced
- ¾ cup Plain bread flour
- ¾ cup   Whole wheat flour
- ¾ tbsp Brown sugar
- ¾ tbsp   Powdered milk
- ¾ tsp Salt
- ½ tsp Instant dry yeast

Directions:
Preparing the Ingredients   Add the ingredients into the bread machine as per the order of the ingredients listed above or follow your bread machine's instruction

manual.   Select the Bake cycle   Select the whole-wheat setting and medium crust function.   When ready, turn the bread out onto a drying rack and allow it to cool, then serve.

95. All-purpose White Bread

Servings: 1 Loaf   Cooking Time: 40 Minutes
Ingredients:
- ¾ cup water at 80 degrees F
- One tablespoon melted butter cooled
- One tablespoon sugar
- ¾ teaspoon salt
- Two tablespoons skim milk powder
- 2 cups white bread flour
- ¾ teaspoon instant yeast

Directions:
Add all of the ingredients to your bread machine, carefully following the instructions of the manufacturer. Set the program of your bread machine to Basic/White Bread and set crust type to Medium.   Press START. Wait until the cycle completes.   Once the loaf is ready, take the bucket out and let the loaf cool for 5 minutes. Gently shake the bucket to remove the loaf.   Put to a cooling rack, slice, and serve.
Nutrition Info: Calories: 140 Cal;Fat: 2 g ;Carbohydrates:27 g ;Protein: 44 g ;Fibre: 2 g

96. Homemade Hot Dog And Hamburger Buns

Servings: 8 - 10   Cooking Time: 1 Hour 35 Minutes
Ingredients:
- 1 1/4 cups milk, slightly warmed
- 1 egg, beaten
- 2 tablespoons butter, unsalted
- 1/4 cup white sugar
- 3/4 teaspoon salt
- 3 3/4 cups bread flour
- 1 1/4 teaspoons active dry yeast
- Flour, for surface

Directions:
Place all ingredients into the pan of the bread maker in the following order, reserving yeast: milk, egg, butter, sugar, salt, flour.   Make a well in the center of the dry ingredients and add the yeast.   Select Dough cycle. When cycle is complete, turn out onto floured surface. Cut dough in half and roll each half out to a 1" thick circle. Cut each half into 6 (3 1/2") rounds with inverted glass as a cutter. (For hot dog buns, cut lengthwise into 1-inch-thick rolls, and cut a slit along the length of the bun for easier separation later.)   Place on a greased baking sheet far apart and brush with melted butter.   Cover and let rise until doubled, about one hour; preheat an oven to 350°F.   Bake for 9 minutes.   Let cool and serve with your favorite meats and toppings!
Nutrition Info: Calories: 233, Sodium: 212 mg, Dietary Fiber: 1.4 g, Fat: 3.8 g, Carbs: 42.5 g, Protein: 6.6 g.

97. Friendship Bread

Servings: 12   Cooking Time: 3 Hours 10 Minutes
Ingredients:
- 1 cup Amish Friendship Bread Starter
- 3 eggs
- 2/3 cup vegetable oil
- 1/4 cup milk
- 1 cup sugar
- 1/2 teaspoon vanilla extract
- 2 teaspoons cinnamon
- 1 1/2 teaspoons baking powder
- 1/2 teaspoon salt
- 1/2 teaspoon baking soda
- 2 cups flour
- 2 small boxes instant vanilla pudding

Directions:
Add all of the wet ingredients into the bread maker pan. Add in dry ingredients, except sugar and cinnamon. Set bread machine on Sweet cycle, light crust color and press Start.   During the last 30 minutes of baking, lift lid and quickly add 1/4 cup sugar and 1/4 teaspoon of cinnamon.   When finished baking, leave in bread machine for 20 minutes to rest.   Remove from baking pan and put loaf on a cooling rack.
Nutrition Info: Calories: 379, Sodium: 296 mg, Dietary Fiber: 1.0 g, Fat: 13.7 g, Carbs: 61.25 g, Protein: 5.3 g.

98. Peasant Bread

Servings: 12   Cooking Time: 3 Hours
Ingredients:
- 2 tablespoons full rounded yeast
- 2 cups white bread flour
- 1 1/2 tablespoons sugar
- 1 tablespoon salt
- 7/8 cup water
- For the topping:
- Olive oil
- Poppy seeds

Directions:
Add water first, then add the dry ingredients to the bread machine, reserving yeast.   Make a well in the center of the dry ingredients and add the yeast.   Choose French cycle, light crust color, and push Start.   When bread is finished, coat the top of loaf with a little olive oil and lightly sprinkle with poppy seeds.   Allow to cool slightly and serve warm with extra olive oil for dipping.
Nutrition Info: Calories: 87, Sodium: 583 mg, Dietary Fiber: 1 g, Fat: 0.3 g, Carbs: 18.2 g, Protein: 2.9 g.

99. Molasses Wheat Bread

Servings: 1 Loaf   Cooking Time: 10 Minutes Or Less
Ingredients:
- 12 slice bread (1½ pound)
- ¾ cup water, at 80°F to 90°F
- ⅓ cup milk, at 80°F
- 1 tablespoon melted butter, cooled
- 3¾ tablespoons honey
- 2 tablespoons molasses

- 2 teaspoons sugar
- 2 tablespoons skim milk powder
- ¾ teaspoon salt
- 2 teaspoons unsweetened cocoa powder
- 1¾ cups whole-wheat flour
- 1¼ cups white bread flour
- 1⅛ teaspoons bread machine yeast or instant yeast

Directions:
Preparing the Ingredients.   Choose the size of bread to prepare. Measure and add the ingredients to the pan in the order as indicated in the ingredient listing. Place the pan in the bread machine and close the lid.   Select the Bake cycle   Turn on the bread maker. Select the White / Basic setting, then select the dough size and crust color. Press start to start the cycle.   When this is done, and the bread is baked, remove the pan from the machine. Let stand a few minutes.   Remove the bread from the pan and leave it on a wire rack to cool for at least 10 minutes.   After this time, proceed to cut it.

100. Toasted Almond Whole Wheat Bread

Servings: 12   Cooking Time: 3 Hours
Ingredients:
- 1 cup, plus 2 tablespoons water
- 3 tablespoons agave nectar
- 2 tablespoons butter, unsalted
- 1 1/2 cups bread flour
- 1 1/2 cups whole wheat flour
- 1/4 cup slivered almonds, toasted
- 1 teaspoon salt
- 1 1/2 teaspoons quick active dry yeast

Directions:
Add all of the ingredients in bread machine pan in the order they appear above, reserving yeast.   Make a well in the center of the dry ingredients and add the yeast. Select the Basic cycle, light or medium crust color, and press Start.   Remove baked bread from pan and cool on a rack before slicing.
Nutrition Info: Calories: 150, Sodium: 209 mg, Dietary Fiber: 2.8 g, Fat: 3.4 g, Carbs: 26.5 g, Protein: 4.4 g.

101. Traditional Italian Bread

Servings: 1 Loaf   Cooking Time: 10 Minutes
Ingredients:
- 12 slice bread (1½ pounds)
- 1 cup water, at 80°F to 90°F
- 1½ tablespoons olive oil
- 1½ tablespoons sugar
- 1⅛ teaspoons salt
- 3 cups white bread flour
- 2⅔ cups white bread flour
- 1½ teaspoons bread machine or instant yeast

Directions:
Preparing the Ingredients.   Place the ingredients in your bread machine as recommended by the manufacturer   Select the Bake cycle   Close the lid, Turn on the bread maker. Select the White / Basic setting, then select the dough size, select light or medium crust.

Press start to start the cycle.   When this is done, and the bread is baked, remove the pan from the machine. Let stand a few minutes.   Remove the bread from the skillet and leave it on a wire rack to cool for at least 10 minutes. Slice and serve.

102. Healthy Whole Wheat Bread

Servings: 10   Cooking Time: 2 Hours
Ingredients:
- Water – 1 ½ cups+2 tbsps.
- Vegetable oil – 2 tbsps.
- Salt – 2 tsps.
- Brown sugar – 1/3 cup.
- Whole wheat flour – 4 ¼ cups.
- Milk powder – 3 tbsps.
- Active dry yeast – 2 tsps.

Directions:
Add water, oil, salt, brown sugar, whole wheat flour, and milk powder to the bread pan. Make a small hole into the flour with your finger and add yeast to the hole. Make sure yeast will not be mixed with any liquids. Select whole wheat setting then select light/medium crust and start. Once loaf is done, remove the loaf pan from the machine. Allow it to cool for 10 minutes. Slice and serve.

103. Flax Bread

Servings: 8 Pcs   Cooking Time: 18 To 20 Minutes
Ingredients:
- ¾ cup of water
- 200 g ground flax seeds
- ½ cup psyllium husk powder
- 1 Tbsp. baking powder
- Seven large egg whites
- 3 Tbsp. butter
- 2 tsp. salt
- ¼ cup granulated stevia
- One large whole egg
- 1 ½ cups whey protein isolate

Directions:
Preheat the oven to 350F.   Combine whey protein isolate, psyllium husk, baking powder, sweetener, and salt.   In another bowl, mix the water, butter, egg and egg whites.   Slowly add psyllium husk mixture to egg mixture and mix well.   Grease the pan lightly with butter and pour in the batter.   Bake in the oven until the bread is set, about 18 to 20 minutes.
Nutrition Info: Calories: 265.5; Fat: 15.68g; Carb: 1.88g; Protein: 24.34 g

104. Autumn Treasures Loaf

Servings: 1 Loaf   Cooking Time: 1 Hour And 30 Minutes
Ingredients:
- 1 cup all-purpose flour
- ½ cup dried fruit, chopped
- ¼ cup pecans, chopped
- ¼ cup of sugar
- Two tablespoons baking powder
- One teaspoon salt
- ¼ teaspoon of baking soda

- ½ teaspoon ground nutmeg
- 1 cup apple juice
- ¼ cup of vegetable oil
- Three tablespoons aquafaba
- One teaspoon of vanilla extract

Directions:
Add all wet ingredients first to the bread pan before the dry ingredients. Turn on the bread machine with the "Quick" or "Cake" setting. Wait for all cycles to be finished. Remove the bread pan from the machine. After 10 minutes, transfer the bread from the pan into a wire rack. Slice the bread only when it has completely cooled down.
Nutrition Info: Calories: 80;Carbohydrates: 12g;Fat: 3g;Protein: 1g

105. English Muffin Bread

Servings: 1 Loaf   Cooking Time: 10 Minutes
Ingredients:
- 12 slice bread (1½ pounds)
- 1¼ cups buttermilk, at 80°F to 90°F
- 1½ tablespoons melted butter, cooled
- 1½ tablespoons sugar
- 1⅛ teaspoons salt
- ⅓ teaspoon baking powder
- 2⅔ cups white bread flour
- 1⅔ teaspoons bread machine or instant yeast

Directions:
Preparing the Ingredients. Place the ingredients in your bread machine as recommended by the manufacturer Select the Bake cycle Close the lid, Turn on the bread maker. Select the White / Basic setting, then select the dough size, select light or medium crust. Press start to start the cycle. When this is done, and the bread is baked, remove the pan from the machine. Let stand a few minutes. Remove the bread from the skillet and leave it on a wire rack to cool for at least 10 minutes. Slice and serve.

106. Everyday White Bread

Servings: 8 – 16 Slices   Cooking Time: 10 Minutes
Ingredients:
- 8 slice bread (1 pound)
- ¾ cup water, at 80°F to 90°F
- 1 tablespoon melted butter, cooled
- 1 tablespoon sugar
- ¾ teaspoon salt
- 2 tablespoons skim milk powder
- 2 cups white bread flour
- ¾ teaspoon bread machine or instant yeast

Directions:
Preparing the Ingredients. Place the ingredients in your bread machine as recommended by the manufacturer. Select the Bake cycle Close the lid, Turn on the bread maker. Select the White / Basic setting, then select the dough size and crust color. Press start to start the cycle. When this is done, and the bread is baked, remove the pan from the machine. Gently shake the bucket to remove the loaf, and turn it out onto a rack to cool.

107. Perfect Sandwich Bread

Servings: 10   Cooking Time: 2 Hours
Ingredients:
- All-purpose flour – 4 cups
- Olive oil – 2 tbsps.
- Yeast – 2 tsps.
- Honey – 1 ½ tsp.
- Warm water – 1 ¾ cups
- Salt – 1 tsp

Directions:
Add water, honey, salt, olive oil, flour, and yeast into the bread machine pan. Select basic/white bread setting then select light/medium crust and start. Once loaf is done, remove the loaf pan from the machine. Allow it to cool for 5 minutes. Slice and serve.

108. Mustard Sour Cream Bread

Servings: 1 Loaf   Cooking Time: 1 Hour
Ingredients:
- 1¼ cups (320 ml) lukewarm milk
- Three tablespoons sunflower oil
- Three tablespoons sour cream
- Two tablespoons dry mustard
- One egg
- ½ sachet sugar vanilla
- 4 cups (690 g) wheat flour
- One teaspoon active dry yeast
- Two tablespoons white sugar
- Two teaspoons sea salt

Directions:
Prepare all of the ingredients for your bread and measuring means (a cup, a spoon, kitchen scales). Carefully measure the ingredients into the pan. Put all the ingredients into a bread bucket in the right order, follow your manual for the bread machine. Cover it. Select the program of your bread machine to BASIC and choose the crust colour to MEDIUM. Press START. Wait until the program completes. When done, take the bucket out and let it cool for 5-10 minutes. Shake the loaf from the pan and let cool for 30 minutes on a cooling rack. Slice, serve and enjoy the taste of fragrant homemade bread.
Nutrition Info: Calories 340;Total Fat 9.2g;Saturated Fat 1.9g;Cholesterol 26g;Sodium 614mg

109. Italian Restaurant Style Breadsticks

Servings: 12 - 16   Cooking Time: 3 Hours
Ingredients:
- 1 1/2 cups warm water
- 2 tablespoons butter, unsalted and melted
- 4 1/4 cups bread flour
- 2 tablespoons sugar
- 1 tablespoon salt
- 1 package active dry yeast
- For the topping:
- 1 stick unsalted butter, melted
- 2 teaspoons garlic powder
- 1 teaspoons salt
- 1 teaspoon parsley

Directions:
Add wet ingredients to your bread maker pan. Mix dry ingredients, except yeast, and add to pan. Make a well in the center of the dry ingredients and add the yeast. Set to Dough cycle and press Start. When the dough is done, roll out and cut into strips; keep in mind that they will double in size after they have risen, so roll them out thinner than a typical breadstick to yield room for them to grow. Place on a greased baking sheet. Cover the dough with a light towel and let sit in a warm area for 45 minutes to an hour. Preheat an oven to 400°F. Bake breadsticks for 6 to 7 minutes. Mix the melted butter, garlic powder, salt and parsley in a small mixing bowl. Brush the bread sticks with half the butter mixture; return to oven and bake for 5 to 8 additional minutes. Remove breadsticks from the oven and brush the other half of the butter mixture. Allow to cool for a few minutes before serving.

Nutrition Info: Calories: 148, Sodium: 450 mg, Dietary Fiber: 1 g, Fat: 2.5 g, Carbs: 27.3 g, Protein: 3.7 g.

110. Gluten-free White Bread

Servings: 14 Slices   Cooking Time: 3 H.
Ingredients:
- 2 eggs
- 1⅓ cups milk
- 6 Tbsp oil
- 1 tsp vinegar
- 3⅝ cups white bread flour
- 1 tsp salt
- 2 Tbsp sugar
- 2 tsp dove farm quick yeast

Directions:
Add each ingredient to the bread machine in the order and at the temperature recommended by your bread machine manufacturer. Close the lid and start the machine on the gluten free bread program, if available. Alternatively use the basic or rapid setting with a dark crust option. When the bread machine has finished baking, remove the bread and put it on a cooling rack.

111. Perfect Cocoa Bread

Servings: 10   Cooking Time: 3 Hours
Ingredients:
- Milk – 1 cup.
- Egg – 1
- Egg yolk – 1
- Olive oil – 3 tbsps.
- Vanilla extract – 1 tsp.
- Salt – 1 tsp.
- Bread flour – 3 cups.
- Brown sugar – ½ cup.
- Cocoa powder – 1/3 cup.
- Vital wheat gluten – 1 tbsp.
- Yeast – 2 ½ tsps.

Directions:
Add all ingredients into the bread machine pan. Select basic setting then select medium crust and start. Once

loaf is done, remove the loaf pan from the machine. Allow it to cool for 10 minutes. Slice and serve.

112. Slider Buns

Servings: 18   Cooking Time: 3 Hours
Ingredients:
- 1 1/4 cups milk
- 1 egg
- 2 tablespoons butter
- 3/4 teaspoon salt
- 1/4 cup white sugar
- 3 3/4 cups all-purpose flour
- 1 package active dry yeast
- Flour, for surface

Directions:
Add all ingredients to the pan of your bread maker in the order listed above. Set bread machine to Dough cycle. Once the Dough cycle is complete, roll dough out on a floured surface to about a 1-inch thickness. Cut out 18 buns with a biscuit cutter or small glass and place them on a greased baking sheet. Let buns rise about one hour or until they have doubled in size. Bake at 350°F for 10 minutes. Brush the tops of baked buns with melted butter and serve.

Nutrition Info: Calories: 130, Sodium: 118 mg, Dietary Fiber: 0.8g, Fat: 2.2 g, Carbs: 23.7 g, Protein: 3.7 g.

113. Southern Cornbread

Servings: 10   Cooking Time: 1 Hour
Ingredients:
- 2 fresh eggs, at room temperature
- 1 cup milk
- 1/4 cup butter, unsalted, at room temperature
- 3/4 cup sugar
- 1 teaspoon salt
- 2 cups unbleached all-purpose flour
- 1 cup cornmeal
- 1 tablespoon baking powder

Directions:
Add all of the ingredients to your bread maker in the order listed. Select the Quick Bread cycle, light crust color, and press Start. Allow to cool for five minutes on a wire rack and serve warm.

Nutrition Info: Calories: 258, Sodium: 295 mg, Dietary Fiber: 1.6 g, Fat: 6.7 g, Carbs: 45.4 g, Protein: 5.5 g.

114. Low-carb Multigrain Bread

Servings: 1 Loaf   Cooking Time: 1 Hour And 30 Minutes
Ingredients:
- ¾ cup whole-wheat flour
- ¼ cup cornmeal
- ¼ cup oatmeal
- Two tablespoons 7-grain cereals
- Two tablespoons baking powder
- One teaspoon salt
- ¼ teaspoon baking soda
- ¾ cup of water

- ¼ cup of vegetable oil
- ¼ cup of orange juice
- Three tablespoons aquafaba

Directions:
In the bread pan, add the wet ingredients first, then the dry ingredients. Press the "Quick" or "Cake" mode of your bread machine. Wait until all cycles are through. Remove the bread pan from the machine. Let the bread rest for 10 minutes in the pan before taking it out to cool down further. Slice the bread after an hour has passed.

Nutrition Info: Calories: 60;Carbohydrates: 9g;Fat: 2g;Protein: 1g

115. Black Forest Loaf

Servings: 1 Loaf   Cooking Time: 3 Hours

Ingredients:
- 1 ½ cups bread flour
- 1 cup whole wheat flour
- 1 cup rye flour
- Three tablespoons cocoa
- One tablespoon caraway seeds
- Two teaspoons yeast
- 1 ½ teaspoons salt
- One ¼ cups water
- 1/3 cup molasses
- 1 ½ tablespoon canola oil

Directions:
Combine the ingredients in the bread pan by putting the wet ingredients first, followed by the dry ones. Press the "Normal" or "Basic" mode and light the bread machine's crust colour setting. After the cycles are completed, take out the bread from the machine. Cooldown and then slice the bread.

Nutrition Info: Calories: 136;Carbohydrates: 27g;Fat: 2g;Protein: 3g

116. Vegan White Bread

Servings: 14 Slices   Cooking Time: 3 H.

Ingredients:
- 1⅓ cups water
- ⅓ cup plant milk (I use silk soy original)
- 1½ tsp salt
- 2 Tbsp granulated sugar
- 2 Tbsp vegetable oil
- 3½ cups all-purpose flour
- 1¾ tsp bread machine yeast

Directions:
Add each ingredient to the bread machine in the order and at the temperature recommended by your bread machine manufacturer. Close the lid, select the basic or white bread, medium crust setting on your bread machine, and press start. When the bread machine has finished baking, remove the bread and put it on a cooling rack.

117. Multigrain Olive Oil White Bread

Servings: 1 Loaf (16 Slices)   Cooking Time: 1 Hour And 30 Minutes

Ingredients:
- For the Dough
- 300 ml water
- 500 grams bakers flour
- 8 grams dried yeast
- 10 ml salt
- 5 ml caster suger
- 40 ml olive oil
- For the Seed mix
- 40 grams sunflower seeds
- 20 grams sesame seeds
- 20 grams flax seeds
- 20 grams quinoa
- 20 grams pumpkin seeds

Directions:
For the water: to 100ml of boiling water add 200ml of cold water. Add the ingredients in the order required by the manufacturer. add the seeds at the time required by your machine. Empty dough onto a floured surface and gently use your finger tips to push some of the air out of it. Shape however you like and place on or in an oiled baking tray. Sprinkle with flour or brush with egg for a glazed finish. Slash the top. Cover and rise for 30 mins. Heat oven to 240C/220C fan/gas 8. Bake for 30-35 mins until browned and crisp.

Nutrition Info: Calories 114.1;Total Fat 3.1 g;Saturated Fat 0.5 g;Polyunsaturated Fat 0.4 g;Monounsaturated Fat 1.9 g;Sodium 83.4 mg;Potassium 0.0 mg;Total Carbohydrate 19.7 g

118. Extra Buttery White Bread

Servings: 16 Slices   Cooking Time: 3 H. 10 Min.

Ingredients:
- 1⅛ cups milk
- 4 Tbsp unsalted butter
- 3 cups bread flour
- 1½ Tbsp white granulated sugar
- 1½ tsp salt
- 1½ tsp bread machine yeast

Directions:
Soften the butter in your microwave. Add each ingredient to the bread machine in the order and at the temperature recommended by your bread machine manufacturer. Close the lid, select the basic or white bread, medium crust setting on your bread machine, and press start. When the bread machine has finished baking, remove the bread and put it on a cooling rack.

119. Honey Whole-wheat Sandwich Bread

Servings: 14 Slices   Cooking Time: 3 H.

Ingredients:
- 4¼ cups whole-wheat flour
- ½ tsp salt
- 1½ cups water
- ¼ cup honey
- 2 Tbsp olive oil, or melted butter
- 2¼ tsp bread machine yeast (1 packet)

Directions:
Add each ingredient to the bread machine in the order and at the temperature recommended by your bread

machine manufacturer. Close the lid, select the whole wheat, low crust setting on your bread machine and press start. When the bread machine has finished baking, remove the bread and put it on a cooling rack.

120. Gluten-free Simple Sandwich Bread

Servings: 1 Loaf   Cooking Time: 10 Minutes
Ingredients:
- 1 1/2 cups sorghum flour
- 1 cup tapioca starch or potato starch (not potato flour)
- 1/2 cup gluten-free millet flour or gluten-free oat flour
- 2 teaspoons xanthan gum
- 1 1/4 teaspoons fine sea salt
- 2 1/2 teaspoons gluten-free yeast for bread machines
- 1 1/4 cups warm water
- 3 tablespoons extra virgin olive oil
- 1 tablespoon honey or raw agave nectar
- 1/2 teaspoon mild rice vinegar or lemon juice
- 2 organic free-range eggs, beaten

Directions:
Preparing the Ingredients   Whisk together the dry ingredients except the yeast and set aside.   Add the liquid ingredients to the bread maker pan first, then gently pour the mixed dry ingredients on top of the liquid. Make a well in the center of the dry ingredients and add the yeast.   Select the Bake cycle   Set for Rapid 1 hour 20 minutes, medium crust color, and press Start.   Transfer to a cooling rack for 15 minutes before slicing to serve.

121. Bagels

Servings: 9   Cooking Time: 1 Hour
Ingredients:
- 1 cup warm water
- 1 1/2 teaspoons salt
- 2 tablespoons sugar
- 3 cups bread flour
- 2 1/4 teaspoons active dry yeast
- 3 quarts boiling water
- 3 tablespoons white sugar
- 1 tablespoon cornmeal
- 1 egg white
- Flour, for surface

Directions:
Place in the bread machine pan in the following order: warm water, salt, sugar, and flour.   Make a well in the center of the dry ingredients and add the yeast.   Select Dough cycle and press Start.   When Dough cycle is complete, remove pan and let dough rest on a lightly floured surface. Stir 3 tablespoons of sugar into the boiling water.   Cut dough into 9 equal pieces and roll each piece into a small ball.   Flatten each ball with the palm of your hand. Poke a hole in the middle of each using your thumb. Twirl the dough on your finger to make the hole bigger, while evening out the dough around the hole.   Sprinkle an ungreased baking sheet with 1 teaspoon cornmeal. Place the bagel on the baking

sheet and repeat until all bagels are formed.   Cover the shaped bagels with a clean kitchen towel and let rise for 10 minutes.   Preheat an oven to 375°F.   Carefully transfer the bagels, one by one, to the boiling water. Boil for 1 minute, turning halfway.   Drain on a clean towel.   Arrange boiled bagels on the baking sheet.   Glaze the tops with egg white and sprinkle any toppings you desire. Bake for 20 to 25 minutes or until golden brown.   Let cool on a wire rack before serving.
Nutrition Info: Calories: 185, Sodium: 394 mg, Dietary Fiber: 1.4 g, Fat: 0.5 g, Carbs: 39.7 g, Protein: 5.2 g.

122. 100 Percent Whole-wheat Bread

Servings: 1 Loaf   Cooking Time: 10 Minutes Or Less
Ingredients:
- 12 slice bread (1½ pound)
- 1⅛ cups water, at 80°F to 90°F
- 2¼ tablespoons melted butter, cooled
- 2¼ tablespoons honey
- 1⅛ teaspoons salt
- 3 cups whole-wheat bread flour
- 2 teaspoons sugar
- 2 tablespoons skim milk powder
- ¾ teaspoon salt
- 1½ teaspoons bread machine or instant yeast

Directions:
Preparing the Ingredients.   Choose the size of bread to prepare. Measure and add the ingredients to the pan in the order as indicated in the ingredient listing. Place the pan in the bread machine and close the lid.   Select the Bake cycle   Turn on the bread maker. Select the Wheat/ Whole setting, then select the dough size and crust color. Press start to start the cycle. When this is done, and the bread is baked, remove the pan from the machine. Let stand a few minutes.   Remove the bread from the pan and leave it on a wire rack to cool for at least 10 minutes. Slice and serve.

123. Classic White Bread I

Servings: 1 Loaf   Cooking Time: 10 Minutes
Ingredients:
- 16 slice bread (2 pounds)
- 1½ cups lukewarm water
- 1 tablespoon + 1 teaspoon olive oil
- 1½ teaspoons sugar
- 1 teaspoon table salt
- ¼ teaspoon baking soda
- 2½ cups all-purpose flour
- 1 cup white bread flour
- 2½ teaspoons bread machine yeast

Directions:
Preparing the Ingredients   Choose the size of bread to prepare. Measure and add the ingredients to the pan in the order as indicated in the ingredient listing. Place the pan in the bread machine and close the lid.   Select the Bake cycle   Close the lid, Turn on the bread maker. Select the White / Basic setting, then select the dough size and crust color. Press start to start the cycle. When this is done, and the bread is baked, remove the

pan from the machine. Let stand a few minutes. Remove the bread from the pan and leave it on a wire rack to cool for at least 10 minutes. After this time, proceed to cut it

124. Mediterranean Semolina Bread

Servings: 1 Loaf (16 Slices)   Cooking Time: 30 Minutes

Ingredients:
- 1 cup lukewarm water (80 degrees F)
- One teaspoon salt
- 2½ tablespoons butter, melted
- 2½ teaspoons white sugar
- 2¼ cups all-purpose flour
- 1/3 cups semolina
- 1½ teaspoons active dry yeast

Directions:
Prepare all of the ingredients for your bread and measuring means (a cup, a spoon, kitchen scales). Carefully measure the ingredients into the pan. Put all the ingredients into a bread bucket in the right order. Follow your manual for the bread machine. Close the cover. Select your bread machine's program to ITALIAN BREAD / SANDWICH mode and choose the crust colour to MEDIUM. Press START. Wait until the program completes. When done, take the bucket out and let it cool for 5-10 minutes. Shake the loaf from the pan and let cool for 30 minutes on a cooling rack. Slice and serve.

Nutrition Info: Calories 243;Total Fat 8.1g;Saturated Fat 4.9g;Cholesterol 20g;Sodium 203mg;Total Carbohydrate 37g;Dietary Fiber 1.5g;Total Sugars 2.8g;Protein 5.3g

125. Oatmeal Walnut Bread

Servings: 1 Loaf   Cooking Time: 1 Hour And 30 Minutes

Ingredients:
- ¾ cup whole-wheat flour
- ¼ cup all-purpose flour
- ½ cup brown sugar
- 1/3 cup walnuts, chopped
- ¼ cup oatmeal
- ¼ teaspoon of baking soda
- Two tablespoons baking powder
- One teaspoon salt
- 1 cup Vegan buttermilk
- ¼ cup of vegetable oil
- Three tablespoons aquafaba

Directions:
Add into the bread pan the wet ingredients then followed by the dry ingredients. Use the "Quick" or "Cake" setting of your bread machine. Allow the cycles to be completed. Take out the pan from the machine. Wait for 10 minutes, then remove the bread from the pan. Once the bread has cooled down, slice it and serve.

Nutrition Info: Calories: 80;Carbohydrates: 11g;Fat: 3g;Protein: 2g

126. Mustard Flavoured General Bread

Servings: 2 Loaves   Cooking Time: 40 Minutes

Ingredients:
- 1¼ cups milk
- Three tablespoons sunflower milk
- Three tablespoons sour cream
- Two tablespoons dry mustard
- One whole egg beaten
- ½ sachet sugar vanilla
- 4 cups flour
- One teaspoon dry yeast
- Two tablespoons sugar
- Two teaspoons salt

Directions:
Take out the bread maker's bucket and pour in milk and sunflower oil stir and then add sour cream and beaten egg. Add flour, salt, sugar, mustard powder, vanilla sugar, and mix well. Make a small groove in the flour and sprinkle the yeast. Transfer the bucket to your bread maker and cover. Set the program of your bread machine to Basic/White Bread and set crust type to Medium. Press START. Wait until the cycle completes. Once the loaf is ready, take the bucket out and let it cool for 5 minutes. Gently shake the bucket to remove the loaf. Transfer to a cooling rack, slice, and serve.

Nutrition Info: Calories: 340 Cal;Fat: 10 g ;Carbohydrates:54 g ;Protein: 10 g ;Fibre: 1 g

127. Buttermilk White Bread

Servings: 1 Loaf   Cooking Time: 25 Minutes

Ingredients:
- 1 1/8 cups water
- Three teaspoon honey
- One tablespoon margarine
- 1 1/2 teaspoon salt
- 3 cups bread flour
- Two teaspoons active dry yeast
- Four teaspoons powdered buttermilk

Directions:
Into the bread machine's pan, place the ingredients in the order suggested by the manufacturer: select medium crust and white bread settings. You can use a few yeasts during the hot and humid months of summer.

Nutrition Info: Calories: 34 calories;Total Carbohydrate: 5.7 g ;Cholesterol: 1 mg ;Total Fat: 1 g ;Protein: 1 g ;Sodium: 313 mg

128. Country White Bread

Servings: 2 Loaves   Cooking Time: 45 Minutes

Ingredients:
- Two teaspoons active dry yeast
- 1 1/2 tablespoon sugar
- 4 cups bread flour
- 1 1/2 teaspoon salt
- One large egg
- 1 1/2 tablespoon butter
- 1 cup warm milk, with a temperature of 110 to 115 degrees F (43 to 46 degrees C)

Directions:
Put all the liquid ingredients in the pan. Add all the dry ingredients except the yeast. Use your hand to form a

hole in the middle of the dry ingredients. Put the yeast in the spot.   Secure the pan in the chamber and close the lid. Choose the basic setting and your preferred crust colour—press start.   Once done, transfer the baked bread to a wire rack. Slice once cooled.
Nutrition Info: Calories: 105 calories;Total Carbohydrate: 0 g ;Total Fat: 0 g ;Protein: 0 g

129. Buttermilk Honey Bread

Servings: 14 Slices   Cooking Time: 3 H. 35 Min.
Ingredients:
- ½ cup water
- ¾ cup buttermilk
- ¼ cup honey
- 3 Tbsp butter, softened and cut into pieces
- 3 cups bread flour
- 1½ tsp salt
- 2¼ tsp yeast (or 1 package)

Directions:
Add each ingredient to the bread machine in the order and at the temperature recommended by your bread machine manufacturer.   Close the lid, select the basic bread, medium crust setting on your bread machine and press start.   When the bread machine has finished baking, remove the bread and put it on a cooling rack.

130. Crusty French Bread

Servings: 1 Loaf   Cooking Time: 10 Minutes
Ingredients:
- 12 slice bread (1½ pound)
- 1 cup water, at 80°F to 90°F
- 1¼ tablespoons olive oil
- 2 tablespoons sugar
- 1¼ teaspoons salt
- 3 cups white bread flour
- 1¼ teaspoons bread machine or instant yeast, or flax seeds (optional)

Directions:
Preparing the Ingredients.   Place the ingredients in your bread machine as recommended by the manufacturer.   Select the Bake cycle   Program the machine for French bread, select light or medium crust, and press Start.   When this is done, and the bread is baked, remove the pan from the machine. Let stand a few minutes.   Remove the bread from the pan and leave it on a wire rack to cool for at least 10 minutes.

131. Chocolate Chip Banana Bread

Servings: 1 Loaf   Cooking Time: 10 Minutes
Ingredients:
- Shortening or gluten-free cooking spray, for preparing the pan
- 250 grams All-Purpose Flour Blend
- 1 teaspoon ground cinnamon
- 1 teaspoon xanthan gum
- 1 teaspoon baking powder
- ½ teaspoon baking soda
- ¼ teaspoon salt
- 2 large eggs
- 1 teaspoon vanilla extract

- 90 grams mini semisweet chocolate chips or nondairy alternative
- 80 grams plain Greek yogurt or nondairy alternative
- 450 grams mashed bananas (about 4 large bananas)
- 8 tablespoons (1 stick) butter or nondairy alternative
- 150 grams light brown sugar

Directions:
Preparing the Ingredients.   Measure and add the ingredients to the pan in the order mentioned above. Place the pan in the bread machine and close the lid. Select the Bake cycle   Close the lid, Turn on the bread maker. Select the White / Basic setting, then select the dough size, select light or medium crust. Press start to start the cycle.   When this is done, and the bread is baked, remove the pan from the machine. Let the bread cool in the pan for at least 20 minutes, then gently transfer it to a wire rack to cool completely

132. Rice Flour Rice Bread

Servings: 16 Slices   Cooking Time: 3 H. 15 Min.
Ingredients:
- 3 eggs
- 1½ cups water
- 3 Tbsp vegetable oil
- 1 tsp apple cider vinegar
- 2¼ tsp active dry yeast
- 3¼ cups white rice flour
- 2½ tsp xanthan gum
- 1½ tsp salt
- ½ cup dry milk powder
- 3 Tbsp white sugar

Directions:
In a medium-size bowl, mix the eggs, water, oil, and vinegar.   In a large bowl, add the yeast, salt, xanthan gum, dry milk powder, rice flour, and sugar. Mix with a whisk until incorporated.   Add each ingredient to the bread machine in the order and at the temperature recommended by your bread machine manufacturer. Close the lid, select the whole wheat, medium crust setting on your bread machine, and press start.   When the bread machine has finished baking, remove the bread and put it on a cooling rack.

133. Coconut Flour Bread

Servings: 12 Pcs   Cooking Time: 15 Minutes
Ingredients:
- 6 eggs
- 1/2 cup coconut flour
- 2 tbsp psyllium husk
- 1/4 cup olive oil
- 1 1/2 tsp salt
- 1 tbsp xanthan gum
- 1 tbsp baking powder
- 2 1/4 tsp yeast

Directions:
Use a small bowl to combine all of the dry ingredients except for the yeast.   In the bread machine pan, add all the wet ingredients.   Add all of your dry ingredients from the small mixing bowl to the bread machine pan.

Top with the yeast.   Set the machine to the basic setting.   When the bread is finished, remove the bread machine pan from the bread machine.   Let cool slightly before transferring to a cooling rack.   It can be stored for four days on the counter and up to 3 months in the freezer.

Nutrition Info: Calories: 174 ;Carbohydrates: 4g ;Protein: 7g ;Fat: 15g

134. Cracked Wheat Bread

Servings: 10   Cooking Time: 1 Hour 20 Minutes

Ingredients:
- 1 1/4 cup plus 1 tablespoon water
- 2 tablespoons vegetable oil
- 3 cups bread flour
- 3/4 cup cracked wheat
- 1 1/2 teaspoons salt
- 2 tablespoons sugar
- 2 1/4 teaspoons active dry yeast

Directions:
Bring water to a boil.   Place cracked wheat in small mixing bowl, pour water over it and stir.   Cool to 80°F. Place cracked wheat mixture into pan, followed by all ingredients (except yeast) in the order listed.   Make a well in the center of the dry ingredients and add the yeast. Select the Basic Bread cycle, medium color crust, and press Start.   Check dough consistency after 5 minutes of kneading. The dough should be a soft, tacky ball. If it is dry and stiff, add water one 1/2 tablespoon at a time until sticky. If it's too wet and sticky, add 1 tablespoon of flour at a time.   Remove bread when cycle is finished and allow to cool before serving.

Nutrition Info: Calories: 232, Sodium: 350 mg, Dietary Fiber: 3.3 g, Fat: 3.3 g, Carbs: 43.7 g, Protein: 6.3 g.

135. Italian White Bread

Servings: 14 Slices   Cooking Time: 3 H.

Ingredients:
- ¾ cup cold water
- 2 cups bread flour
- 1 Tbsp sugar
- 1 tsp salt
- 1 Tbsp olive oil
- 1 tsp active dry yeast

Directions:
Add each ingredient to the bread machine in the order and at the temperature recommended by your bread machine manufacturer.   Close the lid, select the Italian or basic bread, low crust setting on your bread machine, and press start.   When the bread machine has finished baking, remove the bread and put it on a cooling rack.

136. Orange Date Bread

Servings: 1 Loaf   Cooking Time: 1 Hour And 1 30 Minutes

Ingredients:
- 2 cups all-purpose flour
- 1 cup dates, chopped
- ¾ cup of sugar
- ½ cup walnuts, chopped
- Two tablespoons orange rind, grated

- 1 ½ teaspoons baking powder
- One teaspoon baking soda
- ½ cup of orange juice
- ½ cup of water
- One tablespoon vegetable oil
- One teaspoon vanilla extract

Directions:
Put the wet ingredients then the dry ingredients into the bread pan.   Press the "Quick" or "Cake" mode of the bread machine.   Allow all cycles to be finished. Remove the pan from the machine, but keep the bread in the pan for 10 minutes more.   Take out the bread from the pan, and let it cool down completely before slicing.

Nutrition Info: Calories: 80;Carbohydrates: 14g;Fat: 2g;Protein: 1g

137. Pumpkin Raisin Bread

Servings: 1 Loaf   Cooking Time: 1 Hour And 30 Minutes

Ingredients:
- ½ cup all-purpose flour
- ½ cup whole-wheat flour
- ½ cup pumpkin, mashed
- ½ cup raisins
- ¼ cup brown sugar
- Two tablespoons baking powder
- One teaspoon salt
- One teaspoon pumpkin pie spice
- ¼ teaspoon baking soda
- ¾ cup apple juice
- ¼ cup of vegetable oil
- Three tablespoons aquafaba

Directions:
Place all ingredients in the bread pan in this order: apple juice, pumpkin, oil, aquafaba, flour, sugar, baking powder, baking soda, salt, pumpkin pie spice, and raisins. Select the "Quick" or "Cake" mode of your bread machine. Let the machine finish all cycles.   Remove the pan from the machine.   After 10 minutes, transfer the bread to a wire rack.   Slice the bread only when it has completely cooled down.

Nutrition Info: Calories: 70;Carbohydrates: 12g;Fat: 2g;Protein: 1g

138. Whole Wheat Breakfast Bread

Servings: 14 Slices   Cooking Time: 3 H. 5 Min.

Ingredients:
- 3 cups white whole wheat flour
- ½ tsp salt
- 1 cup water
- ½ cup coconut oil, liquified
- 4 Tbsp honey
- 2½ tsp active dry yeast

Directions:
Add each ingredient to the bread machine in the order and at the temperature recommended by your bread machine manufacturer.   Close the lid, select the basic bread, medium crust setting on your bread machine and press start.   When the bread machine has finished baking, remove the bread and put it on a cooling rack.

139. Hawaiian Sandwich Bread

Servings: 14 Slices   Cooking Time: 3 H.

Ingredients:
- ¾ cup pineapple juice
- 1 egg
- 2½ Tbsp olive oil
- 4 level Tbsp sugar
- 1 tsp kosher salt
- 3 level cups bread flour
- ½ cup milk
- 2 level tsp quick rise yeast

Directions:
Add each ingredient to the bread machine in the order and at the temperature recommended by your bread machine manufacturer.   Close the lid, select the basic bread, low crust setting on your bread machine and press start.   When the bread machine has finished baking, remove the bread and put it on a cooling rack.

140. Soft Sandwich Bread

Servings: 14 Slices   Cooking Time: 3 H.

Ingredients:
- 2 Tbsp sugar
- 1 cup water
- 1 Tbsp yeast
- ¼ cup vegetable oil
- 3 cups white flour
- 2 tsp salt

Directions:
Add each ingredient to the bread machine in the order and at the temperature recommended by your bread machine manufacturer.   Close the lid, select the basic bread, low crust setting on your bread machine and press start.   When the bread machine has finished baking, remove the bread and put it on a cooling rack.

141. Almond Flour Bread

Servings: 10 Pcs   Cooking Time: 10 Minutes

Ingredients:
- Four egg whites
- Two egg yolks
- 2 cups almond flour
- 1/4 cup butter, melted
- 2 tbsp psyllium husk powder
- 1 1/2 tbsp baking powder
- 1/2 tsp xanthan gum
- Salt
- 1/2 cup + 2 tbsp warm water
- 2 1/4 tsp yeast

Directions:
Use a mixing bowl to combine all of the dry ingredients except for the yeast.   In the bread machine pan, add all the wet ingredients.   Add all of your dry ingredients from the small mixing bowl to the bread machine pan. Set the machine to the basic setting.   When the bread is finished, remove it to the machine pan from the bread machine.   Let cool slightly before transferring to a cooling rack.   It can be stored for four days on the counter and three months in the freezer.

Nutrition Info: Calories: 110 ;Carbohydrates: 2.4g ;Protein: 4g

142. Healthy Bran Bread

Servings: 1 Loaf   Cooking Time: 10 Minutes

Ingredients:
- 12 slice bread (1½ pounds)
- 1⅛ cups milk, at 80°F to 90°F
- 2¼ tablespoons melted butter, cooled
- 1½ tablespoons unsalted butter, melted
- 3 tablespoons sugar
- 1½ teaspoons salt
- ½ cup wheat bran
- 2⅔ cups white bread flour
- 1½ teaspoon bread machine or instant yeast

Directions:
Preparing the Ingredients.   Measure and add the ingredients to the pan in the order mentioned above. Place the pan in the bread machine and close the lid. Select the Bake cycle   Turn on the bread maker. Select the White / Basic or Whole Wheat setting, then select the dough size and crust color. Press start to start the cycle. When this is done, and the bread is baked, remove the pan from the machine. Let stand a few minutes. Remove the bread from the pan and leave it on a wire rack to cool for at least 10 minutes. Slice and serve.

143. Crisp White Bread

Servings: 1 Loaf (10 Slices)   Cooking Time: 1 Hour And 30 Minutes

Ingredients:
- ¾ cup lukewarm water (80 degrees F)
- One tablespoon butter, melted
- One tablespoon white sugar
- ¾ teaspoon sea salt
- Two tablespoons of milk powder
- 2 cups wheat flour
- ¾ teaspoon active dry yeast

Directions:
Prepare all of the ingredients for your bread and measuring means (a cup, a spoon, kitchen scales). Carefully measure the ingredients into the pan.   Put all the ingredients into a bread bucket in the right order, following the manual for your bread machine.   Close the cover. Select your bread machine program to BASIC / WHITE BREAD and choose the crust colour to MEDIUM.   Press START. Wait until the program completes.   When done, take the bucket out and let it cool for 5-10 minutes.   Shake the loaf from the pan and let cool for 30 minutes on a cooling rack.   Slice and serve.

Nutrition Info: Calories 113;Total Fat 1.4g;Saturated Fat 0.8g;Cholesterol 3g;Sodium 158mg;Total Carbohydrate 21.6g;Dietary Fiber 0.7g;Total Sugars 2.1g;Protein 3.3g

144. Warm Spiced Pumpkin Bread

Servings: One Loaf (12 Slices)   Cooking Time: 60 To 75 Minutes

Ingredients:
- 1½ cups pumpkin purée
- Three eggs, at room temperature
- 1/3 cup melted butter cooled
- 1 cup of sugar

- 3 cups all-purpose flour
- 1½ teaspoons baking powder
- ¾ teaspoon ground cinnamon
- ½ teaspoon baking soda
- ¼ teaspoon ground nutmeg
- ¼ teaspoon ground ginger
- ¼ teaspoon salt
- Pinch ground cloves

Directions:

Lightly grease the bread bucket with butter. Add the pumpkin, eggs, butter, and sugar. Program the machine for Quick/Rapid setting and press Start. Let the wet ingredients be mixed by the paddles until the first fast mixing cycle is finished, about 10 minutes into the process. While the wet ingredients are mixing stir together the flour, baking powder, cinnamon, baking soda, nutmeg ginger, salt, and cloves until well blended. Add the dry ingredients to the bucket when the second fast mixing cycle starts. Scrape down the sides of the bucket once after the dry ingredients are mixed into the wet. When the loaf is finished, remove the bucket from the machine. Let it cool for five minutes. Gently shake the bucket to remove the bread and turn it out onto a rack to cool.

Nutrition Info: Calories: 251;Fat: 7g ;Carbohydrates: 43g;Fibre: 2g;Sodium: 159mg;Protein: 5g

145. Honey White Bread

Servings: 1 Loaf   Cooking Time: 15 Minutes

Ingredients:
- 1 cup milk
- Three tablespoons unsalted butter, melted
- Two tablespoons honey
- 3 cups bread flour
- 3/4 teaspoon salt
- 3/4 teaspoon vitamin c powder
- 3/4 teaspoon ground ginger
- 1 1/2 teaspoons active dry yeast

Directions:

Follow the order as directed in your bread machine manual on how to assemble the ingredients. Use the setting for the Basic Bread cycle.

Nutrition Info: Calories: 172 Cal;Carbohydrates: 28.9 g;Cholesterol: 9 mg;Fat: 3.9 g;Protein: 5 g

146. Mom's White Bread

Servings: 16 Slices   Cooking Time: 3 H.

Ingredients:
- 1 cup and 3 Tbsp water
- 2 Tbsp vegetable oil
- 1½ tsp salt
- 2 Tbsp sugar
- 3¼ cups white bread flour
- 2 tsp active dry yeast

Directions:

Add each ingredient to the bread machine in the order and at the temperature recommended by your bread machine manufacturer. Close the lid, select the basic or white bread, medium crust setting on your bread machine, and press start. When the bread machine has finished baking, remove the bread and put it on a cooling rack.

147. Italian Ciabatta

Servings: 2 Loaves   Cooking Time: 25 Minutes

Ingredients:
- 1½ cups water
- 1½ teaspoons salt
- 1teaspoon white sugar
- 1tablespoon olive oil
- 3¼ cups bread flour
- 1½ teaspoons bread machine yeast

Directions:

Place the ingredients into the pan of the bread machine in the order suggested by the manufacturer. Select the Dough cycle, and Start. Carefully measure the ingredients into the pan. When the cycle is completed, the dough will be a sticky and wet. Do not add more flour. Place the dough on a generously floured board, cover with a large bowl, and let it rest for 15 minutes. Select your bread machine's program to ITALIAN BREAD / SANDWICH mode and choose the crust color to MEDIUM. Lightly flour baking sheets or line them with parchment paper. Using a knife, divide the dough into 2 pieces, and form each into a 3x14-inch oval. Place the loaves on a sheet and dust it lightly with some flour. Cover it, and let it rise in a draft-free place for approximately 45 minutes. Spritz the loaves with water. Place the loaves in the oven, positioned on the middle rack. Bake until golden brown, 25 to 30 minutes. Serve and enjoy!

Nutrition Info: Calories 73;Total Fat 0.9g;Cholesterol 0 mg;Sodium 146.3 mg;Total Carbohydrate 13.7g

148. Beer Bread

Servings: 1 Loaf   Cooking Time: 2.5-3 Hours

Ingredients:
- 3 cups bread flour
- Two tablespoons sugar
- Two ¼ teaspoons yeast
- 1 ½ teaspoons salt
- 2/3 cup beer
- 1/3 cup water
- Two tablespoons vegetable oil

Directions:

Add all ingredients into a pan in this order: water, beer, oil, salt, sugar, flour, and yeast. Start the bread machine with the "Basic" or "Normal" mode on and light to medium crust colour. Let the machine complete all cycles. Take out the pan from the machine. Transfer the beer bread into a wire rack to cool it down for about an hour. Cut into 12 slices, and serve.

Nutrition Info: Calories: 130;Carbohydrates: 25g;Fat: 1g;Protein: 4g

Spice, Nut & Herb Bread

149. Spicy Cajun Bread

Servings: 1 Loaf   Cooking Time: 10 Minutes

Ingredients:
- 12 slice bread (1½ pounds)
- 1⅛ cups water, at 80°F to 90°F
- 1½ tablespoons melted butter, cooled
- 1 tablespoon tomato paste
- 1½ tablespoons sugar
- 1½ teaspoons salt
- 3 tablespoons skim milk powder
- ¾ tablespoon Cajun seasoning
- ¼ teaspoon onion powder
- 3 cups white bread flour
- 1¼ teaspoons bread machine or instant yeast

Directions:
Preparing the Ingredients.   Choose the size of loaf of your preference and then measure the ingredients. Add all of the ingredients mentioned previously in the list. Close the lid after placing the pan in the bread machine.   Select the Bake cycle   Turn on the bread machine. Select the White/Basic setting, select the loaf size, and the crust color. Press start.   When the cycle is finished, carefully remove the pan from the bread maker and let it rest.   Remove the bread from the pan, put in a wire rack to Cool about 10 minutes. Slice

150. Rosemary Cranberry Pecan Bread

Servings: 14 Slices   Cooking Time: 3 H.

Ingredients:
- 1⅓ cups water, plus
- 2 Tbsp water
- 2 Tbsp butter
- 2 tsp salt
- 4 cups bread flour
- ¾ cup dried sweetened cranberries
- ¾ cup toasted chopped pecans
- 2 Tbsp non-fat powdered milk
- ¼ cup sugar
- 2 tsp yeast

Directions:
Add each ingredient to the bread machine in the order and at the temperature recommended by your bread machine manufacturer.   Close the lid, select the basic bread, medium crust setting on your bread machine and press start.   When the bread machine has finished baking, remove the bread and put it on a cooling rack.

151. Basic Pecan Bread

Servings: 1 Loaf

Ingredients:
- 16 slice bread (2 pounds)
- 1⅓ cups lukewarm milk
- 2⅔ tablespoons unsalted butter, melted
- 1 egg, at room temperature
- 2⅔ tablespoons sugar
- 1⅓ teaspoons table salt
- 4 cups white bread flour
- 2 teaspoons bread machine yeast
- 1⅓ cups chopped pecans, toasted
- 12 slice bread (1½ pounds)
- 1 cup lukewarm milk
- 2 tablespoons unsalted butter, melted
- 1 egg, at room temperature
- 2 tablespoons sugar
- 1 teaspoon table salt
- 3 cups white bread flour
- 1½ teaspoons bread machine yeast
- 1 cup chopped pecans, toasted

Directions:
Choose the size of loaf you would like to make and measure your ingredients.   Add all of the ingredients except for the toasted pecans to the bread pan in the order listed above.   Place the pan in the bread machine and close the lid.   Turn on the bread maker. Select the White/Basic or Fruit/Nut (if your machine has this setting) setting, then the loaf size, and finally the crust color. Start the cycle.   When the machine signals to add ingredients, add the toasted pecans. (Some machines have a fruit/nut hopper where you can add the toasted pecans when you start the machine. The machine will automatically add them to the dough during the baking process.)   When the cycle is finished and the bread is baked, carefully remove the pan from the machine. Use a potholder as the handle will be very hot. Let rest for a few minutes.   Remove the bread from the pan and allow to cool on a wire rack for at least 10 minutes before slicing.

Nutrition Info: (Per Serving): Calories 168, fat 4.8 g, carbs 25.6 g, sodium 217 mg, protein 5 g

152. Whole Wheat Raisin Bread

Servings: 10   Cooking Time: 2 Hours

Ingredients:
- Whole wheat flour – 3 ½ cups
- Dry yeast – 2 tsps.
- Eggs – 2, lightly beaten
- Butter – ¼ cup, softened
- Water – ¾ cup
- Milk – 1/3 cup
- Salt – 1 tsp.
- Sugar – 1/3 cup
- Cinnamon – 4 tsps.
- Raisins – 1 cup

Directions:
Add water, milk, butter, and eggs to the bread pan. Add remaining ingredients except for yeast to the bread pan. Make a small hole into the flour with your finger and add yeast to the hole. Make sure yeast will not be mixed with any liquids. Select whole wheat setting then select light/medium crust and start. Once loaf is done, remove the loaf pan from the machine. Allow it to cool for 10 minutes. Slice and serve.

153. Toasted Pecan Bread

Servings: 1 Loaf   Cooking Time: 10 Minutes
Ingredients:
- 12 slice bread (1½ pounds)
- 1 cup milk, at 70°F to 80°F
- 2 tablespoons melted butter, cooled
- 1 egg, at room temperature
- 2 tablespoons sugar
- 1 teaspoon salt
- 3 cups white bread flour
- 1½ teaspoons bread machine or instant yeast
- 1 cup chopped pecans, toasted

Directions:
Preparing the Ingredients.   Add each ingredient to the bread machine except the pecans and raisins in the order and at the temperature recommended by your bread machine manufacturer.   Select the Bake cycle Program the machine for Basic/White bread, select light or medium crust, and press Start.   When the machine signals, add the pecans, or put them in a nut/raisin hopper and the machine will add them automatically When the cycle is finished, carefully remove the pan from the bread maker and let it rest.   Remove the bread from the pan, put in a wire rack to Cool about 5 minutes. Slice

154. Coco-cilantro Flatbread

Servings: 6 Pcs   Cooking Time: 15 Minutes
Ingredients:
- ½ cup Coconut Flour
- 2 tbsp. Flax Meal
- ¼ tsp Baking Soda
- pinch of Salt
- 1 tbsp. Coconut Oil
- 2 tbsp. Chopped Cilantro
- 1 cup Lukewarm Water

Directions:
Whisk together the coconut flour, flax, baking soda, and salt in a bowl.   Add in the water, coconut oil, and chopped cilantro.   Knead it until everything comes together into a smooth dough.   Leave to rest for about 15 minutes.   Divide the dough into six equal-sized portions.   Roll each of it into a ball, then flatten with a rolling pin in between sheets of parchment paper. Refrigerate until ready to use.   To cook, heat in a non-stick pan for 2-3 minutes per side.
Nutrition Info: Kcal per serve 46;Fat: 4 g. (84%);Protein: 1 g. (3%);Carbs: 1 g. (13%)

155. Aromatic Lavender Bread

Servings: 1 Loaf   Cooking Time: 10 Minutes
Ingredients:
- 16 slices bread (2 pounds)
- 1½ cups milk, at 80°F to 90°F
- 2 tablespoons melted butter, cooled
- 2 tablespoons sugar
- 2 teaspoons salt
- 2 teaspoons chopped fresh lavender flowers
- 1 teaspoon lemon zest
- ½ teaspoon chopped fresh thyme
- 4 cups white bread flour
- 1½ teaspoons bread machine or instant yeast

Directions:
Preparing the Ingredients.   Choose the size of loaf of your preference and then measure the ingredients. Add all of the ingredients mentioned previously in the list. Close the lid after placing the pan in the bread machine.   Select the Bake cycle   Turn on the bread machine. Select the White/Basic setting, select the loaf size, and the crust color. Press start.   When the cycle is finished, carefully remove the pan from the bread maker and let it rest.   Remove the bread from the pan, put in a wire rack to Cool about 10 minutes. Slice

156. Onion Bacon Bread

Servings: 22 Slices   Cooking Time: 1 Hour
Ingredients:
- 1 ½ cups lukewarm water (80 degrees F)
- Two tablespoons sugar
- Three teaspoons active dry yeast
- 4 ½ cups wheat flour
- One whole egg
- Two teaspoons kosher salt
- One tablespoon olive oil
- Three small onions, chopped and lightly toasted
- 1 cup bacon, chopped

Directions:
Prepare all of the ingredients for your bread and measuring means (a cup, a spoon, kitchen scales). Carefully measure the ingredients into the pan, except the bacon and onion.   Place all of the ingredients into a bucket in the right order, following the manual for your bread machine.   Close the cover.   Select the program of your bread machine to BASIC and choose the crust colour to MEDIUM.   Press START.   After the machine beeps, add the onion and bacon.   Wait until the program completes.   When done, take the bucket out and let it cool for 5-10 minutes.   Shake the loaf from the pan and let cool for 30 minutes on a cooling rack.   Slice, serve and enjoy the taste of fragrant Homemade Bread.
Nutrition Info: Calories: 391 Cal;Fat: 9.7 g;Cholesterol: 38 g;Sodium: 960 mg;Carbohydrates: 59.9 g;Total Sugars 1.2g;Protein 3.4g;Potassium 43mg

157. Market Seed Bread

Servings: 1 Loaf   Cooking Time: 10 Minutes
Ingredients:
- 12 slice bread (1½ pounds)
- 1 cup plus 2 tablespoons milk, at 80°F to 90°F
- 1½ tablespoons melted butter, cooled
- 1½ tablespoons honey
- ¾ teaspoon salt
- 3 tablespoons flaxseed
- 3 tablespoons sesame seeds
- 1½ tablespoons poppy seeds
- 1¼ cups whole-wheat flour
- 1¾ cups white bread flour
- 1¾ teaspoons bread machine or instant yeast

Directions:
Preparing the Ingredients. Choose the size of loaf of your preference and then measure the ingredients. Add all of the ingredients mentioned previously in the list. Close the lid after placing the pan in the bread machine. Select the Bake cycle   Turn on the bread machine. Select the White/Basic setting, select the loaf size, and the crust color. Press start.   When the cycle is finished, carefully remove the pan from the bread maker and let it rest.   Remove the bread from the pan, put in a wire rack to Cool about 5 minutes. Slice

158. Pumpkin Pie Spice Bread

Servings: 12   Cooking Time: 1 Hour And 20 Minutes
Ingredients:
- Brown sugar – ½ cup
- White sugar – ½ cup
- Canned pumpkin – 1 cup
- Oil – 1/3 cup
- Vanilla – 1 tsp.
- Eggs – 2
- All-purpose flour – 1 ½ cups
- Baking powder – 2 tsp.
- Salt – ¼ tsp.
- Pumpkin pie spice – 1 ½ tsp.
- Chopped walnuts – ½ cup

Directions:
Add everything according to bread machine recommendation.   Select Quick bread cycle and Medium crust. Press Start.   Remove the bread when done.   Cool, slice, and serve.

Nutrition Info:(Per Serving): Calories: 225; Total Fat: 10 g; Saturated Fat: 1 g;   Carbohydrates: 31 g; Cholesterol: 31 mg; Fiber: 1 g; Calcium: 25 mg; Sodium: 145 mg; Protein: 4 g

159. Cardamom Honey Bread

Servings: 1 Loaf   Cooking Time: 10 Minutes
Ingredients:
- 16 slices bread (2 pounds)
- 1⅛ cups lukewarm milk
- 1 egg, at room temperature
- 2 teaspoons unsalted butter, melted
- ¼ cup honey
- 1⅓ teaspoons table salt
- 4 cups white bread flour
- 1⅓ teaspoons ground cardamom
- 1⅔ teaspoons bread machine yeast

Directions:
Preparing the Ingredients. Choose the size of loaf of your preference and then measure the ingredients. Add all of the ingredients mentioned previously in the list. Close the lid after placing the pan in the bread machine. Select the Bake cycle   Turn on the bread machine. Select the White/Basic setting, select the loaf size, and the crust color. Press start.   When the cycle is finished, carefully remove the pan from the bread maker and let it rest.   Remove the bread from the pan, put in a wire rack to Cool about 10 minutes. Slice

160. Multigrain Bread

Servings: 1 Loaf   Cooking Time: 10 Minutes
Ingredients:
- 12 slice bread (1½ pounds)
- 1 cup plus 2 tablespoons water, at 80°F to 90°F
- 2 tablespoons melted butter, cooled
- 1½ tablespoons honey
- 1½ teaspoons salt
- 1 cup plus 2 tablespoons multigrain flour
- 2 cups white bread flour
- 1½ teaspoons bread machine or active dry yeast

Directions:
Preparing the Ingredients. Choose the size of loaf of your preference and then measure the ingredients. Add all of the ingredients mentioned previously in the list. Close the lid after placing the pan in the bread machine. Select the Bake cycle   Turn on the bread machine. Select the White/Basic setting, select the loaf size, and the crust color. Press start.   When the cycle is finished, carefully remove the pan from the bread maker and let it rest.   Remove the bread from the pan, put in a wire rack to Cool about 5 minutes. Slice

161. Sunflower Bread

Servings: 1 Loaf   Cooking Time: 10 Minutes
Ingredients:
- 12 slice bread (1½ pounds)
- 1 cup water, at 80°F to 90°F
- 1 egg, at room temperature
- 3 tablespoons melted butter, cooled
- 3 tablespoons skim milk powder
- 1½ tablespoons honey
- 1½ teaspoons salt
- ¾ cup raw sunflower seeds
- 3 cups white bread flour
- 1 teaspoon bread machine or instant yeast

Directions:
Preparing the Ingredients. Choose the size of loaf of your preference and then measure the ingredients. Add all of the ingredients mentioned previously in the list. Close the lid after placing the pan in the bread machine. Select the Bake cycle   Turn on the bread machine. Select the White/Basic setting, select the loaf size, and the crust color. Press start.   When the cycle is finished, carefully remove the pan from the bread maker and let it rest.   Remove the bread from the pan, put in a wire rack to Cool about 5 minutes. Slice

162. Honeyed Bulgur Bread

Servings: 1 Loaf   Cooking Time: 10 Minutes
Ingredients:
- 12 slice bread (1½ pounds)
- ¾ cup boiling water
- 3 tablespoons bulgur wheat
- 3 tablespoons quick oats
- 2 eggs, at room temperature
- 1½ tablespoons melted butter, cooled
- 2¼ tablespoons honey
- 1 teaspoon salt

- 2¼ cups white bread flour
- 1½ teaspoons bread machine or instant yeast

Directions:
Preparing the Ingredients. Place the water, bulgur, and oats in the bucket of your bread machine for 30 minutes or until the liquid is 80°F to 90°F. Place the remaining ingredients in your bread machine as recommended by the manufacturer. Select the Bake cycle Turn on the bread machine. Select the White/Basic setting, select the loaf size, and the crust color. Press start. When the cycle is finished, carefully remove the pan from the bread maker and let it rest. Remove the bread from the pan, put in a wire rack to Cool about 5 minutes. Slice

163. Chive Bread

Servings: 14 Slices   Cooking Time: 3 H.
Ingredients:
- ⅔ cup milk (70°F to 80°F)
- ¼ cup water (70°F to 80°F)
- ¼ cup sour cream
- 2 Tbsp butter
- 1½ tsp sugar
- 1½ tsp salt
- 3 cups bread flour
- ⅛ tsp baking soda
- ¼ cup minced chives
- 2¼ tsp active dry yeast leaves

Directions:
Add each ingredient to the bread machine in the order and at the temperature recommended by your bread machine manufacturer. Close the lid, select the basic bread, medium crust setting on your bread machine and press start. When the bread machine has finished baking, remove the bread and put it on a cooling rack.

164. Toasted Hazelnut Bread

Servings: 1 Loaf   Cooking Time: 10 Minutes
Ingredients:
- 12 slice bread (1½ pounds)
- 1 cup milk, at 70°F to 80°F
- 1 egg, at room temperature
- 3¾ tablespoons melted butter, cooled
- 3 tablespoons honey
- ¾ teaspoon pure vanilla extract
- ¾ teaspoon salt
- ¾ cup finely ground toasted hazelnuts
- 3 cups white bread flour
- 1½ teaspoons bread machine or instant yeast

Directions:
Preparing the Ingredients. Choose the size of loaf of your preference and then measure the ingredients. Add all of the ingredients mentioned previously in the list. Close the lid after placing the pan in the bread machine. Select the Bake cycle Turn on the bread machine. Select the White/Basic setting, select the loaf size, and the crust color. Press start. When the cycle is finished, carefully remove the pan from the bread maker and let it rest. Remove the bread from the pan, put in a wire rack to Cool about 5 minutes. Slice

165. Double Coconut Bread

Servings: 1 Loaf   Cooking Time: 10 Minutes
Ingredients:
- 12 slice bread (1½ pounds)
- 1 cup milk, at 80°F to 90°F
- 1 egg, at room temperature
- 1½ tablespoons melted butter, cooled
- 2 teaspoons pure coconut extract
- 2½ tablespoons sugar
- ¾ teaspoon salt
- ½ cup sweetened shredded coconut
- 3 cups white bread flour
- 1½ teaspoons bread machine or instant yeast

Directions:
Preparing the Ingredients. Choose the size of loaf of your preference and then measure the ingredients. Add all of the ingredients mentioned previously in the list. Close the lid after placing the pan in the bread machine. Select the Bake cycle Program the machine for Sweet bread, select light or medium crust, and press Start. When the cycle is finished, carefully remove the pan from the bread maker and let it rest. Remove the bread from the pan, put in a wire rack to Cool about 5 minutes. Slice

166. Super Spice Bread

Servings: 1 Loaf
Ingredients:
- 16 slice bread (2 pounds)
- 1⅓ cups lukewarm milk
- 2 eggs, at room temperature
- 2 tablespoons unsalted butter, melted
- 2⅔ tablespoons honey
- 1⅓ teaspoons table salt
- 4 cups white bread flour
- 1⅓ teaspoons ground cinnamon
- ⅔ teaspoon ground cardamom
- ⅔ teaspoon ground nutmeg
- 2¼ teaspoons bread machine yeast
- 12 slice bread (1½ pounds)
- 1 cup lukewarm milk
- 2 eggs, at room temperature
- 1½ tablespoons unsalted butter, melted
- 2 tablespoons honey
- 1 teaspoon table salt
- 3 cups white bread flour
- 1 teaspoon ground cinnamon
- ½ teaspoon ground cardamom
- ½ teaspoon ground nutmeg
- 2 teaspoons bread machine yeast

Directions:
Choose the size of loaf you would like to make and measure your ingredients. Add the ingredients to the bread pan in the order listed above. Place the pan in the bread machine and close the lid. Turn on the bread maker. Select the White/Basic setting, then the loaf size, and finally the crust color. Start the cycle. When the cycle is finished and the bread is baked, carefully remove the pan from the machine. Use a potholder as the handle will be very hot. Let rest for a few

minutes.   Remove the bread from the pan and allow to cool on a wire rack for at least 10 minutes before slicing.
Nutrition Info:(Per Serving):Calories 163, fat 2.8 g, carbs 27.6 g, sodium 197 mg, protein 4.8 g

167. Raisin Seed Bread

Servings: 1 Loaf   Cooking Time: 10 Minutes
Ingredients:
- 12 slice bread (1½ pounds)
- 1 cup plus 2 tablespoons milk, at 80°F to 90°F
- 1½ tablespoons melted butter, cooled
- 1½ tablespoons honey
- ¾ teaspoon salt
- 3 tablespoons flaxseed
- 3 tablespoons sesame seeds
- 1¼ cups whole-wheat flour
- 1¾ cups white bread flour
- 1¾ teaspoons bread machine or instant yeast
- ⅓ cup raisins

Directions:
Preparing the Ingredients.   Choose the size of loaf of your preference and then measure the ingredients. Add all of the ingredients mentioned previously in the list except the raisins.   Close the lid after placing the pan in the bread machine.   Select the Bake cycle Program the machine for Basic/White bread, select light or medium crust, and press Start.   Add the raisins when the bread machine signals, or place the raisins in the raisin/nut hopper and let the machine add them. When the cycle is finished, carefully remove the pan from the bread maker and let it rest.   Remove the bread from the pan, put in a wire rack to Cool about 5 minutes. Slice

168. Nutritious 9-grain Bread

Servings: 10   Cooking Time: 2 Hours
Ingredients:
- Warm water – ¾ cup+2 tbsps.
- Whole wheat flour – 1 cup.
- Bread flour – 1 cup.
- 9-grain cereal – ½ cup., crushed
- Salt – 1 tsp.
- Butter – 1 tbsp.
- Sugar – 2 tbsps.
- Milk powder – 1 tbsp.
- Active dry yeast – 2 tsps.

Directions:
Add all ingredients into the bread machine pan. Select whole wheat setting then select light/medium crust and start. Once loaf is done, remove the loaf pan from the machine. Allow it to cool for 10 minutes. Slice and serve.

169. Parsley Cheddar Bread

Servings: 2 Pcs   Cooking Time: 4 Minutes
Ingredients:
- 1 tbsp butter
- 2 tbsp coconut flour
- One large egg
- 1 tbsp heavy whipping cream
- 2 tbsp water
- 1/4 cup cheddar cheese
- 1/8 tsp garlic powder
- 1/8 tsp onion powder
- 1/8 tsp dried parsley
- 1/8 tsp pink Himalayan salt
- 1/8 tsp black pepper
- 1/4 tsp baking powder

Directions:
Melt the butter by heating on a coffee mug for 20 seconds. Slowly stir in seasonings, baking powder, and coconut flour. Mix well using a fork until smooth.   Whisk in cream, cheese, water, and egg.   Beat well until smooth, then bake for 3 minutes in the microwave.   Allow the bread to cool, then serve.
Nutrition Info: Calories 113;Total Fat 8.4 g;Saturated Fat 12.1 g;Cholesterol 27 mg;Sodium 39 mg;Total Carbs 9.2 g;Sugar 3.1 g Fiber 4.6 g;Protein 8.1 g

170. Caramelized Onion Bread

Servings: 14 Slices   Cooking Time: 3 H. 35 Min.
Ingredients:
- ½ Tbsp butter
- ½ cup onions, sliced
- 1 cup water
- 1 Tbsp olive oil
- 3 cups Gold Medal Better for Bread flour
- 2 Tbsp sugar
- 1 tsp salt
- 1¼ tsp bread machine or quick active dry yeast

Directions:
Melt the butter over medium-low heat in a skillet. Cook the onions in the butter for 10 to 15 minutes until they are brown and caramelized - then remove from the heat.   Add each ingredient except the onions to the bread machine in the order and at the temperature recommended by your bread machine manufacturer. Close the lid, select the basic bread, medium crust setting on your bread machine and press start.   Add ½ cup of onions 5 to 10 minutes before the last kneading cycle ends.   When the bread machine has finished baking, remove the bread and put it on a cooling rack.

171. Rosemary Garlic Dinner Rolls

Servings: 10 Pcs   Cooking Time: 30 Minutes
Ingredients:
- ½ teaspoon baking powder
- 1/3 cup ground flax seed
- 1 cup mozzarella cheese, shredded
- 1 cup almond flour
- One teaspoon rosemary, minced
- A pinch of salt
- 1 oz. cream cheese
- One egg
- beaten
- One tablespoon butter
- One teaspoon garlic, minced

Directions:
Add all ingredients to the Bread Machine.   Select Dough setting. When the time is over, transfer the dough

to the floured surface. Shape it into a ball.   Roll the dough until it becomes a log and slice into six slices. Place on a greased baking sheet.   Combine rosemary, garlic, and butter in a bowl and mix—brush half of this over the biscuits.   Set the heat of the oven to 400F and bake for 15 minutes.   Brush with the remaining mixture and add salt before serving.

Nutrition Info: Calories: 168 Cal;Fat: 12.9g;Carbohydrates: 5.4g;Protein: 10.3g

172. Classic Italian Herb Bread

Servings: 10   Cooking Time: 2 Hours
Ingredients:
- Active dry yeast – ¼ oz.
- Dried Italian seasoning – 4 tsps.
- Sugar – 3 tbsps.
- All-purpose flour – 4 cups
- Olive oil – 1/3 cup
- Water – 1 1/3 cups
- Salt – 2 tsps.

Directions:
Add olive oil and water to the bread pan. Add remaining ingredients except for yeast to the bread pan. Make a small hole in the flour with your finger and add yeast to the hole. Make sure yeast will not be mixed with any liquids. Select basic setting then select light/medium crust and start. Once loaf is done, remove the loaf pan from the machine. Allow it to cool for 10 minutes. Slice and serve.

173. Turmeric Bread

Servings: 14 Slices   Cooking Time: 3 H.
Ingredients:
- 1 tsp dried yeast
- 4 cups strong white flour
- 1 tsp turmeric powder
- 2 tsp beetroot powder
- 2 Tbsp olive oil
- 1.5 tsp salt
- 1 tsp chili flakes
- 1⅜ water

Directions:
Add each ingredient to the bread machine in the order and at the temperature recommended by your bread machine manufacturer.   Close the lid, select the basic bread, medium crust setting on your bread machine and press start.   When the bread machine has finished baking, remove the bread and put it on a cooling rack.

174. Cardamom Cranberry Bread

Servings: 14 Slices   Cooking Time: 3 H.
Ingredients:
- 1¾ cups water
- 2 Tbsp brown sugar
- 1½ tsp salt
- 2 Tbsp coconut oil
- 4 cups flour
- 2 tsp cinnamon
- 2 tsp cardamom

- 1 cup dried cranberries
- 2 tsp yeast

Directions:
Add each ingredient except the dried cranberries to the bread machine in the order and at the temperature recommended by your bread machine manufacturer. Close the lid, select the basic bread, medium crust setting on your bread machine and press start.   Add the dried cranberries 5 to 10 minutes before the last kneading cycle ends.   When the bread machine has finished baking, remove the bread and put it on a cooling rack.

175. French Herb Bread

Servings: 10   Cooking Time: 3 Hours 30 Minutes
Ingredients:
- All-purpose flour – 3 cups
- Instant dry yeast – 2 ½ tsps.
- Sugar – 3 tbsps.
- Garlic powder – ½ tsp.
- Sea salt – 1 ½ tsps.
- Warm water – 1 cup.
- Dried oregano – ½ tsp.
- Dried basil – ½ tsp.
- Dried ground thyme – 1/8 tsp.
- Dried rosemary – 1 tsp.
- Olive oil – 3 tbsps.

Directions:
In a small bowl, mix together dried herbs and olive oil and set aside. Add water salt, sugar, yeast, oil herb mixture, and flour into the bread machine pan. Select French bread setting then select light crust and start. Once loaf is done, remove the loaf pan from the machine. Allow it to cool for 10 minutes. Slice and serve.

176. Cornmeal Whole Wheat Bread

Servings: 10   Cooking Time: 2 Hours
Ingredients:
- Active dry yeast – 2 ½ tsps.
- Water – 1 1/3 cups.
- Sugar – 2 tbsps.
- Egg – 1, lightly beaten
- Butter – 2 tbsps.
- Salt – 1 ½ tsps.
- Cornmeal – ¾ cup.
- Whole wheat flour – ¾ cup.
- Bread flour – 2 ¾ cups.

Directions:
Add all ingredients to the bread machine pan according to the bread machine manufacturer instructions. Select basic bread setting then select medium crust and start. Once loaf is done, remove the loaf pan from the machine. Allow it to cool for 10 minutes. Slice and serve.

177. Delicious Cranberry Bread

Servings: 10   Cooking Time: 3 Hours 27 Minutes
Ingredients:
- Warm water – 1 ½ cups
- Brown sugar – 2 tbsps.
- Salt – 1 ½ tsps.

- Olive oil – 2 tbsps.
- Flour – 4 cups
- Cinnamon – 1 ½ tsps.
- Cardamom – 1 ½ tsps.
- Dried cranberries – 1 cup
- Yeast – 2 tsps.

Directions:
Add all ingredients to the bread machine in the listed order. Select sweet bread setting then select light/medium crust and start. Once loaf is done, remove the loaf pan from the machine. Allow it to cool for 20 minutes. Slice and serve.

178. Fragrant Herb Bread

Servings: 1 Loaf   Cooking Time: 10 Minutes
Ingredients:
- 12 slices bread (1½ pounds)
- 1⅛ cups water, at 80°F to 90°F
- 1½ tablespoons melted butter, cooled
- 1½ tablespoons sugar
- 1 teaspoon salt
- 3 tablespoons skim milk powder
- 1 teaspoon dried thyme
- 1 teaspoon dried chives
- 1 teaspoon dried oregano
- 3 cups white bread flour
- 1¼ teaspoons bread machine or instant yeast

Directions:
Preparing the Ingredients.   Choose the size of loaf of your preference and then measure the ingredients. Add all of the ingredients mentioned previously in the list. Close the lid after placing the pan in the bread machine.   Select the Bake cycle   Turn on the bread machine. Select the White/Basic setting, select the loaf size, and the crust color. Press start.   When the cycle is finished, carefully remove the pan from the bread maker and let it rest.   Remove the bread from the pan, put in a wire rack to Cool about 10 minutes. Slice

179. Pistachio Cherry Bread

Servings: 1 Loaf
Ingredients:
- 16 slice bread (2 pounds)
- 1⅛ cups lukewarm water
- 1 egg, at room temperature
- ¼ cup butter, softened
- ¼ cup packed dark brown sugar
- 1½ teaspoons table salt
- 3¾ cups white bread flour
- ½ teaspoon ground nutmeg
- Dash allspice
- 2 teaspoons bread machine yeast
- 1 cup dried cherries
- ½ cup unsalted pistachios, chopped
- 12 slice bread (1½ pounds)
- ¾ cup lukewarm water
- 1 egg, at room temperature
- 3 tablespoons butter, softened
- 3 tablespoons packed dark brown sugar
- 1⅛ teaspoons table salt

- 2¾ cups white bread flour
- ½ teaspoon ground nutmeg
- Dash allspice
- 1½ teaspoons bread machine yeast
- ¾ cup dried cherries
- ⅓ cup unsalted pistachios, chopped

Directions:
Choose the size of loaf you would like to make and measure your ingredients.   Add all of the ingredients except for the pistachios and cherries to the bread pan in the order listed above.   Place the pan in the bread machine and close the lid.   Turn on the bread maker. Select the White/Basic or Fruit/Nut (if your machine has this setting) setting, then the loaf size, and finally the crust color. Start the cycle.   When the machine signals to add ingredients, add the pistachios and cherries. (Some machines have a fruit/nut hopper where you can add the pistachios and cherries when you start the machine. The machine will automatically add them to the dough during the baking process.)   When the cycle is finished and the bread is baked, carefully remove the pan from the machine. Use a potholder as the handle will be very hot. Let rest for a few minutes.   Remove the bread from the pan and allow to cool on a wire rack for at least 10 minutes before slicing.
Nutrition Info:(Per Serving):Calories 196, fat 5.3 g, carbs 27.8 g, sodium 237 mg, protein 4.4 g

180. Macadamia Bread

Servings: 8 Pcs   Cooking Time: 60 Minutes
Ingredients:
- ¼ cup almond flour
- 1 cup macadamia nuts
- Two tablespoons flax meal
- One teaspoon baking powder
- Two scoops of whey protein powder
- Four eggs
- Two egg whites
- One tablespoon lemon juice
- ¼ cup butter, melted

Directions:
Add all the ingredients to the Bread machine.   Close the lid and choose Express Bake mode. Once done, take out from the machine and cut into at least 16 slices.
Nutrition Info: Calories: 257 Cal;Fat: 22.4g ;Carbohydrates: 4.5g ;Protein: 11.5g

181. Cinnamon Milk Bread

Servings: 1 Loaf
Ingredients:
- 16 slice bread (2 pounds)
- 1⅔ cups lukewarm milk
- 1 egg, at room temperature
- ⅓ cup unsalted butter, melted
- ⅔ cup sugar
- ⅔ teaspoon table salt
- 4 cups white bread flour
- 2 teaspoons ground cinnamon
- 2¼ teaspoons bread machine yeast
- 12 slice bread (1½ pounds)

- 1 cup lukewarm milk
- 1 egg, at room temperature
- ¼ cup unsalted butter, melted
- ½ cup sugar
- ½ teaspoon table salt
- 3 cups white bread flour
- 1½ teaspoons ground cinnamon
- 2 teaspoons bread machine yeast

Directions:
Choose the size of loaf you would like to make and measure your ingredients. Add the ingredients to the bread pan in the order listed above. Place the pan in the bread machine and close the lid. Turn on the bread maker. Select the White/Basic setting, then the loaf size, and finally the crust color. Start the cycle. When the cycle is finished and the bread is baked, carefully remove the pan from the machine. Use a potholder as the handle will be very hot. Let rest for a few minutes. Remove the bread from the pan and allow to cool on a wire rack for at least 10 minutes before slicing.
Nutrition Info:(Per Serving):Calories 187, fat 5.1 g, carbs 33.4 g, sodium 143 mg, protein 4.6 g

182. Spiced Raisin Bread

Servings: 24   Cooking Time: 3 Hours And 25 Minutes
Ingredients:
- Water – 1 cup, plus 2 tbsp.
- Raisins – ¾ cup
- Butter – 2 tbsp., softened
- Brown sugar – 2 tbsp.
- Ground cinnamon – 2 tsp.
- Salt – 1 tsp.
- Ground nutmeg – ¼ tsp.
- Ground cloves – ¼ tsp.
- Orange zest – ¼ tsp., grated
- Bread flour – 3 cups
- Active dry yeast – 2 ¼ tsp.

Directions:
Put all ingredients in the bread machine pan according to its order. Select Basic cycle and choose crust. Press Start. When the bread is done, remove it. Cool, slice, and serve.
Nutrition Info:(Per Serving): Calories: 78; Total Fat: 1 g; Saturated Fat: 1 g; Carbohydrates: 4 g; Cholesterol: 3 mg; Fiber: 1 g; Calcium: 7 mg; Sodium: 106 mg; Protein: 2 g

183. Anise Honey Bread

Servings: 1 Loaf
Ingredients:
- 16 slice bread (2 pounds)
- 1 cup + 1 tablespoon lukewarm water
- 1 egg, at room temperature
- ⅓ cup butter, melted and cooled
- ⅓ cup honey
- ⅔ teaspoon table salt
- 4 cups white bread flour
- 1⅓ teaspoons anise seed
- 1⅓ teaspoons lemon zest
- 2½ teaspoons bread machine yeast

- 12 slice bread (1½ pounds)
- ¾ cup lukewarm water
- 1 egg, at room temperature
- ¼ cup butter, melted and cooled
- ¼ cup honey
- ½ teaspoon table salt
- 3 cups white bread flour
- 1 teaspoon anise seed
- 1 teaspoon lemon zest
- 2 teaspoons bread machine yeast

Directions:
Choose the size of loaf you would like to make and measure your ingredients. Add the ingredients to the bread pan in the order listed above. Place the pan in the bread machine and close the lid. Turn on the bread maker. Select the White/Basic setting, then the loaf size, and finally the crust color. Start the cycle. When the cycle is finished and the bread is baked, carefully remove the pan from the machine. Use a potholder as the handle will be very hot. Let rest for a few minutes. Remove the bread from the pan and allow to cool on a wire rack for at least 10 minutes before slicing.
Nutrition Info:(Per Serving):Calories 157, fat 4.8 g, carbs 29.6 g, sodium 134 mg, protein 4.7 g

184. Seed Bread

Servings: 1 Loaf   Cooking Time: 10 Minutes
Ingredients:
- 3 Tbsp flax seed
- 1 Tbsp sesame seeds
- 1 Tbsp poppy seeds
- ¾ cup water
- 1 Tbsp honey
- 1 Tbsp canola oil
- ½ tsp salt
- 1½ cups bread flour
- 5 Tbsp wholemeal flour
- 1¼ tsp dried active baking yeast

Directions:
Preparing the Ingredients   Add each ingredient to the bread machine in the order and at the temperature recommended by your bread machine manufacturer. Select the Bake cycle   Close the lid, select the basic bread, medium crust setting on your bread machine, and press start. When the bread machine has finished baking, remove the bread and put it on a cooling rack.

185. Hazelnut Honey Bread

Servings: 1 Loaf   Cooking Time: 10 Minutes
Ingredients:
- 16 slices bread (2 pounds)
- 1⅓ cups lukewarm milk
- 2 eggs, at room temperature
- 5 tablespoons unsalted butter, melted
- ¼ cup honey
- 1 teaspoon pure vanilla extract
- 1 teaspoon table salt
- 4 cups white bread flour
- 1 cup toasted hazelnuts, finely ground
- 2 teaspoons bread machine yeast

Directions:
Preparing the Ingredients. Choose the size of loaf of your preference and then measure the ingredients. Add all of the ingredients mentioned previously in the list. Close the lid after placing the pan in the bread machine. Select the Bake cycle Turn on the bread machine. Select the White/Basic setting, select the loaf size, and the crust color. Press start. When the cycle is finished, carefully remove the pan from the bread maker and let it rest. Remove the bread from the pan, put in a wire rack to Cool about 10 minutes. Slice

186. Flaxseed Honey Bread

Servings: 1 Loaf   Cooking Time: 10 Minutes
Ingredients:
- 12 slices bread (1½ pounds)
- 1⅛ cups milk, at 80°F to 90°F
- 1½ tablespoons melted butter, cooled
- 1½ tablespoons honey
- 1 teaspoon salt
- ¼ cup flaxseed
- 3 cups white bread flour
- 1¼ teaspoons bread machine or instant yeast

Directions:
Preparing the Ingredients. Choose the size of loaf of your preference and then measure the ingredients. Add all of the ingredients mentioned previously in the list. Close the lid after placing the pan in the bread machine. Select the Bake cycle. Turn on the bread machine. Select the White/Basic setting, select the loaf size, and the crust color. Press start. When the cycle is finished, carefully remove the pan from the bread maker and let it rest. Remove the bread from the pan, put in a wire rack to Cool about 5 minutes. Slice

187. Healthy Spelt Bread

Servings: 10   Cooking Time: 40 Minutes
Ingredients:
- Milk – 1 ¼ cups.
- Sugar – 2 tbsps.
- Olive oil – 2 tbsps.
- Salt – 1 tsp.
- Spelt flour – 4 cups.
- Yeast – 2 ½ tsps.

Directions:
Add all ingredients to the bread machine pan according to the bread machine manufacturer instructions. Select basic bread setting then select light/medium crust and start. Once loaf is done, remove the loaf pan from the machine. Allow it to cool for 10 minutes. Slice and serve.

188. Quinoa Whole-wheat Bread

Servings: 1 Loaf   Cooking Time: 10 Minutes
Ingredients:
- 12 slice bread (1½ pounds)
- 1 cup milk, at 80°F to 90°F
- ⅔ cup cooked quinoa, cooled
- ¼ cup melted butter, cooled
- 1 tablespoon sugar

- 1 teaspoon salt
- ¼ cup quick oats
- ¾ cup whole-wheat flour
- 1½ cups white bread flour
- 1½ teaspoons bread machine or instant yeast

Directions:
Preparing the Ingredients. Choose the size of loaf of your preference and then measure the ingredients. Add all of the ingredients mentioned previously in the list. Close the lid after placing the pan in the bread machine. Select the Bake cycle Turn on the bread machine. Select the White/Basic setting, select the loaf size, and the crust color. Press start. When the cycle is finished, carefully remove the pan from the bread maker and let it rest. Remove the bread from the pan, put in a wire rack to Cool about 5 minutes. Slice

189. Taco Bread

Servings: 20   Cooking Time: 3 Hours And 48 Minutes
Ingredients:
- Water - 1 ½ cup
- Bread flour – 2 2/3 cups
- Whole wheat flour – 2 cups
- Sugar – 2 tbsp.
- Taco seasoning mix – 3 tbsp.
- Salt 1 /2 tsp.
- Olive oil – 2 tbsp.
- Active dry yeast – 2 tbsp.

Directions:
Add everything according to bread machine recommendation. Select Whole wheat and Medium crust. Press Start. Remove the bread when done. Cool, slice, and serve.

Nutrition Info: (Per Serving): Calories: 127; Total Fat: 1.7 g; Saturated Fat: 0.3 g; Carbohydrates: 24.3 g; Cholesterol: 0 mg; Fiber: 0.9 g; Calcium: 5 mg; Sodium: 237 mg; Protein: 3.2 g

190. Garlic, Herb, And Cheese Bread

Servings: One Loaf (12 Slices)   Cooking Time: 15 Minutes
Ingredients:
- 1/2 cup ghee
- Six eggs
- 2 cups almond flour
- 1 tbsp baking powder
- 1/2 tsp xanthan gum
- 1 cup cheddar cheese, shredded
- 1 tbsp garlic powder
- 1 tbsp parsley
- 1/2 tbsp oregano
- 1/2 tsp salt

Directions:
Lightly beat eggs and ghee before pouring into bread machine pan. Add the remaining ingredients to the pan. Set bread machine to gluten-free. When the bread is finished, remove the bread pan from the bread machine. Let it cool for a while before transferring into a cooling rack. You can store your bread for up to 5 days in the refrigerator.

Nutrition Info: Calories: 156 ; Carbohydrates: 4g;Protein: 5g;Fat: 13g

191. Dilly Onion Bread

Servings: 14 Slices   Cooking Time: 3 H. 5 Min.
Ingredients:
- ¾ cup water (70°F to 80°F)
- 1 Tbsp butter, softened
- 2 Tbsp sugar
- 3 Tbsp dried minced onion
- 2 Tbsp dried parsley flakes
- 1 Tbsp dill weed
- 1 tsp salt
- 1 garlic clove, minced
- 2 cups bread flour
- ⅓ cup whole wheat flour
- 1 Tbsp nonfat dry milk powder
- 2 tsp active dry yeast serving

Directions:
Add each ingredient to the bread machine in the order and at the temperature recommended by your bread machine manufacturer.   Close the lid, select the basic bread, medium crust setting on your bread machine and press start.   When the bread machine has finished baking, remove the bread and put it on a cooling rack.

192. Molasses Candied-ginger Bread

Servings: 1 Loaf   Cooking Time: 10 Minutes
Ingredients:
- 12 slices bread (1½ pounds)
- 1 cup milk, at 80°F to 90°F
- 1 egg, at room temperature
- ¼ cup dark molasses
- 3 tablespoons butter, melted and cooled
- ½ teaspoon salt
- ¼ cup chopped candied ginger
- ½ cup quick oats
- 3 cups white bread flour
- 2 teaspoons bread machine or instant yeast

Directions:
Preparing the Ingredients.   Choose the size of loaf of your preference and then measure the ingredients. Add all of the ingredients mentioned previously in the list. Close the lid after placing the pan in the bread machine. Select the Bake cycle   Turn on the bread machine. Select the White/Basic setting, select the loaf size, and the crust color. Press start.   When the cycle is finished, carefully remove the pan from the bread maker and let it rest.   Remove the bread from the pan, put in a wire rack to Cool about 5 minutes. Slice

193. Sunflower & Flax Seed Bread

Servings: 10   Cooking Time: 3 Hours
Ingredients:
- Water – 1 1/3 cups.
- Butter – 2 tbsps.
- Honey – 3 tbsps.
- Bread flour – 1 ½ cups.
- Whole wheat flour – 1 1/3 cups.

- Salt – 1 tsp.
- Active dry yeast – 1 tsp.
- Flax seeds – ½ cup.
- Sunflower seeds – ½ cup.

Directions:
Add all ingredients except for sunflower seeds into the bread machine pan. Select basic setting then select light/medium crust and press start. Add sunflower seeds just before the final kneading cycle. Once loaf is done, remove the loaf pan from the machine. Allow it to cool for 10 minutes. Slice and serve.

194. Honey-spice Egg Bread

Servings: 1 Loaf   Cooking Time: 10 Minutes
Ingredients:
- 12 slices bread (1½ pounds)
- 1 cup milk, at 80°F to 90°F
- 2 eggs, at room temperature
- 1½ tablespoons melted butter, cooled
- 2 tablespoons honey
- 1 teaspoon salt
- 1 teaspoon ground cinnamon
- ½ teaspoon ground cardamom
- ½ teaspoon ground nutmeg
- 3 cups white bread flour
- 2 teaspoons bread machine or instant yeast

Directions:
Preparing the Ingredients.   Choose the size of loaf of your preference and then measure the ingredients. Add all of the ingredients mentioned previously in the list. Close the lid after placing the pan in the bread machine.   Select the Bake cycle   Turn on the bread machine. Select the White/Basic setting, select the loaf size, and the crust color. Press start.   When the cycle is finished, carefully remove the pan from the bread maker and let it rest.   Remove the bread from the pan, put in a wire rack to Cool about 10 minutes. Slice

195. Mix Seed Raisin Bread

Servings: 1 Loaf   Cooking Time: 10 Minutes
Ingredients:
- 16 slices bread (2 pounds)
- 1½ cups lukewarm milk
- 2 tablespoons unsalted butter, melted
- 2 tablespoons honey
- 1 teaspoon table salt
- 2½ cups white bread flour
- ¼ cup flaxseed
- ¼ cup sesame seeds
- 1½ cups whole-wheat flour
- 2¼ teaspoons bread machine yeast
- ½ cup raisins

Directions:
Preparing the Ingredients.   Choose the size of loaf of your preference and then measure the ingredients. Add all of the ingredients mentioned previously in the list. Close the lid after placing the pan in the bread machine.   Select the Bake cycle   Turn on the bread machine. Select the White/Basic setting, select the loaf size, and the crust color. Press start.   When the cycle is

finished, carefully remove the pan from the bread maker and let it rest. Remove the bread from the pan, put in a wire rack to Cool about 10 minutes. Slice

196. Herb And Parmesan Bread

Servings: 10   Cooking Time: 3 Hours And 25 Minutes
Ingredients:
- Lukewarm water – 1 1/3 cups
- Oil – 2 tbsp.
- Garlic – cloves, crushed
- Fresh herbs – 3 tbsp., chopped (oregano, chives, basil, and rosemary)
- Bread flour – 4 cups
- Salt – 1 tsp.
- Sugar – 1 tbsp.
- Parmesan cheese – 4 tbsp., grated
- Active dry yeast – 2 ¼ tsp.

Directions:
Add everything according to bread machine recommendations. Select Basic cycle and Medium crust. When done, remove the bread. Cool, slice, and serve.
Nutrition Info:(Per Serving): Calories: 105; Total Fat: 5 g; Saturated Fat: 1 g; Carbohydrates: 14 g; Cholesterol: 2 mg; Fiber: 2 g; Calcium: 94 mg; Sodium: 412 mg; Protein: 3 g

197. Chia Seed Bread

Servings: 14 Slices   Cooking Time: 10 Minutes
Ingredients:
- ¼ cup chia seeds
- ¾ cup hot water
- 2⅜ cups water
- ¼ cup oil
- ½ lemon, zest and juice
- 1¾ cups white flour
- 1¾ cups whole wheat flour
- 2 tsp baking powder
- 1 tsp salt
- 1 Tbsp sugar
- 2½ tsp quick rise yeast

Directions:
Preparing the Ingredients   Add the chia seeds to a bowl, cover with hot water, mix well and let them stand until they are soaked and gelatinous, and don't feel warm to touch.   Add each ingredient to the bread machine in the order and at the temperature recommended by your bread machine manufacturer.   Select the Bake cycle Close the lid, select the basic bread, medium crust setting on your bread machine, and press start.   When the mixing blade stops moving, open the machine and mix everything by hand with a spatula.   When the bread machine has finished baking, remove the bread and put it on a cooling rack.

198. Orange Almond Bacon Bread

Servings: 10 Pcs   Cooking Time: 60 Minutes
Ingredients:
- 1 ½ cups almond flour

- One tablespoon baking powder
- 7 oz bacon, diced
- Two eggs
- 1 ½ cups cheddar cheese, shredded
- Four tablespoons butter, melted
- 1/3 cup sour cream

Directions:
Add all ingredients to the bread machine. Close the lid and choose the Sweet Bread mode. After the cooking time is over, remove the machine's bread and rest for about 10 minutes. Enjoy!
Nutrition Info: Calories: 307 Cal ;Fat: 26 g ;Carbohydrate:3 g ;Protein: 14 g

199. Chocolate Mint Bread

Servings: 1 Loaf   Cooking Time: 10 Minutes
Ingredients:
- 12 slices bread (1½ pounds)
- 1 cup milk, at 80°F to 90°F
- ⅛ teaspoon mint extract
- 1½ tablespoons butter, melted and cooled
- ¼ cup sugar
- 1 teaspoon salt
- 1½ tablespoons unsweetened cocoa powder
- 3 cups white bread flour
- 1¾ teaspoons bread machine or instant yeast
- ½ cup semisweet chocolate chips

Directions:
Preparing the Ingredients.   Choose the size of loaf of your preference and then measure the ingredients. Add all of the ingredients mentioned previously in the list. Close the lid after placing the pan in the bread machine. Select the Bake cycle   Turn on the bread machine. Select the White/Basic setting, select the loaf size, and the crust color. Press start.   When the cycle is finished, carefully remove the pan from the bread maker and let it rest.   Remove the bread from the pan, put in a wire rack to Cool about 5 minutes. Slice

200. Italian Pine Nut Bread

Servings: 10   Cooking Time: 3 Hours 30 Minutes
Ingredients:
- Water – 1 cup+ 2 tbsps.
- Bread flour – 3 cups.
- Sugar – 2 tbsps.
- Salt – 1 tsp.
- Active dry yeast – 1 ¼ tsps.
- Basil pesto – 1/3 cup.
- Flour – 2 tbsps.
- Pine nuts – 1/3 cup.

Directions:
In a small bowl, mix basil pesto and flour until well blended. Add pine nuts and stir well. Add water, bread flour, sugar, salt, and yeast into the bread machine pan. Select basic setting then select medium crust and press start. Add basil pesto mixture just before the final kneading cycle. Once loaf is done, remove the loaf pan from the machine. Allow it to cool for 10 minutes. Slice and serve.

201. Anise Lemon Bread

Servings: 1 Loaf   Cooking Time: 10 Minutes

Ingredients:

- 12 slice bread (1½ pounds)
- ¾ cup water, at 80°F to 90°F
- 1 egg, at room temperature
- ¼ cup butter, melted and cooled
- ¼ cup honey
- ½ teaspoon salt
- 1 teaspoon anise seed
- 1 teaspoon lemon zest
- 3 cups white bread flour
- 2 teaspoons bread machine or instant yeast

Directions:

Preparing the Ingredients.   Choose the size of loaf of your preference and then measure the ingredients. Add all of the ingredients mentioned previously in the list. Close the lid after placing the pan in the bread machine. Select the Bake cycle   Turn on the bread machine. Select the White/Basic setting, select the loaf size, and the crust color. Press start.   When the cycle is finished, carefully remove the pan from the bread maker and let it rest.   Remove the bread from the pan, put in a wire rack to Cool about 10 minutes. Slice

202. Egg And Seed Buns

Servings: 8 Pcs   Cooking Time: 50 Minutes

Ingredients:

- Two egg whites
- 1 cup sunflower seeds, ground
- ¼ cup flax seeds, ground
- 5 Tbsp. psyllium husks
- 1 cup boiling water
- 2 tsp. baking powder
- Salt to taste

Directions:

Combine all the dry ingredients.   Add the egg whites and blend until smooth.   Add boiling water and keep whisking.   Line a baking sheet with parchment paper and drop the dough on it one spoonful at a time to form buns.   Bake at 356F for 50 minutes.   Serve.

Nutrition Info: Calories: 91 Cal;Fat: 4.2g;Carb: 12.1g;Protein: 3.3g

203. Olive Bread

Servings: 14 Slices   Cooking Time: 3 H.

Ingredients:

- ½ cup brine from olive jar
- Add warm water (110°F) To make 1½ cup when combined with brine
- 2 Tbsp olive oil
- 3 cups bread flour
- 1⅔ cups whole wheat flour
- 1½ tsp salt
- 2 Tbsp sugar
- 1½ tsp dried leaf basil
- 2 tsp active dry yeast
- ⅔ cup finely chopped Kalamata olives

Directions:

Add each ingredient except the olives to the bread machine in the order and at the temperature recommended by your bread machine manufacturer. Close the lid, select the wheat, medium crust setting on your bread machine and press start.   Add the olives 10 minutes before the last kneading cycle ends.   When the bread machine has finished baking, remove the bread and put it on a cooling rack.

204. Cinnamon Bread

Servings: 1 Loaf   Cooking Time: 10 Minutes

Ingredients:

- 12 slices bread (1½ pounds)
- 1 cup milk, at 80°F to 90°F
- 1 egg, at room temperature
- ¼ cup melted butter, cooled
- ½ cup sugar
- ½ teaspoon salt
- 1½ teaspoons ground cinnamon
- 3 cups white bread flour
- 2 teaspoons bread machine or active dry yeast

Directions:

Preparing the Ingredients.   Choose the size of loaf of your preference and then measure the ingredients. Add all of the ingredients mentioned previously in the list. Close the lid after placing the pan in the bread machine.   Select the Bake cycle   Turn on the bread machine. Select the White/Basic setting, select the loaf size, and the crust color. Press start.   When the cycle is finished, carefully remove the pan from the bread maker and let it rest.   Remove the bread from the pan, put in a wire rack to Cool about 10 minutes. Slice

205. Oatmeal Seed Bread

Servings: 1 Loaf   Cooking Time: 10 Minutes

Ingredients:

- 12 slice bread (1½ pounds)
- 1⅛ cups water, at 80°F to 90°F
- 3 tablespoons melted butter, cooled
- 3 tablespoons light brown sugar
- 1½ teaspoons salt
- 3 tablespoons raw sunflower seeds
- 3 tablespoons pumpkin seeds
- 2 tablespoons sesame seeds
- 1 teaspoon anise seeds
- 1 cup quick oats
- 2¼ cups white bread flour
- 1½ teaspoons bread machine or instant yeast

Directions:

Preparing the Ingredients.   Choose the size of loaf of your preference and then measure the ingredients. Add all of the ingredients mentioned previously in the list. Close the lid after placing the pan in the bread machine. Select the Bake cycle   Turn on the bread machine. Select the White/Basic setting, select the loaf size, and the crust color. Press start.   When the cycle is finished, carefully remove the pan from the bread maker and let it rest.   Remove the bread from the pan, put in a wire rack to Cool about 5 minutes. Slice

206. Whole-wheat Seed Bread

Servings: 1 Loaf   Cooking Time: 10 Minutes
Ingredients:
- 12 slice bread (1½ pounds)
- 1⅛ cups water, at 80°F to 90°F
- 1½ tablespoons honey
- 1½ tablespoons melted butter, cooled
- ¾ teaspoon salt
- 2½ cups whole-wheat flour
- ¾ cup white bread flour
- 3 tablespoons raw sunflower seeds
- 1 tablespoon sesame seeds
- 1½ teaspoons bread machine or instant yeast

Directions:
Preparing the Ingredients.   Choose the size of loaf of your preference and then measure the ingredients. Add all of the ingredients mentioned previously in the list. Close the lid after placing the pan in the bread machine. Select the Bake cycle   Turn on the bread machine. Select the Whole-Wheat/Whole-Grain bread, select the loaf size, and select light or medium crust. Press start. When the cycle is finished, carefully remove the pan from the bread maker and let it rest.   Remove the bread from the pan, put in a wire rack to Cool about 5 minutes. Slice

207. Garlic Herb Bread

Servings: 8   Cooking Time: 3 Hours And 25 Minutes
Ingredients:
- 1% milk – 1 cup, warm
- Light butter - 1 tbsp.
- White sugar – 1 tbsp.
- Salt – 1 ½ tsp.
- Italian seasoning – 1 ½ tsp.
- Garlic powder – 3 tsp.
- White flour – 3 cups
- Active dry yeast – 2 tsp.

Directions:
Add everything according to bread machine recommendations.   Select Basic bread cycle and press Start.   Remove the bread when done.   Cool, slice, and serve.
Nutrition Info:(Per Serving): Calories: 213; Total Fat: 2.8 g; Saturated Fat: 1.4 g; Carbohydrates: 40 g; Cholesterol: 7 mg; Fiber: 1.6 g; Calcium: 46 mg; Sodium: 465 mg; Protein: 6.4 g

208. Pesto Nut Bread

Servings: 14 Slices   Cooking Time: 10 Minutes
Ingredients:
- 1 cup plus 2 Tbsp water
- 3 cups Gold Medal Better for Bread flour
- 2 Tbsp sugar
- 1 tsp salt
- 1¼ tsp bread machine or quick active dry yeast
- For the pesto filling:
- ⅓ cup basil pesto
- 2 Tbsp Gold Medal Better for Bread flour
- ⅓ cup pine nuts

Directions:
Preparing the Ingredients   Add each ingredient to the bread machine in the order and at the temperature recommended by your bread machine manufacturer. Select the Bake cycle   Close the lid, select the basic bread, medium crust setting on your bread machine, and press start.   In a small bowl, combine pesto and 2 Tbsp of flour until well blended. Stir in the pine nuts. Add the filling 5 minutes before the last kneading cycle ends. When the bread machine has finished baking, remove the bread and put it on a cooling rack.

209. Sesame French Bread

Servings: 14 Slices   Cooking Time: 3 H. 15 Min.
Ingredients:
- ⅞ cup water
- 1 Tbsp butter, softened
- 3 cups bread flour
- 2 tsp sugar
- 1 tsp salt
- 2 tsp yeast
- 2 Tbsp sesame seeds toasted

Directions:
Add each ingredient to the bread machine in the order and at the temperature recommended by your bread machine manufacturer.   Close the lid, select the French bread, medium crust setting on your bread machine and press start.   When the bread machine has finished baking, remove the bread and put it on a cooling rack.

210. Coffee Raisin Bread

Servings: 10   Cooking Time: 3 Hours
Ingredients:
- Active dry yeast – 2 ½ tsps.
- Ground cloves – ¼ tsp.
- Ground allspice – ¼ tsp.
- Ground cinnamon – 1 tsp.
- Sugar – 3 tbsps.
- Egg – 1, lightly beaten
- Olive oil – 3 tbsps.
- Strong brewed coffee – 1 cup.
- Bread flour – 3 cups.
- Raisins – ¾ cup.
- Salt – 1 ½ tsps.

Directions:
Add all ingredients except for raisins into the bread machine pan. Select basic setting then select light/medium crust and press start. Add raisins just before the final kneading cycle. Once loaf is done, remove the loaf pan from the machine. Allow it to cool for 10 minutes. Slice and serve.

211. Semolina Bread

Servings: 6 Pcs   Cooking Time: One Hour
Ingredients:
- Almond fine flour, one cup
- Semolina flour, one cup
- Yeast, one teaspoon

- An egg
- Salt, one teaspoon
- Stevia powder, two teaspoons
- Olive oil extra virgin, two teaspoons
- Water warm, one cup
- Sesame seeds, two teaspoons

Directions:
Get a mixing container and combine the almond flour, semolina flour, salt, and stevia powder. In another mixing container, combine the egg extra virgin olive oil, and warm water. By instructions on your machine's manual, pour the ingredients in the bread pan and follow how to mix in the yeast. Put the bread pan in the machine, select the basic bread setting together with the bread size and crust type, if available, then press start once you have closed the machine's lid. When the bread is ready, open the lid and spread the sesame seeds at the top and close for a few minutes. By using oven mitts, remove the pan from the machine. Use a stainless spatula to extract the pan's bread and turn the pan upside down on a metallic rack where the bread will cool off before slicing it.

Nutrition Info: Calories: 100;Carbohydrates: 2.8g;Protein: 5g;Fat: 14g

212. Gingered Spice Bread

Servings: 16   Cooking Time: 3 Hours And 25 Minutes
Ingredients:
- Milk – ¾ cup
- Molasses – 3 tbsp.
- Egg – 1
- Butter – 2 tbsp.
- Salt – ¾ tsp.
- Bread flour – 3 cups
- Ground ginger – 1 tsp.
- Ground cinnamon – ½ tsp.
- Ground cloves – ¼ tsp.
- Bread machine yeast – 2 tsp.

Directions:
Add everything to the bread pan in the order suggested by the manufacturer. Select Basic/White bread cycle, choose Light or Medium crust. Press Start. Remove the bread when done. Cool, slice, and serve.

Nutrition Info:(Per Serving): Calories: 123; Total Fat: 2.4 g; Saturated Fat: 1.3 g; Carbohydrates: 21.6 g; Cholesterol: 18.6 mg; Fiber: 0.8 g; Calcium: 22 mg; Sodium: 131.4 mg; Protein: 3.4 g

213. Nutty Wheat Bread

Servings: 1 Loaf   Cooking Time: 10 Minutes
Ingredients:
- 12 slice bread (1½ pounds)
- 1½ cups water, at 80°F to 90°F
- 2 tablespoons melted butter, cooled
- 1 tablespoon sugar
- 1½ teaspoons salt
- 1¼ cups whole-wheat flour
- 2 cups white bread flour
- 1¼ teaspoons bread machine or instant yeast
- 2 tablespoons chopped almonds

- 2 tablespoons chopped pecans
- 2 tablespoons sunflower seeds

Directions:
Preparing the Ingredients. Place the ingredients, except the almonds, pecans, and seeds, in your bread machine as recommended by the manufacturer. Select the Bake cycle Turn on the bread machine. Select the White/Basic setting, select the loaf size, and the crust color. Press start. When the cycle is finished, carefully remove the pan from the bread maker and let it rest. Remove the bread from the pan, put in a wire rack to Cool about 5 minutes. Slice

214. Savoury Herb Blend Bread

Servings: 16 Pcs   Cooking Time: One Hour
Ingredients:
- 1 cup almond flour
- 1/2 cup coconut flour
- 1 cup parmesan cheese
- 3/4 tsp baking powder
- Three eggs
- 3 tbsp coconut oil
- 1/2 tbsp rosemary
- 1/2 tsp thyme, ground
- 1/2 tsp sage, ground
- 1/2 tsp oregano
- 1/2 tsp garlic powder
- 1/2 tsp onion powder
- 1/4 tsp salt

Directions:
Light beat eggs and coconut oil together before adding to the bread machine pan. Add all the remaining ingredients to the bread machine pan. Set the bread machine to the gluten-free setting. When the bread is finished, remove the bread machine pan from the bread machine. Let cool slightly before transferring to a cooling rack. You can store your bread for up to 7 days.

Nutrition Info: Calories: 170;Carbohydrates: 6g;Protein: 9g;Fat: 15g

215. Pumpkin Coconut Almond Bread

Servings: 12 Slices   Cooking Time: 5 Minutes
Ingredients:
- 1/3 cup vegetable oil
- 3 large eggs
- 1 1/2 cups canned pumpkin puree
- 1 cup sugar
- 1 1/2 teaspoons baking powder
- 1/2 teaspoon baking soda
- 1/4 teaspoon salt
- 1 tablespoon allspice
- 3 cups all-purpose flour
- 1/2 cup coconut flakes, plus a small handful for the topping
- 2/3 cup slivered almonds, plus a tablespoonful for the topping
- Non-stick cooking spray

Directions:

Preparing the Ingredients   Spray bread maker pan with non-stick cooking spray. Mix oil, eggs, and pumpkin in a large mixing bowl.   Mix remaining ingredients together in a separate mixing bowl. Add wet ingredients to bread maker pan, and dry ingredients on top.   Select the Bake cycle   Select Dough cycle and press Start. Open lid and sprinkle top of bread with reserved coconut and almonds.   Set to Rapid for 1 hour 30 minutes and bake. Cool for 10 minutes on a wire rack before serving.

216. Almond Milk Bread

Servings: 1 Loaf
Ingredients:
- 16 slice bread (2 pounds)
- 1 cup lukewarm milk
- 2 eggs, at room temperature
- 2⅔ tablespoons butter, melted and cooled
- ⅓ cup sugar
- 1 teaspoon table salt
- 2⅓ teaspoons lemon zest
- 4 cups white bread flour
- 2¼ teaspoons bread machine yeast
- ½ cup slivered almonds, chopped
- ½ cup golden raisins, chopped
- 12 slice bread (1½ pounds)
- ¾ cup lukewarm milk
- 2 eggs, at room temperature
- 2 tablespoons butter, melted and cooled
- ¼ cup sugar
- 1 teaspoon table salt
- 2 teaspoons lemon zest
- 3 cups white bread flour
- 2 teaspoons bread machine yeast
- ⅓ cup slivered almonds, chopped
- ⅓ cup golden raisins, chopped

Directions:
Choose the size of loaf you would like to make and measure your ingredients.   Add all of the ingredients except for the raisins and almonds to the bread pan in the order listed above.   Place the pan in the bread machine and close the lid.   Turn on the bread maker. Select the White/Basic or Fruit/Nut (if your machine has this setting) setting, then the loaf size, and finally the crust color. Start the cycle.   When the machine signals to add ingredients, add the raisins and almonds. (Some machines have a fruit/nut hopper where you can add the raisins and almonds when you start the machine. The machine will automatically add them to the dough during the baking process.)   When the cycle is finished and the bread is baked, carefully remove the pan from the machine. Use a potholder as the handle will be very hot. Let rest for a few minutes.   Remove the bread from the pan and allow to cool on a wire rack for at least 10 minutes before slicing.
Nutrition Info:(Per Serving):Calories 193, fat 4.6 g, carbs 29.4 g, sodium 214 mg, protein 5.7 g

217. Tuscan Herb Bread

Servings: 10   Cooking Time: 2 Hours

Ingredients:
- Yeast – 2 tsps.
- Bread flour – 2 1/2 cups
- Italian seasoning – 2 tbsps.
- Sugar – 2 tbsps.
- Olive oil – 2 tbsps.
- Warm water – 1 cup
- Salt – 1 tsp.

Directions:
Add olive oil and water to the bread pan. Add remaining ingredients except for yeast to the bread pan. Make a small hole into the flour with your finger and add yeast to the hole. Make sure yeast will not be mixed with any liquids. Select basic setting then select light/medium crust and start. Once loaf is done, remove the loaf pan from the machine. Allow it to cool for 10 minutes. Slice and serve.

218. Cheese Herb Bread

Servings: 10   Cooking Time: 3 Hours 27 Minutes
Ingredients:
- Active dry yeast – 1 ¼ tsps.
- Dried oregano – 1 ¼ tsps.
- Fennel seed – 1 ¼ tsps.
- Dried basil – 1 ¼ tsps.
- Asiago cheese – 2/3 cup, grated
- Bread flour – 3 ¼ cups
- Sugar – 1 tbsp.
- Salt – ¾ tsp.
- Water – 1 cup.

Directions:
Add all ingredients to the bread machine. Select sweet bread setting then select light/medium crust and start. Once loaf is done, remove the loaf pan from the machine. Allow it to cool for 10 minutes. Slice and serve.

219. Healthy Basil Whole Wheat Bread

Servings: 10   Cooking Time: 2 Hours
Ingredients:
- Olive oil – 2 tbsps.
- Basil – 1 tbsp.
- Water – 1 1/3 cups
- Whole wheat flour – 4 cups
- Salt – 2 tsps.
- Sugar – 3 tbsps.
- Active dry yeast – 2 tsps.

Directions:
Add olive oil and water to the bread pan. Add remaining ingredients except for yeast to the bread pan. Make a small hole into the flour with your finger and add yeast to the hole. Make sure yeast will not be mixed with any liquids. Select whole wheat setting then select light/medium crust and start. Once loaf is done, remove the loaf pan from the machine. Allow it to cool for 5 minutes. Slice and serve.

220. Lavender Buttermilk Bread

Servings: 14 Slices   Cooking Time: 3 H.
Ingredients:

- ½ cup water
- ⅞ cup buttermilk
- ¼ cup olive oil
- 3 Tbsp finely chopped fresh lavender leaves
- 1 ¼ tsp finely chopped fresh lavender flowers
- Grated zest of 1 lemon
- 4 cups bread flour
- 2 tsp salt
- 2 ¾ tsp bread machine yeast

Directions:
Add each ingredient to the bread machine in the order and at the temperature recommended by your bread machine manufacturer. Close the lid, select the basic bread, medium crust setting on your bread machine and press start. When the bread machine has finished baking, remove the bread and put it on a cooling rack.

221. Herbed Pesto Bread

Servings: 1 Loaf   Cooking Time: 10 Minutes
Ingredients:
- 12 slices bread (1½ pounds)
- 1 cup water, at 80°F to 90°F
- 2¼ tablespoons melted butter, cooled
- 1½ teaspoons minced garlic
- ¾ tablespoon sugar
- 1 teaspoon salt
- 3 tablespoons chopped fresh parsley
- 1½ tablespoons chopped fresh basil
- ⅓ cup grated Parmesan cheese
- 3 cups white bread flour
- 1¼ teaspoons bread machine or active dry yeast

Directions:
Preparing the Ingredients. Choose the size of loaf of your preference and then measure the ingredients. Add all of the ingredients mentioned previously in the list. Close the lid after placing the pan in the bread machine. Select the Bake cycle   Turn on the bread machine. Select the White/Basic setting, select the loaf size, and the crust color. Press start. When the cycle is finished, carefully remove the pan from the bread maker and let it rest. Remove the bread from the pan, put in a wire rack to Cool about 10 minutes. Slice

222. Fragrant Cardamom Bread

Servings: 1 Loaf   Cooking Time: 10 Minutes
Ingredients:
- 12 slices bread (1½ pounds)
- ¾ cup milk, at 80°F to 90°F
- 1 egg, at room temperature
- 1½ teaspoons melted butter, cooled
- 3 tablespoons honey
- 1 teaspoon salt
- 1 teaspoon ground cardamom
- 3 cups white bread flour
- 1¼ teaspoons bread machine or instant yeast

Directions:
Preparing the Ingredients. Choose the size of loaf of your preference and then measure the ingredients. Add all of the ingredients mentioned previously in the list. Close the lid after placing the pan in the bread machine.

Select the Bake cycle   Turn on the bread machine. Select the White/Basic setting, select the loaf size, and the crust color. Press start. When the cycle is finished, carefully remove the pan from the bread maker and let it rest. Remove the bread from the pan, put in a wire rack to Cool about 10 minutes. Slice

223. Seeded Bread

Servings: 16 Slices   Cooking Time: 40 Minutes
Ingredients:
- Two tablespoons chia seeds
- 1/4 teaspoon salt
- Seven large eggs
- 1/2 teaspoon xanthan gum
- 2 cups almond flour
- One teaspoon baking powder
- 1/2 cup unsalted butter
- Three tablespoons sesame seeds
- Two tablespoons olive oil

Directions:
Add all the ingredients to the Bread machine. Close the lid and choose Bread mode. Once done, take out from the machine and cut into at least 16 slices. This seeded bread can be kept for up to 4-5 days in the fridge.
Nutrition Info: Calories: 101 Cal;Fat: 4 g;Cholesterol:;Carbohydrates: 4 g;Protein: 6 g

224. Herb And Garlic Cream Cheese Bread

Servings: 1 Loaf   Cooking Time: 10 Minutes
Ingredients:
- 12 slices bread (1½ pounds)
- ½ cup water, at 80°F to 90°F
- ½ cup herb and garlic cream cheese, at room temperature
- 1 egg, at room temperature
- 2 tablespoons melted butter, cooled
- 3 tablespoons sugar
- 1 teaspoon salt
- 3 cups white bread flour
- 1½ teaspoons bread machine or instant yeast

Directions:
Preparing the Ingredients. Choose the size of loaf of your preference and then measure the ingredients. Add all of the ingredients mentioned previously in the list. Close the lid after placing the pan in the bread machine. Select the Bake cycle   Turn on the bread machine. Select the White/Basic setting, select the loaf size, and the crust color. Press start. When the cycle is finished, carefully remove the pan from the bread maker and let it rest. Remove the bread from the pan, put in a wire rack to Cool about 10 minutes. Slice

225. Cajun Bread

Servings: 14 Slices   Cooking Time: 10 Minutes
Ingredients:
- ½ cup water
- ¼ cup chopped onion
- ¼ cup chopped green bell pepper
- 2 tsp finely chopped garlic

- 2 tsp soft butter
- 2 cups bread flour
- 1 Tbsp sugar
- 1 tsp Cajun
- ½ tsp salt
- 1 tsp active dry yeast

Directions:
Preparing the Ingredients   Add each ingredient to the bread machine in the order and at the temperature recommended by your bread machine manufacturer. Select the Bake cycle   Close the lid, select the basic bread, medium crust setting on your bread machine and press start.   When the bread machine has finished baking, remove the bread and put it on a cooling rack.

226. Chia Sesame Bread

Servings: 1 Loaf   Cooking Time: 10 Minutes
Ingredients:
- 12 slice bread (1½ pounds)
- 1 cup plus 2 tablespoons water, at 80°F to 90°F
- 1½ tablespoons melted butter, cooled
- 1½ tablespoons sugar
- 1⅛ teaspoons salt
- ½ cup ground chia seeds
- 1½ tablespoons sesame seeds
- 2½ cups white bread flour
- 1½ teaspoons bread machine or instant yeast

Directions:
Preparing the Ingredients.   Choose the size of loaf of your preference and then measure the ingredients. Add all of the ingredients mentioned previously in the list. Close the lid after placing the pan in the bread machine. Select the Bake cycle   Turn on the bread machine. Select the White/Basic setting, select the loaf size, and the crust color. Press start.   When the cycle is finished, carefully remove the pan from the bread maker and let it rest.   Remove the bread from the pan, put in a wire rack to Cool about 5 minutes. Slice

227. Oatmeal Sunflower Bread

Servings: 10   Cooking Time: 3 Hours 30 Minutes
Ingredients:
- Water – 1 cup.
- Honey – ¼ cup.
- Butter – 2 tbsps., softened
- Bread flour – 3 cups.
- Old fashioned oats – ½ cup.
- Milk powder – 2 tbsps.
- Salt – 1 ¼ tsps.
- Active dry yeast – 2 ¼ tsps.
- Sunflower seeds – ½ cup.

Directions:
Add all ingredients except for sunflower seeds into the bread machine pan. Select basic setting then select light/medium crust and press start. Add sunflower seeds just before the final kneading cycle. Once loaf is done, remove the loaf pan from the machine. Allow it to cool for 10 minutes. Slice and serve.

228. Caraway Rye Bread

Servings: 1 Loaf   Cooking Time: 10 Minutes
Ingredients:
- 12 slice bread (1½ pounds)
- 1⅛ cups water, at 80°F to 90°F
- 1¾ tablespoons melted butter, cooled
- 3 tablespoons dark brown sugar
- 1½ tablespoons dark molasses
- 1⅛ teaspoons salt
- 1½ teaspoons caraway seed
- ¾ cup dark rye flour
- 2 cups white bread flour
- 1⅛ teaspoons bread machine or instant yeast

Directions:
Preparing the Ingredients.   Choose the size of loaf of your preference and then measure the ingredients. Add all of the ingredients mentioned previously in the list. Close the lid after placing the pan in the bread machine. Select the Bake cycle   Turn on the bread machine. Select the White/Basic setting, select the loaf size, and the crust color. Press start.   When the cycle is finished, carefully remove the pan from the bread maker and let it rest.   Remove the bread from the pan, put in a wire rack to Cool about 10 minutes. Slice

229. Herb Bread

Servings: 12   Cooking Time: 3 Hours And 25 Minutes
Ingredients:
- Water – 1 cup, plus 2 tbsp.
- Butter – 2 tbsp., softened
- Bread flour – 3 cups.
- Fresh sage leaves – 2 tsp., chopped
- Fresh basil leaves – 1 tbsp., chopped
- Fresh oregano leaves – 1 tbsp., chopped
- Fresh thyme leaves – 2 tsp., chopped
- Fresh parsley - ¼ cup, chopped
- Dry milk – 3 tbsp.
- Sugar – 2 tbsp.
- Salt – 1 tsp.
- Bread machine yeast – 1 ½ tsp.

Directions:
Add everything according to bread machine recommendations.   Select Basic/White cycle and Medium or Light crust.   Remove the bread when done. Cool, slice, and serve.
Nutrition Info:(Per Serving): Calories: 100; Total Fat: 2 g; Saturated Fat: 1 g; Carbohydrates: 21 g; Cholesterol: 5 mg; Fiber: 3 g; Calcium: 75 mg; Sodium: 220 mg; Protein: 1 g

230. Simple Garlic Bread

Servings: 1 Loaf   Cooking Time: 10 Minutes
Ingredients:
- 12 slices bread (1½ pounds)
- 1 cup milk, at 70°F to 80°F
- 1½ tablespoons melted butter, cooled
- 1 tablespoon sugar
- 1½ teaspoons salt
- 2 teaspoons garlic powder

- 2 teaspoons chopped fresh parsley
- 3 cups white bread flour
- 1¾ teaspoons bread machine or instant yeast

Directions:

Preparing the Ingredients. Choose the size of loaf of your preference and then measure the ingredients. Add all of the ingredients mentioned previously in the list. Close the lid after placing the pan in the bread machine. Select the Bake cycle Turn on the bread machine. Select the White/Basic setting, select the loaf size, and the crust color. Press start. When the cycle is finished, carefully remove the pan from the bread maker and let it rest. Remove the bread from the pan, put in a wire rack to Cool about 10 minutes. Slice

231. Grain, Seed And Nut Bread

Servings: 1 Loaf   Cooking Time: 10 Minutes

Ingredients:
- ¼ cup water
- 1 egg
- 3 Tbsp honey
- 1½ tsp butter, softened
- 3¼ cups bread flour
- 1 cup milk
- 1 tsp salt
- ¼ tsp baking soda
- 1 tsp ground cinnamon
- 2½ tsp active dry yeast
- ¾ cup dried cranberries
- ½ cup chopped walnuts
- 1 Tbsp white vinegar
- ½ tsp sugar

Directions:

Preparing the Ingredients. Choose the size of loaf of your preference and then measure the ingredients. Add all of the ingredients mentioned previously in the list. Close the lid after placing the pan in the bread machine. Select the Bake cycle Turn on the bread machine. Select the White/Basic setting, select the loaf size, and the crust color. Press start. When the cycle is finished, carefully remove the pan from the bread maker and let it rest. Remove the bread from the pan, put in a wire rack to Cool about 10 minutes. Slice

232. Pecan Raisin Bread

Servings: 1 Loaf   Cooking Time: 10 Minutes Plus Fermenting Time

Ingredients:
- 1 cup plus 2 Tbsp water (70°F to 80°F)
- 8 tsp butter
- 1 egg
- 6 Tbsp sugar
- ¼ cup nonfat dry milk powder
- 1 tsp salt
- 4 cups bread flour
- 1 Tbsp active dry yeast
- 1 cup finely chopped pecans
- 1 cup raisins

Directions:

Preparing the Ingredients Add each ingredient to the bread machine except the pecans and raisins in the order and at the temperature recommended by your bread machine manufacturer. Select the Bake cycle Close the lid, select the basic bread, medium crust setting on your bread machine, and press start. Just before the final kneading, add the pecans and raisins. When the bread machine has finished baking, remove the bread and put it on a cooling rack.

233. Cracked Black Pepper Bread

Servings: 1 Loaf   Cooking Time: 10 Minutes

Ingredients:
- 12 slice bread (1½ pounds)
- 1⅛ cups water, at 80°F to 90°F
- 1½ tablespoons melted butter, cooled
- 1½ tablespoons sugar
- 1 teaspoon salt
- 3 tablespoons skim milk powder
- 1½ tablespoons minced chives
- ¾ teaspoon garlic powder
- ¾ teaspoon freshly cracked black pepper
- 3 cups white bread flour
- 1¼ teaspoons bread machine or instant yeast

Directions:

Preparing the Ingredients. Choose the size of loaf of your preference and then measure the ingredients. Add all of the ingredients mentioned previously in the list. Close the lid after placing the pan in the bread machine. Select the Bake cycle Turn on the bread machine. Select the White/Basic setting, select the loaf size, and the crust color. Press start. When the cycle is finished, carefully remove the pan from the bread maker and let it rest. Remove the bread from the pan, put in a wire rack to Cool about 10 minutes. Slice

234. Pumpkin Cinnamon Bread

Servings: 14 Slices   Cooking Time: 3 H.

Ingredients:
- 1 cup sugar
- 1 cup canned pumpkin
- ⅓ cup vegetable oil
- 1 tsp vanilla
- 2 eggs
- 1½ cups all-purpose bread flour
- 2 tsp baking powder
- ¼ tsp salt
- 1 tsp ground cinnamon
- ¼ tsp ground nutmeg
- ⅛ tsp ground cloves

Directions:

Add each ingredient to the bread machine in the order and at the temperature recommended by your bread machine manufacturer. Close the lid, select the quick, medium crust setting on your bread machine and press start. When the bread machine has finished baking, remove the bread and put it on a cooling rack.

235. Lavender Bread

Servings: 8 Slices   Cooking Time: 1 Hour

Ingredients:

- ¾ cup lukewarm milk (80 degrees F)
- One tablespoon butter, melted
- One tablespoon brown sugar
- ¾ teaspoon salt
- One teaspoon fresh lavender flower, chopped
- ¼ teaspoon lemon zest
- ¼ teaspoon fresh thyme, chopped
- 2 cups all-purpose flour, sifted
- ¾ teaspoon active dry yeast

Directions:

Prepare all of the ingredients for your bread and measuring means (a cup, a spoon, kitchen scales). Carefully measure the ingredients into the pan.   Place all of the ingredients into a bucket in the right order, following the manual for your bread machine.   Close the cover.   Select the program of your bread machine to BASIC and choose the crust colour to MEDIUM. Press START.   Wait until the program completes. When done, take the bucket out and let it cool for 5-10 minutes.   Shake the loaf from the pan and let cool for 30 minutes on a cooling rack.   Slice, serve and enjoy the taste of fragrant Homemade Bread.

Nutrition Info: Calories 133; Total Fat 1.8g; Saturated Fat 1g; Cholesterol 4g; Sodium 228mg; Total Carbohydrate 25.3g; Dietary Fiber 0.9g; Total Sugars 1.2g; Protein 3.4g; Potassium 43mg

Fruit And Vegetable Bread

236. Cocoa Date Bread

Servings: 1 Loaf
Ingredients:
- 16 slice bread (2 pounds)
- 1 cup lukewarm water
- ½ cup lukewarm milk
- 2 tablespoons unsalted butter, melted
- 5 tablespoons honey
- 3 tablespoons molasses
- 1 tablespoon sugar
- 3 tablespoons skim milk powder
- 1 teaspoon table salt
- 2 cups white bread flour
- 2½ cups whole-wheat flour
- 1 tablespoon cocoa powder, unsweetened
- 1½ teaspoons bread machine yeast
- 1 cup dates, chopped
- 12 slice bread (1½ pounds)
- ¾ cup lukewarm water
- ½ cup lukewarm milk
- 2 tablespoons unsalted butter, melted
- ¼ cup honey
- 3 tablespoons molasses
- 1 tablespoon sugar
- 2 tablespoons skim milk powder
- 1 teaspoon table salt
- 1¼ cups white bread flour
- 2¼ cups whole-wheat flour
- 1 tablespoon cocoa powder, unsweetened
- 1½ teaspoons bread machine yeast
- ¾ cup dates, chopped

Directions:
Choose the size of loaf you would like to make and measure your ingredients. Add all of the ingredients except for the dates to the bread pan in the order listed above. Place the pan in the bread machine and close the lid. Turn on the bread maker. Select the White/Basic or Fruit/Nut (if your machine has this setting) setting, then the loaf size, and finally the crust color. Start the cycle. When the machine signals to add ingredients, add the dates. (Some machines have a fruit/nut hopper where you can add the dates when you start the machine. The machine will automatically add them to the dough during the baking process.) When the cycle is finished and the bread is baked, carefully remove the pan from the machine. Use a potholder as the handle will be very hot. Let rest for a few minutes. Remove the bread from the pan and allow to cool on a wire rack for at least 10 minutes before slicing.
Nutrition Info:(Per Serving):Calories 221, fat 2.7 g, carbs 38.6 g, sodium 227 mg, protein 4.8 g

237. Harvest Fruit Bread

Servings: 14 Slices   Cooking Time: 3 H.
Ingredients:
- 1 cup plus 2 Tbsp water (70°F to 80°F)

- 1 egg
- 3 Tbsp butter, softened
- ¼ cup packed brown sugar
- 1½ tsp salt
- ¼ tsp ground nutmeg
- Dash allspice
- 3¾ cups plus 1 Tbsp bread flour
- 2 tsp active dry yeast
- 1 cup dried fruit (dried cherries, cranberries and/or raisins)
- ⅓ cup chopped pecans

Directions:
Add each ingredient except the fruit and pecans to the bread machine in the order and at the temperature recommended by your bread machine manufacturer. Close the lid, select the basic bread, medium crust setting on your bread machine, and press start. Just before the final kneading, add the fruit and pecans. When the bread machine has finished baking, remove the bread and put it on a cooling rack.

238. Orange Bread

Servings: 1 Loaf   Cooking Time: 10 Minutes
Ingredients:
- 16 slice bread (2 pounds)
- 1¼ cups lukewarm milk
- ¼ cup orange juice
- ¼ cup sugar
- 1½ tablespoons unsalted butter, melted
- 1¼ teaspoons table salt
- 4 cups white bread flour
- Zest of 1 orange
- 1¾ teaspoons bread machine yeast

Directions:
Preparing the Ingredients. Choose the size of loaf of your preference and then measure the ingredients. Add all of the ingredients mentioned previously in the list. Close the lid after placing the pan in the bread machine Select the Bake cycle Turn on the bread machine. Select the White/Basic setting, select the loaf size, and the crust color. Press start. When the cycle is finished, carefully remove the pan from the bread maker and let it rest. Remove the bread from the pan, put in a wire rack to cool. Cool completely, about 10 minutes. Slice

239. Light Corn Bread

Servings: 1 Loaf   Cooking Time: 10 Minutes
Ingredients:
- 12 slice bread (1½ pounds)
- ¾ cup milk, at 80°F to 90°F
- 1 egg, at room temperature
- 2¼ tablespoons butter, melted and cooled
- 2¼ tablespoons honey
- ¾ teaspoon salt
- ⅓ cup cornmeal
- 2⅔ cups white bread flour
- 1¾ teaspoons bread machine or instant yeast

Directions:
Preparing the Ingredients. Choose the size of loaf of your preference and then measure the ingredients. Add all of the ingredients mentioned previously in the list. Close the lid after placing the pan in the bread machine. Select the Bake cycle Turn on the bread machine. Select the White/Basic setting, select the loaf size, and the crust color. Press start. When the cycle is finished, carefully remove the pan from the bread maker and let it rest. Remove the bread from the pan, put in a wire rack to Cool about 5 minutes. Slice

240. Zucchini Bread

Servings: 12 Slices   Cooking Time: 10 Minutes
Ingredients:
- 1/2 teaspoon salt
- 1 cup sugar
- 1 tablespoon pumpkin pie spice
- 1 tablespoon baking powder
- 1 teaspoon pure vanilla extract
- 1/3 cup milk
- 1/2 cup vegetable oil
- 2 eggs
- 2 cups bread flour
- 1 1/2 teaspoons active dry yeast or bread machine yeast
- 1 cup shredded zucchini, raw and unpeeled
- 1 cup of chopped walnuts (optional)

Directions:
Preparing the Ingredients   Add all of the ingredients for the zucchini bread into the bread maker pan in the order listed above, reserving yeast.   Make a well in the center of the dry ingredients and add the yeast.   Select the Bake cycle   Select Wheat bread cycle, medium crust color, and press Start.   Transfer to a cooling rack for 10 to 15 minutes before slicing to serve.

241. Garlic Olive Bread

Servings: 1 Loaf   Cooking Time: 10 Minutes
Ingredients:
- 12 slice bread (1½ pounds)
- 1 cup lukewarm milk
- 1½ tablespoons unsalted butter, melted
- 1 teaspoon garlic, minced
- 1½ tablespoons sugar
- 1 teaspoon table salt
- 3 cups white bread flour
- 1 teaspoon bread machine yeast
- ⅓ cup black olives, chopped
- 16 slice bread (2 pounds)
- 1⅓ cups lukewarm milk
- 2 tablespoons unsalted butter, melted
- 1⅓ teaspoons garlic, minced
- 2 tablespoons sugar
- 1⅓ teaspoons table salt
- 4 cups white bread flour
- 1½ teaspoons bread machine yeast
- ½ cup black olives, chopped

Directions:

Preparing the Ingredients   Choose the size of loaf of your preference and then measure the ingredients. Add all of the ingredients mentioned previously in the list, except for the olives. Close the lid after placing the pan in the bread machine.   Select the Bake   Turn on the bread machine. White/Basic or Fruit/Nut (if your machine has this setting) setting, select the loaf size, and the crust color. Press start.   When the machine signals to add ingredients, add the olives. When the cycle is finished, carefully remove the pan from the bread maker and let it rest.   Remove the bread from the pan, put in a wire rack to cool for at least 10 minutes, and slice.

242. Zucchini Lemon Bread

Servings: 1 Loaf
Ingredients:
- 16 slice bread (2 pounds)
- ⅔ cup lukewarm milk
- 1 cup finely shredded zucchini
- ⅓ teaspoon lemon juice, at room temperature
- 4 teaspoons olive oil
- 4 teaspoons sugar
- 1⅓ teaspoons table salt
- 1 cup whole-wheat flour
- 2 cups white bread flour
- 1 cup quick oats
- 2¼ teaspoons bread machine yeast
- 12 slice bread (1½ pounds)
- ½ cup lukewarm milk
- ¾ cup finely shredded zucchini
- ¼ teaspoon lemon juice, at room temperature
- 1 tablespoon olive oil
- 1 tablespoon sugar
- 1 teaspoon table salt
- ¾ cup whole-wheat flour
- 1½ cups white bread flour
- ¾ cup quick oats
- 2¼ teaspoons bread machine yeast

Directions:
Choose the size of loaf you would like to make and measure your ingredients.   Add the ingredients to the bread pan in the order listed above.   Place the pan in the bread machine and close the lid.   Turn on the bread maker. Select the White/Basic setting, then the loaf size, and finally the crust color. Start the cycle. When the cycle is finished and the bread is baked, carefully remove the pan from the machine. Use a potholder as the handle will be very hot. Let rest for a few minutes.   Remove the bread from the pan and allow to cool on a wire rack for at least 10 minutes before slicing.
Nutrition Info: (Per Serving): Calories 127, fat 2 g, carbs 23.4 g, sodium 194 mg, protein 4.1 g

243. Pineapple Carrot Bread

Servings: 12 Slices   Cooking Time: 5 Minutes
Ingredients:
- 1 (8-ounce) can crushed pineapple, with juice
- 1/2 cup carrots, shredded
- 2 eggs
- 2 tablespoons butter

- 4 cups bread flour
- 3 tablespoons sugar
- 1 teaspoon salt
- 3/4 teaspoon ground ginger
- 1 1/4 teaspoons active dry yeast

Directions:
Preparing the Ingredients   Add all of the ingredients (except yeast) to the bread maker pan in the order listed above.   Make a well in the center of the dry ingredients and add the yeast.   Select the Bake cycle   Select the Basic bread cycle and press Start.   Transfer baked loaf to a cooling rack for 15 minutes before slicing to serve.

244. Honey Banana Bread

Servings: 1 Loaf
Ingredients:
- 16 slice bread (2 pounds)
- ⅔ cup lukewarm milk
- 1⅓ cups banana, mashed
- 1 egg, beaten
- 2 tablespoons unsalted butter, melted
- ¼ cup honey
- 1⅓ teaspoons pure vanilla extract
- ⅔ teaspoon table salt
- 1⅓ cups whole-wheat flour
- 1⅔ cups white bread flour
- 2 teaspoons bread machine yeast
- 12 slice bread (1½ pounds)
- ½ cup lukewarm milk
- 1 cup banana, mashed
- 1 egg, beaten
- 1½ tablespoons unsalted butter, melted
- 3 tablespoons honey
- 1 teaspoon pure vanilla extract
- ½ teaspoon table salt
- 1 cup whole-wheat flour
- 1¼ cups white bread flour
- 1½ teaspoons bread machine yeast

Directions:
Choose the size of loaf you would like to make and measure your ingredients.   Add the ingredients to the bread pan in the order listed above.   Place the pan in the bread machine and close the lid.   Turn on the bread maker. Select the Sweet setting, then the loaf size, and finally the crust color. Start the cycle.   When the cycle is finished and the bread is baked, carefully remove the pan from the machine. Use a potholder as the handle will be very hot. Let rest for a few minutes.   Remove the bread from the pan and allow to cool on a wire rack for at least 10 minutes before slicing.
Nutrition Info:(Per Serving):Calories 153, fat 3.4 g, carbs 27.1 g, sodium 131 mg, protein 4.2 g

245. Blueberry Bread

Servings: 10   Cooking Time: 2 Hours
Ingredients:
- Milk – ¾ cup.
- Egg – 1
- Water – 3 tbsps.
- Butter – 2 tbsps.

- Sugar – 3 tbsps.
- Salt – ¾ tsp.
- Ground nutmeg – ¼ tsp.
- Dried blueberries – 1/3 cup.
- Bread flour – 3 cups.
- Active dry yeast – 1 tsp.

Directions:
Add all ingredients into the bread machine pan. Select basic setting then select medium crust and start. Once loaf is done, remove the loaf pan from the machine. Allow it to cool for 10 minutes. Slice and serve.

246. Peaches And Cream Bread

Servings: 1 Loaf   Cooking Time: 10 Minutes
Ingredients:
- 12 slice bread (1½ pounds)
- ¾ cup canned peaches, drained and chopped
- ⅓ cup heavy whipping cream, at 80°F to 90°F
- 1 egg, at room temperature
- 1 tablespoon melted butter, cooled
- 2¼ tablespoons sugar
- 1⅛ teaspoons salt
- ⅓ teaspoon ground cinnamon
- ⅛ teaspoon ground nutmeg
- ⅓ cup whole-wheat flour
- 2⅔ cups white bread flour
- 1⅛ teaspoons bread machine or instant yeast

Directions:
Preparing the Ingredients.   Choose the size of loaf of your preference and then measure the ingredients. Add all of the ingredients mentioned previously in the list. Close the lid after placing the pan in the bread machine.   Select the Bake cycle   Turn on the bread machine. Select the White/Basic setting, select the loaf size, and the crust color. Press start.   When the cycle is finished, carefully remove the pan from the bread maker and let it rest.   Remove the bread from the pan, put in a wire rack to Cool completely, about 10 minutes.

247. Sun Vegetable Bread

Servings: 8 Pcs   Cooking Time: 1 Hour And 30 Minutes
Ingredients:
- 2 cups (250 g) wheat flour
- 2 cups (250 g) whole-wheat flour
- Two teaspoons yeast
- 1½ teaspoons salt
- One tablespoon sugar
- One tablespoon paprika dried slices
- Two tablespoons dried beets
- One tablespoon dried garlic
- 1½ cups water
- One tablespoon vegetable oil

Directions:
The set baking program, which should be 4 hours, crust colour, is medium.   Be sure to look at the kneading phase of the dough to get a smooth and soft bun.
Nutrition Info: Calories 253;Total Fat 2.6g;Saturated Fat 0.5g;Cholesterol 0g;Sodium 444mg;Total Sugars 0.6g;Protein 7.2g

248. Savory Sweet Potato Pan Bread

Servings: 1 Loaf   Cooking Time: 10 Minutes

Ingredients:
- 8 wedges
- 1½ cups uncooked shredded dark-orange sweet potato (about ½ potato) ½ cup sugar
- ¼ cup vegetable oil
- 2 eggs
- ¾ cup all-purpose flour
- ¾ cup whole wheat flour
- 2 teaspoons dried minced onion
- 1 teaspoon dried rosemary leaves, crumbled
- 1 teaspoon baking soda
- ½ teaspoon salt
- ¼ teaspoon baking powder
- 2 teaspoons sesame seed

Directions:
Preparing the Ingredients.   Choose the size of loaf of your preference and then measure the ingredients. Add all of the ingredients mentioned previously in the list. Close the lid after placing the pan in the bread machine.   Select the Bake cycle   Turn on the bread machine. Select the White/Basic setting, select the loaf size, and the crust color. Press start.   When the cycle is finished, carefully remove the pan from the bread maker and let it rest.   Remove the bread from the pan, put in a wire rack to Cool about 10 minutes. Serve warm.

249. Onion Chive Bread

Servings: 1 Loaf

Ingredients:
- 16 slice bread (2 pounds)
- 1¼ cups lukewarm water
- ¼ cup unsalted butter, melted
- 2 tablespoons sugar
- 1½ teaspoons table salt
- 4¼ cups white bread flour
- ¼ cup dried minced onion
- 2 tablespoons fresh chives, chopped
- 2¼ teaspoons bread machine yeast
- 12 slice bread (1½ pounds)
- 1 cup lukewarm water
- 3 tablespoons unsalted butter, melted
- 1½ tablespoons sugar
- 1⅛ teaspoons table salt
- 3⅛ cups white bread flour
- 3 tablespoons dried minced onion
- 1½ tablespoons fresh chives, chopped
- 1⅔ teaspoons bread machine yeast

Directions:
Choose the size of loaf you would like to make and measure your ingredients.   Add the ingredients to the bread pan in the order listed above.   Place the pan in the bread machine and close the lid.   Turn on the bread maker. Select the White/Basic setting, then the loaf size, and finally the crust color. Start the cycle. When the cycle is finished and the bread is baked, carefully remove the pan from the machine. Use a potholder as the handle will be very hot. Let rest for a few minutes.   Remove the bread from the pan and allow to cool on a wire rack for at least 10 minutes before slicing.

Nutrition Info: (Per Serving): Calories 147, fat 3 g, carbs 26.2 g, sodium 223 mg, protein 4.6 g

250. Ginger-topped Pumpkin Bread

Servings: 2 Loaves (24 Slices Each)   Cooking Time: 10 Minutes

Ingredients:
- 1 can (15 oz) pumpkin (not pumpkin pie mix)
- 1⅔ cups granulated sugar
- ⅔ cup unsweetened applesauce
- ½ cup milk
- 2 teaspoons vanilla
- 1 cup fat-free egg product or 2 eggs plus 4 egg whites 3 cups all-purpose flour
- 2 teaspoons baking soda
- 1 teaspoon salt
- 1 teaspoon ground cinnamon
- ½ teaspoon baking powder
- ½ teaspoon ground cloves
- glaze and topping
- ⅔ cup powdered sugar
- 2 to 3 teaspoons warm water
- ¼ teaspoon vanilla
- 3 tablespoons finely chopped crystallized ginger

Directions:
Preparing the Ingredients.   Choose the size of loaf of your preference and then measure the ingredients. Add all of the ingredients mentioned previously in the list. Close the lid after placing the pan in the bread machine.   Select the Bake cycle   Turn on the bread machine. Select the White/Basic setting, select the loaf size, and the crust color. Press start.   When the cycle is finished, carefully remove the pan from the bread maker and let it rest.   Remove the bread from the pan, put in a wire rack to cool for at least 2 hours. In small bowl, mix powdered sugar, water and ¼ teaspoon vanilla until thin enough to drizzle. Drizzle over loaves. Sprinkle with ginger. Wrap tightly and store at room temperature up to 4 days, or refrigerate up to 10 days.

251. Garlic Onion Pepper Bread

Servings: 10   Cooking Time: 2 Hours

Ingredients:
- Water – ½ cup.
- Onion – ¼ cup., chopped
- Bell pepper – ¼ cup., chopped
- Garlic – 2 tsps., chopped
- Butter – 2 tsps.
- Bread flour – 2 cups.
- Sugar – 1 tbsp.
- Cajun seasoning – 1 tsp.
- Salt – ½ tsp.
- Active dry yeast – 1 tsp.

Directions:
Add all ingredients into the bread machine pan. Select basic bread setting then select medium crust and press start. Once loaf is done, remove the loaf pan from the machine. Allow it to cool for 10 minutes. Slice and serve.

252. Apple-fig Bread With Honey Glaze

Servings: 1 Loaf   Cooking Time: 10 Minutes

Ingredients:
- 1½ cups all-purpose flour
- 1½ teaspoons ground cinnamon
- 1 teaspoon baking powder
- ½ teaspoon salt
- ½ teaspoon ground nutmeg
- ¼ teaspoon ground allspice
- ⅔ cup granulated sugar
- ½ cup vegetable oil
- 1 egg
- 1 egg yolk
- 1½ teaspoons vanilla
- ½ cup milk
- 1 cup chopped peeled apples
- ½ cup dried figs, chopped glaze
- ⅓ to ½ cup powdered sugar
- 2 tablespoons honey
- 1 tablespoon butter, softened
- Dash ground allspice

Directions:
Preparing the Ingredients.   Choose the size of loaf of your preference and then measure the ingredients. Add all of the ingredients mentioned previously in the list. Close the lid after placing the pan in the bread machine Select the Bake cycle   Turn on the bread machine. Select the White/Basic setting, select the loaf size, and the crust color. Press start.   When the cycle is finished, carefully remove the pan from the bread maker and let it rest.   Remove the bread from the pan, put in a wire rack to cool. Cool completely, about 2 hours. In small bowl, beat ⅓ cup powdered sugar, the honey, butter and dash of allspice until smooth, slowly adding additional powdered sugar for desired glaze consistency. Spread glaze over top of loaf. Let stand until set. (Glaze will remain slightly tacky to the touch.) Wrap tightly and store in refrigerator.

253. Plum Orange Bread

Servings: 1 Loaf   Cooking Time: 10 Minutes

Ingredients:
- 12 slice bread (1½ pounds)
- 1⅛ cup water, at 80°F to 90°F
- 2¼ tablespoons melted butter, cooled
- 3 tablespoons sugar
- ¾ teaspoon salt
- ¾ teaspoon orange zest
- ⅓ teaspoon ground cinnamon
- Pinch ground nutmeg
- 1¾ cups plus 2 tablespoons whole-wheat flour
- 1⅛ cups white bread flour
- 1½ teaspoons bread machine or instant yeast
- 1 cup chopped fresh plums

Directions:
Preparing the Ingredients.   Choose the size of loaf of your preference and then measure the ingredients. Add all of the ingredients mentioned previously in the list, except for the plums. Close the lid after placing the pan in the bread machine.   Select the Bake cycle   Turn on the bread machine. White/Basic or Fruit/Nut (if your machine has this setting) setting, select the loaf size, and the crust color. Press start.   When the machine signals to add ingredients, add the plums. When the cycle is finished, carefully remove the pan from the bread maker and let it rest.   Remove the bread from the pan, put in a wire rack to cool for at least 10 minutes, and slice.

254. Delicious Apple Bread

Servings: 10   Cooking Time: 3 Hours 27 Minutes

Ingredients:
- Buttermilk – 1 cup.
- Apple juice concentrate – ¼ cup.
- Butter – 1 ½ tbsps.
- Brown sugar – 3 tbsps.
- Ground cinnamon – 1 ½ tsp.
- Apples – 1 cup., peeled and chopped
- Salt – 1 tsp.
- Bread flour – 3 ½ cups.
- Vital wheat gluten – 4 tsps.
- Yeast – 2 tsps.

Directions:
Add all ingredients to the bread machine as listed order. Select sweet bread setting then select light/medium crust and start. Once loaf is done, remove the loaf pan from the machine. Allow it to cool for 15 minutes. Slice and serve.

255. Poppy Seed–lemon Bread

Servings: 1 Loaf   Cooking Time: 10 Minutes

Ingredients:
- 1 cup sugar
- ¼ cup grated lemon peel
- 1 cup milk
- ¾ cup vegetable oil
- 2 tablespoons poppy seed
- 2 teaspoons baking powder
- ½ teaspoon salt
- 2 eggs, slightly beaten

Directions:
Preparing the Ingredients.   Choose the size of loaf of your preference and then measure the ingredients. Add all of the ingredients mentioned previously in the list. Close the lid after placing the pan in the bread machine Select the Bake cycle   Turn on the bread machine. Select the White/Basic setting, select the loaf size, and the crust color. Press start.   When the cycle is finished, carefully remove the pan from the bread maker and let it rest.   Remove the bread from the pan, put in a wire rack to cool completely, about 2 hours. Wrap tightly and store at room temperature up to 4 days, or refrigerate.

256. Banana Whole-wheat Bread

Servings: 1 Loaf   Cooking Time: 10 Minutes

Ingredients:
- 12 slice bread (1½ pounds)
- ½ cup milk, at 80°F to 90°F
- 1 cup mashed banana
- 1 egg, at room temperature
- 1½ tablespoons melted butter, cooled

- 3 tablespoons honey
- 1 teaspoon pure vanilla extract
- ½ teaspoon salt
- 1 cup whole-wheat flour
- 1¼ cups white bread flour
- 1½ teaspoons bread machine or instant yeast

Directions:

Preparing the Ingredients. Choose the size of loaf of your preference and then measure the ingredients. Add all of the ingredients mentioned previously in the list. Close the lid after placing the pan in the bread machine Select the Bake cycle. Turn on the bread machine. Select the Sweet bread setting, select the loaf size, and the crust color. Press start. When the cycle is finished, carefully remove the pan from the bread maker and let it rest. Shake the bucket to remove the loaf, and turn it out onto a rack to cool.

257. Zucchini Spice Bread

Servings: 1 Loaf

Ingredients:

- 16 slice bread (2 pounds)
- 2 eggs, at room temperature
- ⅔ cup unsalted butter, melted
- ⅔ teaspoon table salt
- 1 cup shredded zucchini
- ⅔ cup light brown sugar
- 3 tablespoons sugar
- 2 cups all-purpose flour
- ⅔ teaspoon baking powder
- ⅔ teaspoon baking soda
- ⅓ teaspoon ground allspice
- 1⅓ teaspoons ground cinnamon
- ⅔ cup chopped pecans
- 12 slice bread (1½ pounds)
- 2 eggs, at room temperature
- ½ cup unsalted butter, melted
- ½ teaspoon table salt
- ¾ cup shredded zucchini
- ½ cup light brown sugar
- 2 tablespoons sugar
- 1½ cups all-purpose flour
- ½ teaspoon baking powder
- ½ teaspoon baking soda
- ¼ teaspoon ground allspice
- 1 teaspoon ground cinnamon
- ½ cup chopped pecans

Directions:

Choose the size of loaf you would like to make and measure your ingredients. Add the ingredients to the bread pan in the order listed above. Place the pan in the bread machine and close the lid. Turn on the bread maker. Select the Quick/Rapid setting, then the loaf size, and finally the crust color. Start the cycle. When the cycle is finished and the bread is baked, carefully remove the pan from the machine. Use a potholder as the handle will be very hot. Let rest for a few minutes. Remove the bread from the pan and allow to cool down on a wire rack for at least 10 minutes or more before slicing.

Nutrition Info:(Per Serving):Calories 167, fat 8.3 g, carbs 19.7 g, sodium 223 mg, protein 3.2 g

258. Chocolate-pistachio Bread

Servings: 2/3 Cup (24 Slices)   Cooking Time: 10 Minutes

Ingredients:

- ⅔ cup granulated sugar
- ½ cup butter, melted
- ¾ cup milk
- 1 egg
- 1½ cups all-purpose flour
- 1 cup chopped pistachio nuts
- ½ cup semisweet chocolate chips
- ⅓ cup unsweetened baking cocoa
- 2 teaspoons baking powder
- ¼ teaspoon salt
- Decorator sugar crystals, if desired

Directions:

Preparing the Ingredients. Choose the size of loaf of your preference and then measure the ingredients. Add all of the ingredients mentioned previously in the list. Close the lid after placing the pan in the bread machine. Select the Bake cycle Turn on the bread machine. Select the White/Basic setting, select the loaf size, and the crust color. Press start. When the cycle is finished, carefully remove the pan from the bread maker and let it rest. Remove the bread from the pan, put in a wire rack to cool for at least 2 hours. Wrap tightly and store at room temperature up to 4 days, or refrigerate.

259. Basil Tomato Bread

Servings: 14 Slices   Cooking Time: 10 Minutes

Ingredients:

- 2¼ tsp dried active baking yeast
- 1⅝ cups bread flour
- 3 Tbsp wheat bran
- 5 Tbsp quinoa
- 3 Tbsp dried milk powder
- 1 Tbsp dried basil
- 25g sun-dried tomatoes, chopped
- 1 tsp salt
- 1⅛ cups water
- 1 cup boiling water to cover tomatoes

Directions:

Preparing the Ingredients. Cover dried tomatoes with boiling water in a bowl. Soak for 10 minutes, drain, and cool to room temperature. Snip tomatoes into small pieces, using scissors. Add each ingredient to the bread machine in the order and at the temperature recommended by your bread machine manufacturer. Select the Bake cycle Close the lid, select the basic bread, medium crust setting on your bread machine and press start. When the bread machine has finished baking, remove the bread and put it on a cooling rack.

260. Cornmeal Bread

Servings: 14 Slices   Cooking Time: 2 H. 10 Min.

Ingredients:

- 2½ tsp active dry yeast
- 1⅓ cup water
- 2 Tbsp dark or light brown sugar
- 1 large beaten egg
- 2 Tbsp softened butter
- 1½ tsp salt
- ¾ cup cornmeal
- ¾ cup whole wheat flour
- 2¾ cups white bread flour

Directions:
Add each ingredient to the bread machine in the order and at the temperature recommended by your bread machine manufacturer. Close the lid, select the basic bread, medium crust setting on your bread machine, and press start. When the bread machine has finished baking, remove the bread and put it on a cooling rack.

261. Gluten-free Glazed Lemon-pecan Bread

Servings: 1 Loaf   Cooking Time: 10 Minutes

Ingredients:
- 12 slice bread (1½ pounds)
- ½ cup white rice flour
- ½ cup tapioca flour
- ½ cup potato starch
- ¼ cup sweet white sorghum flour
- ¼ cup garbanzo and fava flour
- 1 teaspoon xanthan gum
- 1 teaspoon gluten-free baking powder
- 1 teaspoon baking soda
- ½ teaspoon salt
- 2 eggs
- ½ cup sunflower or canola oil or melted ghee
- ¼ cup almond milk, soymilk or regular milk
- ½ teaspoon cider vinegar
- 1 tablespoon grated lemon peel
- ¼ cup fresh lemon juice
- ⅔ cup granulated sugar
- ½ cup chopped pecans
- glaze
- 2 tablespoons fresh lemon juice
- 1 cup gluten-free powdered sugar

Directions:
Preparing the Ingredients. Choose the size of loaf of your preference and then measure the ingredients. Add all of the ingredients mentioned previously in the list. Close the lid after placing the pan in the bread machine. Select the Bake cycle. Turn on the bread machine. Select the White/Basic setting, select the loaf size, and the crust color. Press start. When the cycle is finished, carefully remove the pan from the bread maker and let it rest. Remove the bread from the pan, put in a wire rack to Cool about 10 minutes. In small bowl, stir all glaze ingredients until smooth. With fork, poke holes in top of loaf; drizzle glaze over loaf. Serve warm.

262. Cinnamon Apple Bread

Servings: 1 Loaf

Ingredients:
- 16 slice bread (2 pounds)
- 1⅓ cups lukewarm milk
- 3⅓ tablespoons butter, melted
- 2⅔ tablespoons sugar
- 2 teaspoons table salt
- 1⅓ teaspoons cinnamon, ground
- A pinch ground cloves
- 4 cups white bread flour
- 2¼ teaspoons bread machine yeast
- 1⅓ cups peeled apple, finely diced
- 12 slice bread (1½ pounds)
- 1 cup lukewarm milk
- 2½ tablespoons butter, melted
- 2 tablespoons sugar
- 1½ teaspoons table salt
- 1 teaspoon cinnamon, ground
- Pinch ground cloves
- 3 cups white bread flour
- 2¼ teaspoons bread machine yeast
- 1 cup peeled apple, finely diced

Directions:
Choose the size of loaf you would like to make and measure your ingredients. Add all of the ingredients except for the apples to the bread pan in the order listed above. Place the pan in the bread machine and close the lid. Turn on the bread maker. Select the White/Basic or Fruit/Nut (if your machine has this setting) setting, then the loaf size, and finally the crust color. Start the cycle. When the machine signals to add ingredients, add the apples. (Some machines have a fruit/nut hopper where you can add the apples when you start the machine. The machine will automatically add them to the dough during the baking process.) When the cycle is finished and the bread is baked, carefully remove the pan from the machine. Use a potholder as the handle will be very hot. Let rest for a few minutes. Remove the bread from the pan and allow to cool on a wire rack for at least 10 minutes before slicing.
Nutrition Info:(Per Serving):Calories 174, fat 2.3 g, carbs 26.4 g, sodium 286 mg, protein 4.6 g

263. Yeasted Pumpkin Bread

Servings: 1 Loaf   Cooking Time: 10 Minutes

Ingredients:
- 8 slice bread (1 pounds)
- ⅓ cup milk, at 80°F to 90°F
- ⅔ cup canned pumpkin
- 2 tablespoons melted butter, cooled
- ⅔ teaspoon grated ginger
- 2¾ tablespoons sugar
- ½ teaspoon salt
- ⅔ teaspoon ground cinnamon
- ¼ teaspoon ground cloves
- 2 cups white bread flour
- 1⅛ teaspoons bread machine or instant yeast

Directions:
Preparing the Ingredients. Choose the size of loaf of your preference and then measure the ingredients. Add all of the ingredients mentioned previously in the list. Close the lid after placing the pan in the bread machine.

Select the Bake cycle   Turn on the bread machine. Select the White/Basic setting, select the loaf size, and the crust color. Press start.   When the cycle is finished, carefully remove the pan from the bread maker and let it rest.   Remove the bread from the pan, put in a wire rack to Cool about 10 minutes. Slice

264. Fresh Blueberry Bread

Servings: 1 Loaf   Cooking Time: 10 Minutes
Ingredients:
- 12 to 16 slices (1½ to 2 pounds)
- 1 cup plain Greek yogurt, at room temperature
- ½ cup milk, at room temperature
- 3 tablespoons butter, at room temperature
- 2 eggs, at room temperature
- ½ cup sugar
- ¼ cup light brown sugar
- 1 teaspoon pure vanilla extract
- ½ teaspoon lemon zest
- 2 cups all-purpose flour
- 1 tablespoon baking powder
- ¾ teaspoon salt
- ¼ teaspoon ground nutmeg
- 1 cup blueberries

Directions:
Preparing the Ingredients.   Place the yogurt, milk, butter, eggs, sugar, brown sugar, vanilla, and zest in your bread machine.   Select the Bake cycle.   Program the machine for Quick/Rapid bread and press Start. While the wet ingredients are mixing, stir together the flour, baking powder, salt, and nutmeg in a medium bowl. After the first fast mixing is done and the machine signals, add the dry ingredients. When the second mixing cycle is complete, stir in the blueberries. When the loaf is done, remove the bucket from the machine. Let the loaf cool for 5 minutes. Gently shake the bucket to remove the loaf, and turn it out onto a rack to cool.

265. Strawberry Shortcake Bread

Servings: 1 Loaf   Cooking Time: 10 Minutes
Ingredients:
- 12 slice bread (1½ pounds)
- 1⅛ cups milk, at 80°F to 90°F
- 3 tablespoons melted butter, cooled
- 3 tablespoons sugar
- 1½ teaspoons salt
- ¾ cup sliced fresh strawberries
- 1 cup quick oats
- 2¼ cups white bread flour
- 1½ teaspoons bread machine or instant yeast

Directions:
Preparing the Ingredients.   Choose the size of loaf of your preference and then measure the ingredients. Add all of the ingredients mentioned previously in the list. Close the lid after placing the pan in the bread machine.   Select the Bake cycle   Turn on the bread machine. Select the White/Basic setting, select the loaf size, and the crust color. Press start.   When the cycle is finished, carefully remove the pan from the bread maker

and let it rest.   Remove the bread from the pan, put in a wire rack to cool for at least 2 hours, and slice.

266. Chocolate-cherry Bread

Servings: 1 Loaf   Cooking Time: 10 Minutes
Ingredients:
- 1½ teaspoons baking powder
- ½ teaspoon baking soda
- ¼ teaspoon salt
- ¾ cup sugar
- ½ cup butter, softened
- 2 eggs
- 1 teaspoon almond extract
- 1 teaspoon vanilla
- 1 container (8 oz) sour cream
- ½ cup chopped dried cherries
- ½ cup bittersweet or dark chocolate chips

Directions:
Preparing the Ingredients.   Choose the size of loaf of your preference and then measure the ingredients. Add all of the ingredients mentioned previously in the list. Close the lid after placing the pan in the bread machine.   Select the Bake cycle   Turn on the bread machine. Select the White/Basic setting, select the loaf size, and the crust color. Press start.   When the cycle is finished, carefully remove the pan from the bread maker and let it rest.   Remove the bread from the pan, put in a wire rack to cool for at least 2 hours. Wrap tightly and store at room temperature up to 4 days, or refrigerate.

267. Tomato Herb Bread

Servings: 1 Loaf   Cooking Time: 10 Minutes
Ingredients:
- 8 slice bread (1 pounds)
- ½ cup tomato sauce, at 80°F to 90°F
- ½ tablespoon olive oil
- ½ tablespoon sugar
- 1 tablespoon dried basil
- ½ tablespoon dried oregano
- ½ teaspoon salt
- 2 tablespoons grated Parmesan cheese
- 1½ cups white bread flour
- 1⅛ teaspoons bread machine or instant yeast

Directions:
Preparing the Ingredients.   Choose the size of loaf of your preference and then measure the ingredients. Add all of the ingredients mentioned previously in the list. Close the lid after placing the pan in the bread machine. Select the Bake cycle   Turn on the bread machine. Select the White/Basic setting, select the loaf size, and the crust color. Press start.   When the cycle is finished, carefully remove the pan from the bread maker and let it rest.   Remove the bread from the pan, put in a wire rack to Cool about 5 minutes. Slice

268. Confetti Bread

Servings: 1 Loaf   Cooking Time: 10 Minutes
Ingredients:
- 8 slice bread (1 pounds)

- ⅓ cup milk, at 80°F to 90°F
- 2 tablespoons water, at 80°F to 90°F
- 2 teaspoons melted butter, cooled
- ⅔ teaspoon white vinegar
- 4 teaspoons sugar
- ⅔ teaspoon salt
- 4 teaspoons grated Parmesan cheese
- ⅓ cup quick oats
- 1⅔ cups white bread flour
- 1 teaspoon bread machine or instant yeast
- ⅓ cup finely chopped zucchini
- ¼ cup finely chopped yellow bell pepper
- ¼ cup finely chopped red bell pepper
- 4 teaspoons chopped chives

Directions:
Preparing the Ingredients. Place the ingredients, except the vegetables, in your bread machine as recommended by the manufacturer. Select the Bake cycle Program the machine for Basic/White bread, select light or medium crust, and press Start. When the machine signals, add the chopped vegetables; if your machine has no signal, add the vegetables just before the second kneading is finished. When the cycle is finished, carefully remove the pan from the bread maker and let it rest. Remove the bread from the pan, put in a wire rack to Cool about 10 minutes. Slice

269. Tomato Bread

Servings: 8 Pcs   Cooking Time: 1 Hour And 30 Minutes
Ingredients:
- Three tablespoons tomato paste
- 1½ cups (340 ml) water
- 4 1/3 cups (560 g) flour
- 1½ tablespoon vegetable oil
- Two teaspoons sugar
- Two teaspoons salt
- 1 ½ teaspoons dry yeast
- ½ teaspoon oregano, dried
- ½ teaspoon ground sweet paprika

Directions:
Dilute the tomato paste in warm water. If you do not like the tomato flavour, reduce the amount of tomato paste, but putting less than one tablespoon does not make sense because the colour will fade. Prepare the spices. I added a little more oregano and Provencal herbs to the oregano and paprika (this bread also begs for kicks). Sift the flour to enrich it with oxygen. Add the spices to the flour and mix well. Pour the vegetable oil into the bread maker container. Add the tomato/water mixture, sugar, salt, the flour with spices, and then the yeast. Turn on the bread maker (the Basic program – I have the WHITE BREAD – the crust Medium). After the end of the baking cycle, turn off the bread maker. Remove the bread container and take out the hot bread. Place it on the grate for cooling for 1 hour. Enjoy!
Nutrition Info: Calories 281; Total Fat 3.3g; Saturated Fat 0.6g; Cholesterol 0g; Sodium 590mg; Total Carbohydrate 54.3g; Dietary Fiber 2.4g; Total Sugars 1.9g; Protein 7.6g

270. Cranberry & Golden Raisin Bread

Servings: 14 Slices   Cooking Time: 10 Minutes
Ingredients:
- 1⅓ cups water
- 4 Tbsp sliced butter
- 3 cups flour
- 1 cup old fashioned oatmeal
- ⅓ cup brown sugar
- 1 tsp salt
- 4 Tbsp dried cranberries
- 4 Tbsp golden raisins
- 2 tsp bread machine yeast

Directions:
Preparing the Ingredients   Add each ingredient except cranberries and golden raisins to the bread machine one by one, according to the manufacturer's instructions. Select the Bake cycle   Close the lid, select the sweet or basic bread, medium crust setting on your bread machine and press start. Add the cranberries and golden raisins 5 to 10 minutes before the last kneading cycle ends. When the bread machine has finished baking, remove the bread and put it on a cooling rack.

271. Gluten-free Best-ever Banana Bread

Servings: 1 Loaf   Cooking Time: 10 Minutes
Ingredients:
- 16 slices bread
- ½ cup tapioca flour
- ½ cup white rice flour
- ½ cup potato starch
- ¼ cup garbanzo and fava flour
- ¼ cup sweet white sorghum flour
- 1 teaspoon xanthan gum
- ½ teaspoon guar gum
- 1 teaspoon gluten-free baking powder
- 1 teaspoon baking soda
- 1 teaspoon salt
- 1 teaspoon ground cinnamon
- ¾ cup packed brown sugar
- 1 cup mashed very ripe bananas (2 medium)
- ½ cup ghee (measured melted)
- ¼ cup almond milk, soymilk or regular milk
- 1 teaspoon gluten-free vanilla
- 2 eggs

Directions:
Preparing the Ingredients. Choose the size of loaf of your preference and then measure the ingredients. Add all of the ingredients mentioned previously in the list. Close the lid after placing the pan in the bread machine. Select the Bake cycle   Turn on the bread machine. Select the White/Basic setting, select the loaf size, and the crust color. Press start. When the cycle is finished, carefully remove the pan from the bread maker and let it rest. Remove the bread from the pan, put in a wire rack to Cool about 1 hour.

272. Carrot Coriander Bread

Servings: 14 Slices   Cooking Time: 3 H.

Ingredients:
- 2-3 freshly grated carrots,
- 1⅛ cup lukewarm water
- 2 Tbsp sunflower oil
- 4 tsp freshly chopped coriander
- 2½ cups unbleached white bread flour
- 2 tsp ground coriander
- 1 tsp salt
- 5 tsp sugar
- 4 tsp easy blend dried yeast

Directions:
Add each ingredient to the bread machine in the order and at the temperature recommended by your bread machine manufacturer. Close the lid, select the basic bread, medium crust setting on your bread machine, and press start. When the bread machine has finished baking, remove the bread and put it on a cooling rack.

273. Raisin Candied Fruit Bread

Servings: 1 Loaf   Cooking Time: 10 Minutes

Ingredients:
- 16 slice bread (2 pounds)
- 1 egg, beaten
- 1½ cups + 1 tablespoon lukewarm water
- ⅔ teaspoon ground cardamom
- 1¼ teaspoons table salt
- 2 tablespoons sugar
- ⅓ cup butter, melted
- 4 cups bread flour
- 1¼ teaspoons bread machine yeast
- ½ cup raisins
- ½ cup mixed candied fruit

Directions:
Preparing the Ingredients. Choose the size of loaf of your preference and then measure the ingredients. Add all of the ingredients mentioned previously in the list, except for the candied fruits and raisins. Close the lid after placing the pan in the bread machine. Select the Bake cycle   Turn on the bread machine. White/Basic or Fruit/Nut (if your machine has this setting) setting, select the loaf size, and the crust color. Press start. When the machine signals to add ingredients, add the candied fruits and raisins. When the cycle is finished, carefully remove the pan from the bread maker and let it rest. Remove the bread from the pan, put in a wire rack to cool for at least 10 minutes, and slice.

274. Cinnamon Pumpkin Bread

Servings: 1 Loaf

Ingredients:
- 16 slice bread (2 pounds)
- 2 cups pumpkin puree
- 4 eggs, slightly beaten
- ½ cup unsalted butter, melted
- 1¼ cups sugar
- ½ teaspoon table salt
- 4 cups white bread flour
- 1 teaspoon cinnamon, ground
- ¾ teaspoon baking soda
- ½ teaspoon nutmeg, ground

- ½ teaspoon ginger, ground
- Pinch ground cloves
- 2 teaspoons baking powder
- 12 slice bread (1½ pounds)
- 1½ cups pumpkin puree
- 3 eggs, slightly beaten
- ⅓ cup unsalted butter, melted
- 1 cup sugar
- ¼ teaspoon table salt
- 3 cups white bread flour
- ¾ teaspoon cinnamon, ground
- ½ teaspoon baking soda
- ¼ teaspoon nutmeg, ground
- ¼ teaspoon ginger, ground
- Pinch ground cloves
- 1½ teaspoons baking powder

Directions:
Choose the size of loaf you would like to make and measure your ingredients. Add the ingredients to the bread pan in the order listed above. Place the pan in the bread machine and close the lid. Turn on the bread maker. Select the Quick/Rapid setting, then the loaf size, and finally the crust color. Start the cycle. When the cycle is finished and the bread is baked, carefully remove the pan from the machine. Use a potholder as the handle will be very hot. Let rest for a few minutes. Remove the bread from the pan and allow to cool on a wire rack for at least 10 minutes before slicing.

Nutrition Info: (Per Serving):Calories 246, fat 6.7 g, carbs 37.6 g, sodium 146 mg, protein 5.2 g

275. Curd Onion Bread With Sesame Seeds

Servings: 8 Pcs   Cooking Time: 1 Hour And 30 Minutes

Ingredients:
- ¾ cup of water
- 3 2/3 cups wheat flour
- ¾ cup cottage cheese
- Two tablespoons softened butter
- Two tablespoon sugar
- 1 ½ teaspoons salt
- 1 ½ tablespoon sesame seeds
- Two tablespoons dried onions
- One ¼ teaspoons dry yeast

Directions:
Put the products in the bread maker according to its instructions. Bake on the BASIC program.

Nutrition Info: Calories 277;Total Fat 4.7g;Saturated Fat 2.3g;Cholesterol 9g;Sodium 547mg;Total Carbohydrate 48.4g;Dietary Fiber 1.9g;Total Sugars 3.3g;Protein 9.4g

276. Banana Split Loaf

Servings: 12   Cooking Time: 1 Hour

Ingredients:
- 2 eggs
- 1/3 cup butter, melted
- 2 tablespoons whole milk
- 2 overripe bananas, mashed
- 2 cups all-purpose flour
- 2/3 cups sugar

- 1 1/4 teaspoons baking powder
- 1/2 teaspoon baking soda
- 1/2 teaspoon salt
- 1 cup chopped walnuts
- 1/2 cup chocolate chips

Directions:
Pour eggs, butter, milk and bananas into the bread maker pan and set aside. Stir together all dry ingredients in a large mixing bowl. Add dry ingredients to bread maker pan. Set to Basic setting, medium crust color, and press Start. Remove bread and place on a cooling rack before serving.

Nutrition Info: Calories: 260, Sodium: 203 mg, Dietary Fiber: 1.6 g, Fat: 11.3 g, Carbs: 35.9 g, Protein: 5.2 g.

277. Honey Potato Flakes Bread

Servings: 1 Loaf
Ingredients:
- 16 slice bread (2 pounds)
- 1⅓ cups lukewarm milk
- 2⅔ tablespoons unsalted butter, melted
- 4 teaspoons honey
- 2 teaspoons table salt
- 4 cups white bread flour
- 1½ teaspoons dried thyme
- ⅔ cup instant potato flakes
- 2½ teaspoons bread machine yeast
- 12 slice bread (1½ pounds)
- 1¼ cups lukewarm milk
- 2 tablespoons unsalted butter, melted
- 1 tablespoon honey
- 1½ teaspoons table salt
- 3 cups white bread flour
- 1 teaspoon dried thyme
- ½ cup instant potato flakes
- 2 teaspoons bread machine yeast

Directions:
Choose the size of loaf you would like to make and measure your ingredients. Add the ingredients to the bread pan in the order listed above. Place the pan in the bread machine and close the lid. Turn on the bread maker. Select the White/Basic setting, then the loaf size, and finally the crust color. Start the cycle. When the cycle is finished and the bread is baked, carefully remove the pan from the machine. Use a potholder as the handle will be very hot. Let rest for a few minutes. Remove the bread from the pan and allow to cool on a wire rack for at least 10 minutes before slicing.

Nutrition Info: (Per Serving):Calories 157, fat 3.1 g, carbs 27.8 g, sodium 294 mg, protein 4.8 g

278. Tomato Onion Bread

Servings: 12 Slices   Cooking Time: 1 Hour And 30 Minutes
Ingredients:
- 2 cups all-purpose flour
- 1 cup wholemeal flour
- ½ cup of warm water
- 4¾ ounces (140 ml) milk

- Three tablespoons olive oil
- Two tablespoons sugar
- One teaspoon salt
- Two teaspoons dry yeast
- ½ teaspoon baking powder
- Five sun-dried tomatoes
- One onion
- ¼ teaspoon black pepper

Directions:
Prepare all the necessary products. Finely chop the onion and sauté in a frying pan. Cut up the sun-dried tomatoes (10 halves). Pour all liquid ingredients into the bowl, then cover with flour and put in the tomatoes and onions. Pour in the yeast and baking powder without touching the liquid. Select the baking mode and start. You can choose the Bread with Additives program, and then the bread maker will knead the dough at low speeds. I chose the usual baking mode the kneading was very active, and the vegetables practically dissolved in the dough. For children who like to find something in the food and carefully remove it from it (for example, pieces of onions), this is an ideal option! Enjoy!

Nutrition Info: Calories 241;Total Fat 6.4g;Saturated Fat 1.1g;Sodium 305mg;Total Carbohydrate 40g;Total Sugars 6.8g;Protein 6.7g

279. Potato Bread

Servings: 14 Slices   Cooking Time: 3 H. 10 Min.
Ingredients:
- ¾ cup milk
- ½ cup water
- 2 Tbsp canola oil
- 1½ tsp salt
- 3 cups bread flour
- ½ cup instant potato flakes
- 1 Tbsp sugar
- ¼ tsp white pepper
- 2 tsp active dry yeast

Directions:
Add each ingredient to the bread machine in the order and at the temperature recommended by your bread machine manufacturer. Close the lid, select the basic bread, medium crust setting on your bread machine, and press start. When the bread machine has finished baking, remove the bread and put it on a cooling rack.

280. Olive Bread With Italian Herbs

Servings: 8 Pcs   Cooking Time: 1 Hour And 50 Minutes
Ingredients:
- 1 cup (250 ml) water
- ½ cup brine from olives
- Four tablespoons butter
- Three tablespoons sugar
- Two teaspoons salt
- 4 cups flour
- Two teaspoons dry yeast
- ½ cup olives
- One teaspoon Italian herbs

Directions:

Add all liquid products. Then add the butter. Fill with brine and water. Add salt and sugar. Gently pour in the flour and pour the dry yeast in the corners on top of the flour. Send the form to the bread maker and wait for the signal before the last dough kneading to add the olives and herbs. In the meantime, cut olives into 2-3 parts. After the bread maker signals, add it and the Italian herbs into the dough. Then wait again for the bread maker to signal that the bread is ready. Cooled Bread has an exciting structure, not to mention the smell and taste. Bon Appetit!

Nutrition Info: Calories: 332 Cal;Fat: 7.5 g;Cholesterol: 15 g;Sodium: 749 mg;Carbohydrates: 55.5 g;Fiber: 3

281. Savory Onion Bread

Servings: 1 Loaf   Cooking Time: 10 Minutes
Ingredients:
- 12 slice bread (1½ pounds)
- 1 cup water, at 80°F to 90°F
- 3 tablespoons melted butter, cooled
- 1½ tablespoons sugar
- 1⅛ teaspoons salt
- 3 tablespoons dried minced onion
- 1½ tablespoons chopped fresh chives
- 3 cups plus 2 tablespoons white bread flour
- 1⅔ teaspoons bread machine or instant yeast

Directions:
Preparing the Ingredients. Place the ingredients in your bread machine as recommended by the manufacturer. Select the Bake cycle   Turn on the bread machine. Select the White/Basic setting, select the loaf size, and the crust color. Press start. When the cycle is finished, carefully remove the pan from the bread maker and let it rest. Remove the bread from the pan, put in a wire rack to Cool about 5 minutes. Slice

282. Potato Honey Bread

Servings: 1 Loaf   Cooking Time: 10 Minutes
Ingredients:
- 12 slice bread (1½ pounds)
- ¾ cup lukewarm water
- ½ cup finely mashed potatoes, at room temperature
- 1 egg, at room temperature
- ¼ cup unsalted butter, melted
- 2 tablespoons honey
- 1 teaspoon table salt
- 3 cups white bread flour
- 2 teaspoons bread machine yeast

Directions:
Preparing the Ingredients. Choose the size of loaf of your preference and then measure the ingredients. Add all of the ingredients mentioned previously in the list. Close the lid after placing the pan in the bread machine. Select the Bake cycle   Turn on the bread machine. Select the White/Basic setting, select the loaf size, and the crust color. Press start. When the cycle is finished, carefully remove the pan from the bread maker and let it

rest. Remove the bread from the pan, put in a wire rack to Cool about 10 minutes. Slice

283. Cinnamon Raisin Breadsticks

Servings: 16   Cooking Time: 3 Hours
Ingredients:
- 1 cup milk
- 2 tablespoons water
- 1 tablespoon oil
- 3/4 teaspoon salt
- 2 tablespoons brown sugar
- 3 cups bread flour
- 1 teaspoon cinnamon
- 1 tablespoon active dry yeast
- 1/2 cup raisins
- Vanilla icing, for glaze

Directions:
Preheat oven to 475°F. Mix the cinnamon into the bread flour. Add milk, water, oil, salt and brown sugar to the bread maker pan, then add the flour/cinnamon mixture. Make a well in the center of the dry ingredients and add the yeast. Set on Dough cycle and press Start. Take out the dough out and punch down; let rest for 10 minutes. Roll dough into a 12-by-8-inch rectangle. Sprinkle raisins on one half of the dough and gently press them into the dough. Fold the dough in half and gently roll and stretch dough back out into a rectangle. Cut into strips, then twist. Line a baking sheet with parchment paper and bake for 4 minutes. Place on 2 baking sheets that have been lined with parchment paper. Reduce oven temperature to 350°F. Brush breadsticks lightly with water and return to oven and bake 20-25 minutes. Cool on a wire rack. Glaze with vanilla icing and serve.

Nutrition Info: Calories: 121, Sodium: 117 mg, Dietary Fiber: 1 g, Fat: 1.4 g, Carbs: 23.7 g, Protein: 3.4 g.

284. Cranberry Orange Pecan Bread

Servings: 16   Cooking Time: 2 Hours 50 Minutes
Ingredients:
- 1 cup water
- 1/4 cup orange juice
- 2 teaspoons salt
- 1/3 cup sugar
- 2 1/2 tablespoons nonfat dry milk
- 2 1/2 tablespoons butter, cubed
- 4 cups bread flour
- 2 1/2 teaspoons orange zest
- 2 1/2 teaspoons bread machine yeast
- 1/2 cup dried cranberries
- 1/2 cup pecans, chopped

Directions:
Set aside cranberries and pecans, then place all other ingredients in the bread maker pan in order listed. Choose Sweet cycle, light crust and press Start. Add cranberries and pecans at the end of the kneading cycle. Transfer to a plate and let cool 10 minutes before slicing with a bread knife.

Nutrition Info: Calories: 247 Sodium: 311 Dietary Fiber: 2.6 g, Fat: 11.5 g, Carbs: 31.5 g, Protein: 5.4 g.

285. Black Olive Bread

Servings: 1 Loaf   Cooking Time: 10 Minutes

Ingredients:
- 12 slices (1½ pounds)
- 1 cup milk, at 80°F to 90°F
- 1½ tablespoons melted butter, cooled
- 1 teaspoon minced garlic
- 1½ tablespoons sugar
- 1 teaspoon salt
- 3 cups white bread flour
- 1 teaspoon bread machine or instant yeast
- ⅓ cup chopped black olives

Directions:
Preparing the Ingredients.   Choose the size of loaf of your preference and then measure the ingredients. Add all of the ingredients mentioned previously in the list. Close the lid after placing the pan in the bread machine.   Select the Bake cycle   Turn on the bread machine. Select the White/Basic setting, select the loaf size, and the crust color. Press start.   When the cycle is finished, carefully remove the pan from the bread maker and let it rest.   Remove the bread from the pan, put in a wire rack to cool for at least 10 minutes.

286. Cranberry Walnut Wheat Bread

Servings: 14 Slices   Cooking Time: 10 Minutes

Ingredients:
- 1 cup warm water
- 1 tablespoon molasses
- 2 tablespoons butter
- 1 teaspoon salt
- 2 cups 100% whole wheat flour
- 1 cup unbleached flour
- 2 tablespoons dry milk
- 1 cup cranberries
- 1 cup walnuts, chopped
- 2 teaspoons active dry yeast

Directions:
Preparing the Ingredients   Add the liquid ingredients to the bread maker pan. Add the dry ingredients, except the yeast, walnuts and cranberries.   Make a well in the center of the bread flour and add the yeast. Insert the pan into your bread maker and secure the lid.   Select the Bake cycle   Select Wheat Bread setting, choose your preferred crust color, and press Start. Add cranberries and walnuts after first kneading cycle is finished. Remove the bread from the oven and turn it out of the pan onto a cooling rack and allow it to cool completely before slicing.

287. Caramelized Onion Focaccia Bread

Servings: 4   Cooking Time: 10 Minutes

Ingredients:
- 3/4 cup water
- 2 tablespoons olive oil
- 1 tablespoon sugar
- 1 teaspoon salt
- 2 cups flour
- 1 1/2 teaspoons yeast
- 3/4 cup mozzarella cheese, shredded
- 2 tablespoons parmesan cheese, shredded
- Onion topping:
- 3 tablespoons butter
- 2 medium onions
- 2 cloves garlic, minced

Directions:
Preparing the Ingredients   Place all ingredients, except cheese and onion topping, in your bread maker in the order listed above.   Grease a large baking sheet.   Pat dough into a 12-inch circle on the pan; cover and let rise in warm place for about 30 minutes.   Melt butter in large frying pan over medium-low heat. Cook onions and garlic in butter 15 minutes, stirring often, until onions are caramelized.   Preheat an oven to 400°F.   Make deep depressions across the dough at 1-inch intervals with the handle of a wooden spoon.   Spread the onion topping over dough and sprinkle with cheeses.   Bake 15 to 20 minutes or until golden brown. Cut into wedges and serve warm.

288. Garden Vegetable Bread

Servings: 14 Slices   Cooking Time: 3 H.

Ingredients:
- ½ cup warm buttermilk (70°F to 80°F)
- 3 Tbsp water (70°F to 80°F)
- 1 Tbsp canola oil
- ⅔ cup shredded zucchini
- ¼ cup chopped red sweet pepper
- 2 Tbsp chopped green onions
- 2 Tbsp grated parmesan cheese
- 2 Tbsp sugar
- 1 tsp salt
- ½ tsp lemon-pepper seasoning
- ½ cup old-fashioned oats
- 2½ cup bread flour
- 1½ tsp active dry yeast
- Peppercorns

Directions:
Add each ingredient to the bread machine in the order and at the temperature recommended by your bread machine manufacturer.   Close the lid, select the basic bread, medium crust setting on your bread machine and press start.   When the bread machine has finished baking, remove the bread and put it on a cooling rack.

289. Oatmeal Zucchini Bread

Servings: 1 Loaf   Cooking Time: 10 Minutes

Ingredients:
- 8 slice bread (1 pounds)
- ⅓ cup milk, at 80°F to 90°F
- ½ cup finely shredded zucchini
- ¼ teaspoon freshly squeezed lemon juice, at room temperature
- 2 teaspoons olive oil
- 2 teaspoons sugar
- ⅔ teaspoon salt
- ½ cup quick oats
- ½ cup whole-wheat flour
- 1 cup white bread flour

- 1½ teaspoons bread machine or instant yeast

Directions:

Preparing the Ingredients. Choose the size of loaf of your preference and then measure the ingredients. Add all of the ingredients mentioned previously in the list. Close the lid after placing the pan in the bread machine. Select the Bake cycle Turn on the bread machine. Select the White/Basic setting, select the loaf size, and the crust color. Press start. When the cycle is finished, carefully remove the pan from the bread maker and let it rest. Remove the bread from the pan, put in a wire rack to Cool about 10 minutes. Slice

290. Olive Rosemary Bread

Servings: 10   Cooking Time: 3 Hours 27 Minutes

Ingredients:
- Water – 1 cup.
- Olives – 1 cup., pitted and quartered
- Salt – 1 tsp.
- Sugar – 1 tbsp.
- Olive oil – 2 tbsps.
- Bread flour – 3 ¼ cups.
- Rosemary – ¼ cup., chopped
- Instant yeast – 1 ¼ tsp.

Directions:

Add all ingredients into the bread machine pan. Select sweet bread setting then select medium crust and start. Once loaf is done, remove the loaf pan from the machine. Allow it to cool for 10 minutes. Slice and serve.

291. Hot Red Pepper Bread

Servings: 1 Loaf   Cooking Time: 10 Minutes

Ingredients:
- 12 slice bread (1½ pounds)
- 1¼ cups milk, at 80°F to 90°F
- ¼ cup red pepper relish
- 2 tablespoons chopped roasted red pepper
- 3 tablespoons melted butter, cooled
- 3 tablespoons light brown sugar
- 1 teaspoon salt
- 3 cups white bread flour
- 1½ teaspoons bread machine or instant yeast

Directions:

Preparing the Ingredients. Choose the size of loaf of your preference and then measure the ingredients. Add all of the ingredients mentioned previously in the list. Close the lid after placing the pan in the bread machine. Select the Bake cycle Turn on the bread machine. Select the White/Basic setting, select the loaf size, and the crust color. Press start. When the cycle is finished, carefully remove the pan from the bread maker and let it rest. Remove the bread from the pan, put in a wire rack to Cool about 10 minutes. Slice

292. Beetroot Bread

Servings: 1 Loaf

Ingredients:
- 16 slice bread (2 pounds)
- 1 cup lukewarm water

- 1 cup grated raw beetroot
- 2 tablespoons unsalted butter, melted
- 2 tablespoons sugar
- 2 teaspoons table salt
- 4 cups white bread flour
- 1⅔ teaspoons bread machine yeast
- 12 slice bread (1½ pounds)
- ¾ cups lukewarm water
- ¾ cup grated raw beetroot
- 1½ tablespoons unsalted butter, melted
- 1½ tablespoons sugar
- 1¼ teaspoons table salt
- 3 cups white bread flour
- 1¼ teaspoons bread machine yeast

Directions:

Choose the size of loaf you would like to make and measure your ingredients. Add the ingredients to the bread pan in the order listed above. Place the pan in the bread machine and close the lid. Turn on the bread maker. Select the White/Basic setting, then the loaf size, and finally the crust color. Start the cycle. When the cycle is finished and the bread is baked, carefully remove the pan from the machine. Use a potholder as the handle will be very hot. Let rest for a few minutes. Remove the bread from the pan and allow to cool on a wire rack for at least 10 minutes before slicing.

Nutrition Info:(Per Serving):Calories 143, fat 2.3 g, carbs 26.4 g, sodium 268 mg, protein 4 g

293. Squash Carrot Bread

Servings: 8 Pcs   Cooking Time: 1 Hour And 30 Minutes

Ingredients:
- One small zucchini
- One baby carrot
- 1 cup whey
- 1 ½ cups (180 g) white wheat flour
- ¾ cup (100 g) whole wheat flour
- ¾ cup (100 g) rye flour
- Two tablespoons vegetable oil
- One teaspoon yeast, fresh
- One teaspoon salt
- ½ teaspoon sugar

Directions:

Cut/dice carrots and zucchini to about 8-10 mm (1/2 inch) in size. In a frying pan, heat the vegetable oil, then fry the vegetables over medium heat until soft. If desired, season the vegetables with salt and pepper. Transfer the vegetables to a flat plate so that they cool down more quickly. While still hot, they cannot be added to the dough. Now dissolve the yeast in the serum. Send all kinds of flour, serum with yeast, as well as salt and sugar to the bakery. Knead the dough in the dough for the Rolls program. At the very end of the batch, add the vegetables to the dough. After adding vegetables, the dough will become moister at the end of the fermentation, which will last about an hour before doubling the dough's volume, shift it onto a thickly floured surface. Form into a loaf and put it in an oiled form. Cover the form with a food film and leave for 1 to 1 1/3 hours. Preheat oven to 450°F and put bread in it. Bake the bread for 15 minutes, and then gently remove it from the mould. Lay it on the grate and bake for 15-20 minutes more

Nutrition Info: Calories 220; Total Fat 4.3g; Saturated Fat 0.8g; Cholesterol 0g; Sodium 313mg; Total Carbohydrate 39.1g; Dietary Fiber 4.1g; Total Sugars 2.7g; Protein 6.6g

294. Mushroom Leek Bread

Servings: 10   Cooking Time: 2 Hours

Ingredients:
- Butter – 2 tbsps.
- Mushrooms – 2 cups., sliced
- Leeks – ¾ cup., sliced
- Dried thyme – 1 ½ tsps.
- Water – 1 1/3 cup.
- Salt – 1 ½ tsps.
- Honey – 2 tbsps.
- Whole wheat flour – 1 ¼ cups.
- Bread flour – 3 cups.
- Yeast – 1 tsp.

Directions:
Heat butter into the saucepan over medium-high heat. Add leeks, mushrooms, and thyme and sauté until tender. Transfer mushroom leek mixture into the bread machine pan. Add remaining ingredients into the bread machine pan. Select basic setting then select medium crust and start. Once loaf is done, remove the loaf pan from the machine. Allow it to cool for 10 minutes. Slice and serve.

295. Cranberry Orange Breakfast Bread

Servings: 14 Slices   Cooking Time: 10 Minutes

Ingredients:
- 1⅛ cup orange juice
- 2 Tbsp vegetable oil
- 2 Tbsp honey
- 3 cups bread flour
- 1 Tbsp dry milk powder
- ½ tsp ground cinnamon
- ½ tsp ground allspice
- 1 tsp salt
- 1 (.25 ounce) package active dry yeast
- 1 Tbsp grated orange zest
- 1 cup sweetened dried cranberries
- ⅓ cup chopped walnuts

Directions:
Preparing the Ingredients.   Add each ingredient to the bread machine in the order and at the temperature recommended by your bread machine manufacturer. Select the Bake cycle   Close the lid, select the basic bread, low crust setting on your bread machine, and press start.   Add the cranberries and chopped walnuts 5 to 10 minutes before last kneading cycle ends.   When the bread machine has finished baking, remove the bread and put it on a cooling rack.

296. Mashed Potato Bread

Servings: 1 Loaf   Cooking Time: 10 Minutes

Ingredients:

- 12 slice bread (1½ pounds)
- ¾ cup water, at 80°F to 90°F
- ½ cup finely mashed potatoes, at room temperature
- 1 egg, at room temperature
- ¼ cup melted butter, cooled
- 2 tablespoons honey
- 1 teaspoon salt
- 3 cups white bread flour
- 2 teaspoons bread machine or instant yeast

Directions:
Preparing the Ingredients.   Choose the size of loaf of your preference and then measure the ingredients. Add all of the ingredients mentioned previously in the list. Close the lid after placing the pan in the bread machine. Select the Bake cycle   Turn on the bread machine. Select the White/Basic setting, select the loaf size, and the crust color. Press start.   When the cycle is finished, carefully remove the pan from the bread maker and let it rest.   Remove the bread from the pan, put in a wire rack to Cool about 10 minutes. Slice

297. Zucchini Bread

Servings: 2 Loaves   Cooking Time: 10 Minutes

Ingredients:
- 3 cups shredded zucchini (2 to 3 medium)
- 1⅔ cups sugar
- ⅔ cup vegetable oil
- 2 teaspoons vanilla
- 4 eggs
- 3 cups all-purpose or whole wheat flour
- 2 teaspoons baking soda
- 1 teaspoon salt
- 1 teaspoon ground cinnamon
- ½ teaspoon baking powder
- ½ teaspoon ground cloves
- ½ cup chopped nuts
- ½ cup raisins, if desired

Directions:
Preparing the Ingredients.   Choose the size of loaf of your preference and then measure the ingredients. Add all of the ingredients mentioned previously in the list. Close the lid after placing the pan in the bread machine.   Select the Bake cycle   Turn on the bread machine. Select the White/Basic setting, select the loaf size, and the crust color. Press start.   When the cycle is finished, carefully remove the pan from the bread maker and let it rest.   Remove the bread from the pan, put in a wire rack to cool for at least 2 hours before slicing. Wrap tightly and store at room temperature up to 4 days, or refrigerate up to 10 days.

298. Strawberry Oat Bread

Servings: 1 Loaf   Cooking Time: 10 Minutes

Ingredients:
- 16 slice bread (2 pounds)
- 1½ cups lukewarm milk
- ¼ cup unsalted butter, melted
- ¼ cup sugar
- 2 teaspoons table salt

- 1½ cups quick oats
- 3 cups white bread flour
- 2 teaspoons bread machine yeast
- 1 cup strawberries, sliced

Directions:
Preparing the Ingredients. Choose the size of loaf of your preference and then measure the ingredients. Add all of the ingredients mentioned previously in the list, except for the strawberries. Close the lid after placing the pan in the bread machine. Select the Bake cycle Turn on the bread machine. White/Basic or Fruit/Nut (if your machine has this setting) setting, select the loaf size, and the crust color. Press start. When the machine signals to add ingredients, add the strawberries. When the cycle is finished, carefully remove the pan from the bread maker and let it rest. Remove the bread from the pan, put in a wire rack to cool for at least 10 minutes, and slice.

299. Potato Dill Bread

Servings: 14 Slices   Cooking Time: 40 Min.
Ingredients:
- 1 (.25 oz) package active dry yeast
- ½ cup water
- 1 Tbsp sugar
- 1 tsp salt
- 2 Tbsp melted butter
- 1 package or bunch fresh dill
- ¾ cup room temperature mashed potatoes
- 2¼ cups bread flour

Directions:
Add each ingredient to the bread machine in the order and at the temperature recommended by your bread machine manufacturer. Close the lid, select the basic bread, medium crust setting on your bread machine, and press start. When the bread machine has finished baking, remove the bread and put it on a cooling rack.

300. Blueberry-basil Loaf

Servings: 1 Loaf   Cooking Time: 10 Minutes
Ingredients:
- 12 slice bread (1½ pounds)
- 1¼ cups fresh blueberries
- 1 tablespoon all-purpose flour
- 2¼ cups all-purpose flour
- 1 cup granulated sugar
- 2 teaspoons baking powder
- 1 teaspoon grated lemon peel
- ½ teaspoon salt
- 1 cup buttermilk
- 6 tablespoons butter, melted
- 1 teaspoon vanilla
- 2 eggs
- ¼ cup coarsely chopped fresh basil leaves
- Topping
- ½ cup packed brown sugar
- ¼ cup butter, melted
- 2⁄3 cup all-purpose flour

Directions:

Preparing the Ingredients. Choose the size of loaf of your preference and then measure the ingredients. Add all of the ingredients mentioned previously in the list. Close the lid after placing the pan in the bread machine. Select the Bake cycle Turn on the bread machine. Select the White/Basic setting, select the loaf size, and the crust color. Press start. When the cycle is finished, carefully remove the pan from the bread maker and let it rest. Remove the bread from the pan, put in a wire rack to Cool about 1 hour.

301. Cheese Onion Garlic Bread

Servings: 10   Cooking Time: 3 Hours
Ingredients:
- Cheddar cheese – 1 cup., shredded
- Dried onion – 3 tbsps., minced
- Garlic powder – 2 tsps.
- Active dry yeast – 2 tsps.
- Margarine – 2 tbsps.
- Sugar – 2 tbsps.
- Milk Powder – 2 tbsps.
- Bread flour – 3 cups.
- Warm water – 1 1/8 cups.
- Salt – 1 ½ tsps.

Directions:
Add water, salt, flour, milk powder, sugar, margarine, and yeast into the bread machine pan. Select basic setting then select medium crust and press start. Add cheese, dried onion, and garlic powder just before the final kneading cycle. Once loaf is done, remove the loaf pan from the machine. Allow it to cool for 10 minutes. Slice and serve.

302. Australian Vegetable Bread

Servings: 8 Pcs   Cooking Time: 1 Hour And 50 Minutes
Ingredients:
- 4 cups (4 * 1 cup) all-purpose flour
- 4 tablespoons (4 * 1 tbsp) sugar
- 2 teaspoons (4 * ½ tsp) salt
- 2 tablespoons (4 * ½ tbsp) olive oil
- 1 teaspoon (4 * ¼ tsp) yeast
- liquid (3 parts juice + 1-part water)

Directions:
Knead in the bread maker four types of dough (3 species with different colors with juice and one kind with water). Take juices of mixed vegetables for colored liquid: for Bordeaux - juice of beet for red color - tomato juice for green color - juice or puree of spinach for white dough - water. While the following kind of dough is kneaded, the previous lump stands warm to raise. Use the Pasta Dough program on your bread maker. The finished white dough was rolled into a large cake, the color dough of each kind was divided into four pieces each. In a white cake, lay the colored scones: roll them into small rolls and wrap them in 3 layers in a different order - you get four rolls. Then completely cover the colored cakes with white dough, create the desired form for the bucket, put it in the bread machine. The program BAKING set the time to 60 minutes. The focus was that the loaf resembles plain white bread (as if bread with a surprise) However,

the colored dough was foolish and sometimes decided to get out.

Nutrition Info: Calories 225;Total Fat 3.3g;Saturated Fat 0.5g;Cholesterol 0g;Sodium 466mg;Total Carbohydrate 43.1g;Dietary Fiber 1.4g

303. Golden Butternut Squash Raisin Bread

Servings: 1 Loaf   Cooking Time: 10 Minutes

Ingredients:
- 16 slice bread (2 pounds)
- 2 cups cooked mashed butternut squash, at room temperature
- 1 cup (2 sticks) butter, at room temperature
- 3 eggs, at room temperature
- 1 teaspoon pure vanilla extract
- 2 cups sugar
- ½ cup light brown sugar
- 3 cups all-purpose flour
- 1 teaspoon baking soda
- 1 teaspoon ground cinnamon
- ½ teaspoon ground cloves
- ½ teaspoon ground nutmeg
- ½ teaspoon salt
- ½ teaspoon baking powder
- ½ cup golden raisins

Directions:
Preparing the Ingredients.   Place the butternut squash, butter, eggs, vanilla, sugar, and brown sugar in your bread machine.   Select the Bake cycle   Program the machine for Quick/Rapid bread and press Start. While the wet ingredients are mixing, stir together the flour, baking soda, cinnamon, cloves, nutmeg, salt, and baking powder in a small bowl.   After the first fast mixing is done and the machine signals, add the dry ingredients and raisins.   When the cycle is finished, carefully remove the pan from the bread maker and let it rest.   Remove the bread from the pan, put in a wire rack to Cool about 5 minutes. Slice

304. Ginger-carrot-nut Bread

Servings: 1 Loaf   Cooking Time: 10 Minutes

Ingredients:
- 2 eggs
- ¾ cup packed brown sugar
- 1⁄3 cup vegetable oil
- ½ cup milk
- 1 teaspoon vanilla
- 2 cups all-purpose flour
- 2 teaspoons baking powder
- 1 teaspoon ground ginger
- ½ teaspoon salt
- 1 cup shredded carrots (2 medium)
- ½ cup chopped nuts

Directions:
Preparing the Ingredients.   Choose the size of loaf of your preference and then measure the ingredients. Add all of the ingredients mentioned previously in the list. Close the lid after placing the pan in the bread machine   Select the Bake cycle   Turn on the bread machine. Select the White/Basic setting, select the

loaf size, and the crust color. Press start.   When the cycle is finished, carefully remove the pan from the bread maker and let it rest.   Remove the bread from the pan, put in a wire rack to cool. Cool completely, about 10 minutes. Wrap tightly and store at room temperature up to 4 days, or refrigerate.

305. Cinnamon-raisin Bread

Servings: 14 Slices   Cooking Time: 10 Minutes

Ingredients:
- 1 cup water
- 2 Tbsp butter, softened
- 3 cups Gold Medal Better for Bread flour
- 3 Tbsp sugar
- 1½ tsp salt
- 1 tsp ground cinnamon
- 2½ tsp bread machine yeast
- ¾ cup raisins

Directions:
Preparing the Ingredients   Add each ingredient except the raisins to the bread machine in the order and at the temperature recommended by your bread machine manufacturer.   Select the Bake cycle   Close the lid, select the sweet or basic bread, medium crust setting on your bread machine and press start.   Add raisins 10 minutes before the last kneading cycle ends.   When the bread machine has finished baking, remove the bread and put it on a cooling rack.

306. Lemon-lime Blueberry Bread

Servings: 1 Loaf   Cooking Time: 10 Minutes

Ingredients:
- 12 slice bread (1½ pounds)
- ¾ cup plain yogurt, at room temperature
- ½ cup water, at 80°F to 90°F
- 3 tablespoons honey
- 1 tablespoon melted butter, cooled
- 1½ teaspoons salt
- ½ teaspoon lemon extract
- 1 teaspoon lime zest
- 1 cup dried blueberries
- 3 cups white bread flour
- 2¼ teaspoons bread machine or instant yeast

Directions:
Preparing the Ingredients.   Choose the size of loaf of your preference and then measure the ingredients. Add all of the ingredients mentioned previously in the list. Close the lid after placing the pan in the bread machine   Select the Bake cycle   Turn on the bread machine. Select the White/Basic setting, select the loaf size, and the crust color. Press start.   When the cycle is finished, carefully remove the pan from the bread maker and let it rest.   Remove the bread from the pan, put in a wire rack to cool. Cool completely, about 10 minutes. Slice

307. Oatmeal-streusel Bread

Servings: 1 Loaf   Cooking Time: 10 Minutes

Ingredients:
- Streusel

- ¼ cup packed brown sugar
- ¼ cup chopped walnuts, toasted
- 2 teaspoons ground cinnamon
- Bread
- 1 cup all-purpose flour
- ½ cup whole wheat flour
- ½ cup old-fashioned oats
- 2 tablespoons ground flaxseed or flaxseed meal
- 1 teaspoon baking powder
- ½ teaspoon salt
- ¼ teaspoon baking soda
- ¾ cup packed brown sugar
- ⅔ cup vegetable oil
- 2 eggs
- ¼ cup sour cream
- 2 teaspoons vanilla
- ½ cup milk
- Icing
- ¾ to 1 cup powdered sugar
- 1 tablespoon milk
- 2 teaspoons light corn syrup

Directions:
Preparing the Ingredients.   Choose the size of loaf of your preference and then measure the ingredients. Add all of the ingredients mentioned previously in the list. Close the lid after placing the pan in the bread machine Select the Bake cycle.   Turn on the bread machine. Select the White/Basic setting, select the loaf size, and the crust color. Press start.   When the cycle is finished, carefully remove the pan from the bread maker and let it rest.   Remove the bread from the pan, put in a wire rack to Cool completely, about 2 hours.   In small bowl, beat all icing ingredients, adding enough of the powdered sugar for desired drizzling consistency. Drizzle icing over bread. Let stand until set. Wrap tightly and store at room temperature up to 4 days, or refrigerate. To toast walnuts, bake in ungreased shallow pan at 350°F for 7 to 11 minutes, stirring occasionally, until light brown.

308. Chai-spiced Bread

Servings: 1 Loaf   Cooking Time: 10 Minutes
Ingredients:
- ¾ cup granulated sugar
- ½ cup butter, softened
- ½ cup cold brewed tea or water
- ⅓ cup milk
- 2 teaspoons vanilla
- 2 eggs
- 2 cups all-purpose flour
- 2 teaspoons baking powder
- ¾ teaspoon ground cardamom
- ½ teaspoon salt
- ¼ teaspoon ground cinnamon
- ⅛ teaspoon ground cloves
- glaze
- 1 cup powdered sugar
- ¼ teaspoon vanilla
- 3 to 5 teaspoons milk
- Additional ground cinnamon

Directions:

Preparing the Ingredients.   Choose the size of loaf of your preference and then measure the ingredients. Add all of the ingredients mentioned previously in the list. Close the lid after placing the pan in the bread machine. Select the Bake cycle   Turn on the bread machine. Select the White/Basic setting, select the loaf size, and the crust color. Press start.   When the cycle is finished, carefully remove the pan from the bread maker and let it rest.   Remove the bread from the pan, put in a wire rack to cool for at least 2 hours, and slice. Wrap tightly and store at room temperature up to 4 days, or refrigerate.

309. Pretty Borscht Bread

Servings: 1 Loaf   Cooking Time: 10 Minutes
Ingredients:
- 12 slice bread (1½ pounds)
- ¾ cups water, at 80°F to 90°F
- ¾ cup grated raw beetroot
- 1½ tablespoons melted butter, cooled
- 1½ tablespoons sugar
- 1¼ teaspoons salt
- 3 cups white bread flour
- 1¼ teaspoons bread machine or instant yeast

Directions:
Preparing the Ingredients.   Place the ingredients in your bread machine as recommended by the manufacturer.   Program the machine for Basic/White bread, select light or medium crust, and press Start. Select the Bake cycle   When the loaf is done, remove the bucket from the machine.   Let the loaf cool for 5 minutes.   Gently shake the bucket to remove the loaf, and turn it out onto a rack to cool.

310. Apple Spice Bread

Servings: 1 Loaf   Cooking Time: 10 Minutes
Ingredients:
- 16 slice bread (2 pounds)
- 1⅓ cup milk, at 80°F to 90°F
- 3⅓ tablespoons melted butter, cooled
- 2⅔ tablespoons sugar
- 2 teaspoons salt
- 1⅓ teaspoons ground cinnamon
- Pinch ground cloves
- 4 cups white bread flour
- 2¼ teaspoons bread machine or active dry yeast
- 1⅓ cups finely diced peeled apple

Directions:
Preparing the Ingredients.   Choose the size of loaf of your preference and then measure the ingredients. Add all of the ingredients mentioned previously in the list, except for the apple. Close the lid after placing the pan in the bread machine.   Select the Bake cycle   Turn on the bread machine. White/Basic or Fruit/Nut (if your machine has this setting) setting, select the loaf size, and the crust color. Press start.   When the machine signals to add ingredients, add the apple. When the cycle is finished, carefully remove the pan from the bread maker and let it rest.   Remove the bread from the pan, put in a wire rack to cool for at least 10 minutes, and slice.

311. Cinnamon Pull-apart Bread

Servings: 16   Cooking Time: 3 Hours

Ingredients:
- 1/3 cup whole milk
- 4 tablespoons unsalted butter
- 1/4 cup warm water
- 1 teaspoon pure vanilla extract
- 2 large eggs
- 3 cups all-purpose flour
- 1/4 cup sugar
- 1/2 teaspoon salt
- 2 1/4 teaspoons active dry yeast
- For the Filling:
- 4 tablespoons unsalted butter, melted until browned (will smell like warm caramel)
- 1 cup sugar
- 2 teaspoons ground cinnamon
- Pinch of ground nutmeg

Directions:
Add milk and butter to a saucepan and heat on medium-low until the butter melts; add liquid to the bread maker. Add the rest of the ingredients (except yeast) in the order listed.   Make a well in the center of the dry ingredients and add the yeast.   Select Dough cycle and press Start. When the dough is done, roll it out into a big sheet of dough, and brush the dough with the browned butter. Combine sugar cinnamon and nutmeg in a mixing bowl and sprinkle over buttered dough.   Cut the dough into long thin strips and cut the strips into squares. Stack in threes, and place the dough squares next to one another in a greased bread pan.   Let rise in a warm place until doubled in size; cover with plastic wrap and refrigerate overnight to bake for breakfast.   Preheat an oven to 350°F.   Bake for 30 to 35 minutes, until the top is very golden brown.   When bread is done, transfer to a plate to cool and serve warm.

Nutrition Info: Calories: 210, Sodium: 126 mg, Dietary Fiber: 0.9 g, Fat: 6.8 g, Carbs: 34.3 g, Protein: 3.7 g.

312. Sauerkraut Rye Bread

Servings: 1 Loaf   Cooking Time: 10 Minutes

Ingredients:
- 12 slice bread (1½ pounds)
- 1 cup water, at 80°F to 90°F
- 1½ tablespoons melted butter, cooled
- ⅓ cup molasses
- ½ cup drained sauerkraut
- ⅓ teaspoon salt
- 1½ tablespoons unsweetened cocoa powder
- Pinch ground nutmeg
- ¾ cup rye flour
- 2 cups white bread flour
- 1⅔ teaspoons bread machine or instant yeast

Directions:
Preparing the Ingredients.   Choose the size of loaf of your preference and then measure the ingredients. Add all of the ingredients mentioned previously in the list. Close the lid after placing the pan in the bread machine. Select the Bake cycle   Turn on the bread machine.

Select the White/Basic setting, select the loaf size, and the crust color. Press start.   When the cycle is finished, carefully remove the pan from the bread maker and let it rest.   Remove the bread from the pan, put in a wire rack to Cool about 5 minutes. Slice

313. Gluten-free Cinnamon Raisin Bread

Servings: 12 Slices   Cooking Time: 5 Minutes

Ingredients:
- 3/4 cup almond milk
- 2 tablespoons flax meal
- 6 tablespoons warm water
- 1 1/2 teaspoons apple cider vinegar
- 2 tablespoons butter
- 1 1/2 tablespoons honey
- 1 2/3 cups brown rice flour
- 1/4 cup corn starch
- 2 tablespoons potato starch
- 1 1/2 teaspoons xanthan gum
- 1 tablespoon cinnamon
- 1/2 teaspoon salt
- 1 teaspoon active dry yeast
- 1/2 cup raisins

Directions:
Preparing the Ingredients   Mix together flax and water and let stand for 5 minutes.   Combine dry ingredients in a separate bowl, except for yeast.   Add wet ingredients to the bread machine.   Add the dry mixture on top and make a well in the middle of the dry mixture.   Add the yeast to the well.   Select the Bake cycle   Set to Gluten Free, light crust color, and press Start.   After first kneading and rise cycle, add raisins.   Remove to a cooling rack when baked and let cool for 15 minutes before slicing.

314. Perfect Sweet Potato Bread

Servings: 10   Cooking Time: 3 Hours

Ingredients:
- Sweet potato – 1, mashed
- Milk powder – 2 tbsps.
- Salt – 1 ½ tsps.
- Brown sugar – 1/3 cup.
- Butter – 2 tbsps., softened
- Cinnamon – ½ tsp.
- Bread flour – 4 cups.
- Vanilla extract – 1 tsp.
- Warm water – ½ cup.

Directions:
Add water, vanilla, bread flour, cinnamon, butter, brown sugar, salt, yeast, milk powder, and sweet potato into the bread machine pan. Select white bread setting then select light crust and press start. Once loaf is done, remove the loaf pan from the machine. Allow it to cool for 10 minutes. Slice and serve.

315. Potato Thyme Bread

Servings: 1 Loaf   Cooking Time: 10 Minutes

Ingredients:
- 12 slice bread (1½ pounds)

- 1¼ cups milk, at 80°F to 90°F
- 2 tablespoons melted butter, cooled
- 1 tablespoon honey
- 1½ teaspoons salt
- 1 teaspoon dried thyme
- ½ cup instant potato flakes
- 3 cups white bread flour
- 2 teaspoons bread machine or instant yeast

Directions:
Preparing the Ingredients. Choose the size of loaf of your preference and then measure the ingredients. Add all of the ingredients mentioned previously in the list. Close the lid after placing the pan in the bread machine. Select the Bake cycle Turn on the bread machine. Select the White/Basic setting, select the loaf size, and the crust color. Press start. When the cycle is finished, carefully remove the pan from the bread maker and let it rest. Remove the bread from the pan, put in a wire rack to Cool about 5 minutes. Slice

316. Brown Sugar Date Nut Swirl Bread

Servings: 16   Cooking Time: 2 Hours 30 Minutes
Ingredients:
- 1 cup milk
- 1 large egg
- 4 tablespoons butter
- 4 tablespoons sugar
- 1 teaspoon salt
- 4 cups flour
- 1 2/3 teaspoons yeast
- For the filling:
- 1/2 cup packed brown sugar
- 1 cup walnuts, chopped
- 1 cup medjool dates, pitted and chopped
- 2 teaspoons cinnamon
- 2 teaspoons clove spice
- 1 1/3 tablespoons butter
- Powdered sugar, sifted

Directions:
Add wet ingredients to the bread maker pan. Mix flour, sugar and salt and add to pan. Make a well in the center of the dry ingredients and add the yeast. Select the Dough cycle and press Start. Punch the dough down and allow it to rest in a warm place. Mix the brown sugar with walnuts, dates and spices; set aside. Roll the dough into a rectangle, on a lightly floured surface. Baste with a tablespoon of butter, add the filling. Start from the short side and roll the dough to form a jelly roll shape. Place the roll into a greased loaf pan and cover. Let it rise in a warm place, until nearly doubled in size; about 30 minutes. Bake at 350°F for approximately 30 minutes. Cover with foil during the last 10 minutes of cooking. Transfer to a cooling rack for 15 minutes; sprinkle with the powdered sugar and serve.
Nutrition Info: Calories: 227, Sodium: 197 mg, Dietary Fiber: 1.5 g, Fat: 8.3 g, Carbs: 33.1 g, Protein: 5.5 g.

317. Pineapple Coconut Bread

Servings: 1 Loaf   Cooking Time: 10 Minutes
Ingredients:
- 6 tablespoons butter, at room temperature
- 2 eggs, at room temperature
- ½ cup coconut milk, at room temperature
- ½ cup pineapple juice, at room temperature
- 1 cup sugar
- 1½ teaspoons coconut extract
- 2 cups all-purpose flour
- ¾ cup shredded sweetened coconut
- 1 teaspoon baking powder
- ½ teaspoon salt

Directions:
Preparing the Ingredients. Place the butter, eggs, coconut milk, pineapple juice, sugar, and coconut extract in your bread machine. Program the machine for Quick/Rapid bread and press Start. While the wet ingredients are mixing, stir together the flour, coconut, baking powder, and salt in a small bowl. Select the Bake cycle After the first fast mixing is done and the machine signals, add the dry ingredients. When the cycle is finished, carefully remove the pan from the bread maker and let it rest. Remove the bread from the pan, put in a wire rack to cool for at least 10 minutes, and slice.

318. Brown Bread With Raisins

Servings: 1 Loaf   Cooking Time: 10 Minutes
Ingredients:
- 32 slices
- 1 cup all-purpose flour
- 1 cup whole wheat flour
- 1 cup whole-grain cornmeal
- 1 cup raisins
- 2 cups buttermilk
- ¾ cup molasses
- 2 teaspoons baking soda
- 1 teaspoon salt

Directions:
Preparing the Ingredients. Choose the size of loaf of your preference and then measure the ingredients. Add all of the ingredients mentioned previously in the list. Close the lid after placing the pan in the bread machine. Select the Bake cycle Turn on the bread machine. Select the White/Basic setting, select the loaf size, and the crust color. Press start. When the cycle is finished, carefully remove the pan from the bread maker and let it rest. Remove the bread from the pan, put in a wire rack to Cool completely, about 30 minutes.

319. Cranberry Honey Bread

Servings: 1 Loaf
Ingredients:
- 16 slice bread (2 pounds)
- 1¼ cups + 1 tablespoon lukewarm water
- ¼ cup unsalted butter, melted
- 3 tablespoons honey or molasses
- 4 cups white bread flour
- ½ cup cornmeal

- 2 teaspoons table salt
- 2½ teaspoons bread machine yeast
- ¾ cup cranberries, dried
- 12 slice bread (1½ pounds)
- 1 cup + 1 tablespoon lukewarm water
- 2 tablespoons unsalted butter, melted
- 3 tablespoons honey or molasses
- 3 cups white bread flour
- ⅓ cup cornmeal
- 1½ teaspoons table salt
- 2 teaspoons bread machine yeast
- ½ cup cranberries, dried

Directions:

Choose the size of loaf you would like to make and measure your ingredients. Add all of the ingredients except for the dried cranberries to the bread pan in the order listed above. Place the pan in the bread machine and close the lid. Turn on the bread maker. Select the White/Basic or Fruit/Nut (if your machine has this setting) setting, then the loaf size, and finally the crust color. Start the cycle. When the machine signals to add ingredients, add the dried cranberries. (Some machines have a fruit/nut hopper where you can add the dried cranberries when you start the machine. The machine will automatically add them to the dough during the baking process.) When the cycle is finished and the bread is baked, carefully remove the pan from the machine. Use a potholder as the handle will be very hot. Let rest for a few minutes. Remove the bread from the pan and allow to cool on a wire rack for at least 10 minutes before slicing.

Nutrition Info:(Per Serving):Calories 174, fat 2.6 g, carbs 33.6 g, sodium 310 mg, protein 4 g

320. Sweet Potato Bread

Servings: 1 Loaf   Cooking Time: 10 Minutes
Ingredients:
- 12 slice bread (1½ pounds)
- ⅓ cup + 2 tablespoons lukewarm water
- ¾ cup plain sweet potatoes, peeled and mashed
- 1½ tablespoons unsalted butter, melted
- ¼ cup dark brown sugar
- 1 teaspoon table salt
- 3 cups bread flour
- ⅛ teaspoon ground nutmeg
- ⅛ teaspoon cinnamon
- ¾ teaspoon vanilla extract
- 1½ tablespoons dry milk powder
- 1½ teaspoons bread machine yeast

Directions:

Preparing the Ingredients. Choose the size of loaf of your preference and then measure the ingredients. Add all of the ingredients mentioned previously in the list. Close the lid after placing the pan in the bread machine. Select the Bake cycle Turn on the bread machine. Select the Quick/Rapid setting, select the loaf size, and the crust color. Press start. When the cycle is finished, carefully remove the pan from the bread maker and let it rest. Remove the bread from the pan, put in a wire rack to Cool about 5 minutes. Slice

321. Fruit Raisin Bread

Servings: 14 Slices   Cooking Time: 3 H. 5 Min.
Ingredients:
- 1 egg
- 1 cup water plus 2 Tbsp
- ½ tsp ground cardamom.
- 1 tsp salt
- 1½ Tbsp sugar
- ¼ cup butter, softened
- 3 cups bread flour
- 1 tsp bread machine yeast
- ⅓ cup raisins
- ⅓ cup mixed candied fruit

Directions:

Add each ingredient except the raisins and fruitcake mix to the bread machine in the order and at the temperature recommended by your bread machine manufacturer. Close the lid, select the basic bread, medium crust setting on your bread machine, and press start. Add raisins and fruit at the fruit/nut beep or 5 to 10 minutes before the last kneading cycle ends. When the bread machine has finished baking, remove the bread and put it on a cooling rack.

322. Monkey Bread

Servings: 12 - 15   Cooking Time: 2 Hours
Ingredients:
- 1 cup water
- 1 cup butter, unsalted
- 2 tablespoons butter, softened
- 3 cups all-purpose flour
- 1 teaspoon ground cinnamon
- 1 teaspoon salt
- 1/4 cup white sugar
- 2 1/2 teaspoons active dry yeast
- 1 cup brown sugar, packed
- 1 cup raisins
- Flour, for surface

Directions:

Add ingredients, except 1 cup butter, brown sugar, raisins and yeast, to bread maker pan in order listed above. Make a well in the center of the dry ingredients and add the yeast. Make sure that no liquid comes in contact with the yeast. Select Dough cycle and press Start. Place finished dough on floured surface and knead 10 times. Melt one cup of butter in small saucepan. Stir in brown sugar and raisins and mix until smooth. Remove from heat. Cut dough into one inch chunks. Drop one chunk at a time into the butter sugar mixture. Thoroughly coat dough pieces, then layer them loosely in a greased Bundt pan. Let rise in a warm, draft-free space; about 15 to 20 minutes. Bake at 375°F for 20 to 25 minutes or until golden brown. Remove from oven, plate, and serve warm.

Nutrition Info: Calories: 294, Sodium: 265. Mg, Dietary Fiber: 1.3 g, Fat: 14.1 g, Carbs: 40 g, Protein: 3.3 g.

323. French Onion Bread

Servings: 1 Loaf   Cooking Time: 10 Minutes
Ingredients:
- 12 slice bread (1½ pounds)
- 1¼ cups milk, at 80°F to 90°F
- ¼ cup melted butter, cooled
- 3 tablespoons light brown sugar
- 1 teaspoon salt
- 3 tablespoons dehydrated onion flakes
- 2 tablespoons chopped fresh chives
- 1 teaspoon garlic powder
- 3 cups white bread flour
- 1 teaspoon bread machine or instant yeast

Directions:
Preparing the Ingredients.   Choose the size of loaf of your preference and then measure the ingredients. Add all of the ingredients mentioned previously in the list. Close the lid after placing the pan in the bread machine. Select the Bake cycle   Turn on the bread machine. Select the White/Basic setting, select the loaf size, and the crust color. Press start.   When the cycle is finished, carefully remove the pan from the bread maker and let it rest.   Remove the bread from the pan, put in a wire rack to Cool about 5 minutes. Slice

324. Blueberries 'n Orange Bread

Servings: 1 Loaf   Cooking Time: 10 Minutes
Ingredients:
- 18 slices bread
- 3 cups Original Bisquick mix
- ½ cup granulated sugar
- 1 tablespoon grated orange peel
- ½ cup milk
- 3 tablespoons vegetable oil
- 2 eggs
- 1 cup fresh or frozen (rinsed and drained) blueberries glaze
- ½ cup powdered sugar
- 3 to 4 teaspoons orange juice
- Additional grated orange peel, if desired

Directions:
Preparing the Ingredients.   Choose the size of loaf of your preference and then measure the ingredients. Add all of the ingredients mentioned previously in the list. Close the lid after placing the pan in the bread machine.   Select the Bake cycle   Program the machine for Basic/White bread, select light or medium crust, and press Start. When the loaf is done, remove the bucket from the machine. Let the loaf cool for 5 minutes. Gently shake the bucket to remove the loaf, and turn it out onto a rack to cool. Cool completely, about 45 minutes.   In small bowl, mix powdered sugar and orange juice until smooth and thin enough to drizzle. Drizzle glaze over bread; sprinkle with additional orange peel.

325. Yeasted Carrot Bread

Servings: 1 Loaf   Cooking Time: 10 Minutes
Ingredients:
- 12 slice bread (1½ pounds)
- ¾ cup milk, at 80°F to 90°F
- 3 tablespoons melted butter, cooled
- 1 tablespoon honey
- 1½ cups shredded carrot
- ¾ teaspoon ground nutmeg
- ½ teaspoon salt
- 3 cups white bread flour
- 2¼ teaspoons bread machine or active dry yeast

Directions:
Preparing the Ingredients.   Choose the size of loaf of your preference and then measure the ingredients. Add all of the ingredients mentioned previously in the list. Close the lid after placing the pan in the bread machine. Select the Bake cycle   Turn on the bread machine. Select the Quick/Rapid setting, select the loaf size, and the crust color. Press start.   When the cycle is finished, carefully remove the pan from the bread maker and let it rest.   Remove the bread from the pan, put in a wire rack to Cool about 5 minutes. Slice

Cheese & Sweet Bread

326. Cheese Jalapeno Bread

Servings: 10   Cooking Time: 2 Hours

Ingredients:
- Monterey jack cheese – ¼ cup, shredded
- Active dry yeast – 2 tsps.
- Butter – 1 ½ tbsps.
- Sugar – 1 ½ tbsps.
- Milk – 3 tbsps.
- Flour – 3 cups.
- Water – 1 cup.
- Jalapeno pepper – 1, minced
- Salt – 1 ½ tsps.

Directions:
Add all ingredients to the bread machine pan according to the bread machine manufacturer instructions. Select basic bread setting then select light/medium crust and start. Once loaf is done, remove the loaf pan from the machine. Allow it to cool for 10 minutes. Slice and serve.

327. Crunchy Wheat-and-honey Twist

Servings: 1 Loaf   Cooking Time: 10 Minutes Plus Fermenting Time

Ingredients:
- 16 slice bread (2 pounds)
- Bread dough
- ¾ cup plus 2 tablespoons water
- 2 tablespoons honey
- 1 tablespoon butter, softened
- 1¼ cups whole wheat flour
- 1 cup bread flour
- ⅓ cup slivered almonds, toasted
- 1 teaspoon salt
- 1 teaspoon bread machine or fast-acting dry yeast
- Topping
- Butter, melted
- 1 egg, slightly beaten
- 2 tablespoons sugar
- ¼ teaspoon ground cinnamon

Directions:
Preparing the Ingredients.   Measure carefully, placing all bread dough ingredients in bread machine pan in the order recommended by the manufacturer.   Select Dough/Manual cycle. Do not use delay cycle.   Remove dough from pan, using lightly floured hands. Cover and let rest 10 minutes on lightly floured surface.   Grease large cookie sheet with shortening. Divide dough in half. Roll each half into 15-inch rope. Place ropes side by side on cookie sheet; twist together gently and loosely. Pinch ends to seal. Brush melted butter lightly over dough. Select the Bake cycle   Cover and let rise in warm place 45 to 60 minutes or until doubled in size.   Dough is ready if indentation remains when touched.   Heat oven to 375°F. Brush egg over dough. Mix sugar and cinnamon; sprinkle over dough. Bake 25 to 30 minutes or until twist is golden brown and sounds hollow when tapped. Remove from cookie sheet to cooling rack; cool

20 minutes.   To toast almonds, bake in ungreased shallow pan at 350°F for 6 to 10 minutes, stirring occasionally, until light brown.

328. Delicious Sour Cream Bread

Servings: 1 Loaf   Cooking Time: 10 Minutes Plus Fermenting Time

Ingredients:
- 12 slice bread (1½ pounds)
- ½ cup + 1 tablespoon lukewarm water
- ½ cup + 1 tablespoon sour cream, at room temperature
- 2¼ tablespoons butter, at room temperature
- 1 tablespoon maple syrup
- ¾ teaspoon table salt
- 2¾ cups white bread flour
- 1⅔ teaspoons bread machine yeast

Directions:
Preparing the Ingredients.   Choose the size of loaf of your preference and then measure the ingredients. Add all of the ingredients mentioned previously in the list. Close the lid after placing the pan in the bread machine. Select the Bake cycle   Turn on the bread machine. Select the Basic/White setting, select the loaf size, and the crust color. Press start.   When the cycle is finished, carefully remove the pan from the bread maker and let it rest.   Remove the bread from the pan, put in a wire rack to Cool about 5 minutes. Slice

329. Allspice Currant Bread

Servings: 1 Loaf

Ingredients:
- 16 slice bread (2 pounds)
- 1½ cups lukewarm water
- 2 tablespoons unsalted butter, melted
- ¼ cup sugar
- ¼ cup skim milk powder
- 2 teaspoons table salt
- 4 cups white bread flour
- 1½ teaspoons dried lemon zest
- ¾ teaspoon ground allspice
- ¼ teaspoon ground nutmeg
- 2½ teaspoons bread machine yeast
- 1 cup dried currants
- 12 slice bread (1½ pounds)
- 1⅛ cups lukewarm water
- 1½ tablespoons unsalted butter, melted
- 3 tablespoons sugar
- 3 tablespoons skim milk powder
- 1½ teaspoons table salt
- 3 cups white bread flour
- 1 teaspoon dried lemon zest
- ½ teaspoon ground allspice
- ¼ teaspoon ground nutmeg
- 2½ teaspoons bread machine yeast
- ¾ cup dried currants

Directions:

Choose the size of loaf you would like to make and measure your ingredients. Add all of the ingredients except for the dried currants to the bread pan in the order listed above. Place the pan in the bread machine and close the lid. Turn on the bread maker. Select the White/Basic or Fruit/Nut (if your machine has this setting) setting, then the loaf size, and finally the crust color. Start the cycle. When the machine signals to add ingredients, add the dried currants. (Some machines have a fruit/nut hopper where you can add the dried currants when you start the machine. The machine will automatically add them to the dough during the baking process.) When the cycle is finished and the bread is baked, carefully remove the pan from the machine. Use a potholder as the handle will be very hot. Let rest for a few minutes. Remove the bread from the pan and allow to cool on a wire rack for at least 10 minutes before slicing.

Nutrition Info:(Per Serving):Calories 168, fat 2.5 g, carbs 32.3 g, sodium 306 mg, protein 4.8 g

330. Double Cheese Bread

Servings: 8 Pcs   Cooking Time: 15 Minutes

Ingredients:
- ¾ cup plus one tablespoon milk, at 80°F to 90°F
- Two teaspoons butter, melted and cooled
- Four teaspoons sugar
- 2/3 teaspoon salt
- 1/3 teaspoon freshly ground black pepper
- Pinch cayenne pepper
- 1 cup (4 ounces) shredded aged sharp Cheddar cheese
- 1/3 cup shredded or grated Parmesan cheese
- 2 cups white bread flour
- ¾ teaspoon instant yeast

Directions:
Place the ingredients in your machine as recommended on it. Make a program on the machine for Basic White bread, select light or medium crust, and press Start. When the loaf is finished, remove the bucket from the machine. Let the loaf cool for a minute. Gently shake the bucket and remove the loaf and turn it out onto a rack to cool.

Nutrition Info: Calories: 183 calories;Total Carbohydrate: 28 g ;Total Fat: 4g ;Protein: 6 g ;Sodium: 344 mg

331. Easy Apple Coffee Cake

Servings: 10 Servings   Cooking Time: 10 Minutes Plus Fermenting Time

Ingredients:
- 2/3 cup water
- 3 tablespoons butter, softened
- 2 cups bread flour
- 3 tablespoons granulated sugar
- 1 teaspoon salt
- 1½ teaspoons bread machine or fast-acting dry yeast
- 1 cup canned apple pie filling
- Powdered sugar, if desired

Directions:
Preparing the Ingredients. Choose the size of loaf of your preference and then measure the ingredients. Add all of the ingredients mentioned previously in the list, except for pie filling and powdered sugar. Close the lid after placing the pan in the bread machine. Remove dough from pan, using lightly floured hands. Cover and let rest 10 minutes on floured surface. Select the Bake cycle Select Dough/Manual cycle. Do not use delay cycle. Grease large cookie sheet. Roll dough into 13×8-inch rectangle on lightly floured surface. Place on cookie sheet. Spoon pie filling lengthwise down center third of rectangle. On each 13-inch side, using sharp knife, make cuts from filling to edge of dough at 1-inch intervals. Fold ends up over filling. Fold strips diagonally over filling, alternating sides and overlapping in center. Cover and let rise in warm place 30 to 45 minutes or until doubled in size. Dough is ready if indentation remains when touched. Heat oven to 375°F. Bake 30 to 35 minutes or until golden brown. Remove from cookie sheet to cooling rack; cool. Sprinkle with powdered sugar.

332. Onion, Garlic, Cheese Bread

Servings: 1 Loaf   Cooking Time: 40 Minutes

Ingredients:
- Three tablespoons dried minced onion
- 3 cups bread flour
- Two teaspoons Garlic powder
- Two teaspoons Active dry yeast
- Two tablespoons White sugar
- Two tablespoons Margarine
- Two tablespoons Dry milk powder
- 1 cup shredded sharp cheddar cheese
- 1 1/8 cups warm water
- 1 1/2 teaspoon salt

Directions:
In the order suggested by the manufacturer, put the flour, water, powdered milk, margarine or butter, salt, and yeast in the bread pan. Press the basic cycle with a light crust. When the manufacturer directs the sound alerts, add two teaspoons of the onion flakes, the garlic powder, and shredded cheese. After the last knead, sprinkle the remaining onion flakes over the dough.

Nutrition Info: Calories: 204 calories;Total Carbohydrate: 29 g ;Total Fat: 6 g ;Protein: 8 g

333. Cottage Cheese Bread

Servings: 1 Loaf   Cooking Time: 45 Minutes

Ingredients:
- 1/2 cup water
- 1 cup cottage cheese
- Two tablespoons margarine
- One egg
- One tablespoon white sugar
- 1/4 teaspoon baking soda
- One teaspoon salt
- 3 cups bread flour
- 2 1/2 teaspoons active dry yeast

Directions:

Into the bread machine, place the ingredients according to the ingredients list's order, then push the start button. In case the dough looks too sticky, feel free to use up to half a cup more bread flour.

Nutrition Info: Calories: 171 calories;Total Carbohydrate: 26.8 g ;Cholesterol: 18 mg ;Total Fat: 3.6 g ;Protein: 7.3 g ;Sodium: 324 mg

334. Cocoa Banana Bread

Servings: 1 Loaf   Cooking Time: 10 Minutes Plus Fermenting Time

Ingredients:
- 12 slice bread (1½ pounds)
- 3 bananas, mashed
- 2 eggs, at room temperature
- ¾ cup packed light brown sugar
- ½ cup unsalted butter, melted
- ½ cup sour cream, at room temperature
- ¼ cup sugar
- 1½ teaspoons pure vanilla extract
- 1 cup all-purpose flour
- ½ cup quick oats
- 2 tablespoons unsweetened cocoa powder
- 1 teaspoon baking soda

Directions:
Preparing the Ingredients.   Choose the size of loaf of your preference and then measure the ingredients. Add all of the ingredients mentioned previously in the list. Close the lid after placing the pan in the bread machine. Select the Bake cycle   Turn on the bread machine. Select the Quick/Rapid setting, select the loaf size, and the crust color. Press start.   When the cycle is finished, carefully remove the pan from the bread maker and let it rest.   Remove the bread from the pan, put in a wire rack to Cool about 5 minutes. Slice

335. Mozzarella Cheese And Salami Loaf

Servings: 1 Loaf   Cooking Time: 45 Minutes

Ingredients:
- ¾ cup water, set at 80 degrees F
- 1/3 cup mozzarella cheese, shredded
- Four teaspoons sugar
- 2/3 teaspoon salt
- 2/3 teaspoon dried basil
- Pinch of garlic powder
- 2 cups + 2 tablespoons white bread flour
- One teaspoon instant yeast
- ½ cup hot salami, finely diced

Directions:
Add the listed ingredients to your bread machine (except salami), following the manufactures instructions.   Set the bread machine's program to Basic/White Bread and the crust type to light. Press Start.   Let the bread machine work and wait until it beeps. This your indication to add the remaining ingredients at this point, add the salami.   Wait until the remaining bake cycle completes.   Once the loaf is done, take the bucket out from the bread machine and let it rest for 5 minutes. Gently shake the bucket and remove the loaf, transfer the loaf to a cooling rack and slice.   Serve and enjoy!

Nutrition Info: Calories: 164 calories;Total Carbohydrate: 28 g ;Total Fat: 3 g ;Protein: 6 g ;Sugar: 2 g

336. Buttermilk Pecan Bread

Servings: 1 Loaf

Ingredients:
- 16 slice bread (2 pounds)
- 1 cup buttermilk, at room temperature
- 1 cup butter, at room temperature
- 1⅓ tablespoons instant coffee granules
- 3 eggs, at room temperature
- 1 cup sugar
- 3 cups all-purpose flour
- ⅔ tablespoon baking powder
- ⅔ teaspoon table salt
- 1⅓ cups chopped pecans
- 12 slice bread (1½ pounds)
- ¾ cup buttermilk, at room temperature
- ¾ cup butter, at room temperature
- 1 tablespoon instant coffee granules
- 3 eggs, at room temperature
- ¾ cup sugar
- 2 cups all-purpose flour
- ½ tablespoon baking powder
- ½ teaspoon table salt
- 1 cup chopped pecans

Directions:
Choose the size of loaf you would like to make and measure your ingredients.   Add the ingredients to the bread pan in the order listed above.   Place the pan in the bread machine and close the lid.   Turn on the bread maker. Select the Quick/Rapid setting, then the loaf size, and finally the crust color. Start the cycle. When the cycle is finished and the bread is baked, carefully remove the pan from the machine. Use a potholder as the handle will be very hot. Let rest for a few minutes.   Remove the bread from the pan and allow to cool on a wire rack for at least 10 minutes before slicing.

Nutrition Info:(Per Serving):Calories 262, fat 14.3 g, carbs 26.4 g, sodium 217 mg, protein 4.7 g

337. Delicious Pumpkin Bread

Servings: 10   Cooking Time: 2 Hours

Ingredients:
- All-purpose flour – 3 cups.
- Ground ginger – ¼ tsp.
- Ground nutmeg – ¼ tsp.
- Ground cinnamon – ¾ tsp.
- Baking soda – ½ tsp.
- Baking powder – 1 ½ tsps.
- Granulated sugar – 1 cup.
- Pumpkin puree – 1 ½ cups.
- Eggs – 3
- Olive oil – 1/3 cup
- Salt – ¼ tsp.

Directions:
Add all ingredients into the bread machine pan. Select basic setting then select light crust and press start. Once

loaf is done, remove the loaf pan from the machine. Allow it to cool for 10 minutes. Slice and serve.

338. Vanilla Almond Milk Bread

Servings: 1 Loaf   Cooking Time: 10 Minutes Plus Fermenting Time

Ingredients:
- 12 slice bread (1½ pounds)
- ½ cup plus 1 tablespoon milk, at 80°F to 90°F
- 3 tablespoons melted butter, cooled
- 3 tablespoons sugar
- 1 egg, at room temperature
- 1½ teaspoons pure vanilla extract
- ⅓ teaspoon almond extract
- 2½ cups white bread flour
- 1½ teaspoons bread machine or instant yeast

Directions:
Preparing the Ingredients.   Choose the size of loaf of your preference and then measure the ingredients. Add all of the ingredients mentioned previously in the list. Close the lid after placing the pan in the bread machine. Select the Bake cycle   Turn on the bread machine. Select the Sweet setting, select the loaf size, and the crust color. Press start.   When the cycle is finished, carefully remove the pan from the bread maker and let it rest. Remove the bread from the pan, put in a wire rack to Cool about 5 minutes. Slice

339. Barmbrack Bread

Servings: 1 Loaf   Cooking Time: 10 Minutes Plus Fermenting Time

Ingredients:
- 8 slices bread (1 pound)
- ⅔ cup water, at 80°F to 90°F
- 1 tablespoon melted butter, cooled
- 2 tablespoons sugar
- 2 tablespoons skim milk powder
- 1 teaspoon salt
- 1 teaspoon dried lemon zest
- ¼ teaspoon ground allspice
- ⅛ teaspoon ground nutmeg
- 2 cups white bread flour
- 1½ teaspoons bread machine or active dry yeast
- ½ cup dried currants

Directions:
Preparing the Ingredients.   Place the ingredients, except the currants, in your bread machine as recommended by the manufacturer.   Select the Bake cycle   Program the machine for Basic/White bread, select light or medium crust, and press Start.   Add the currants when your machine signals or when the second kneading cycle starts. When the cycle is finished, carefully remove the pan from the bread maker and let it rest. Remove the bread from the pan, put in a wire rack to Cool about 5 minutes. Slice

340. Date And Nut Bread

Servings: 1 Loaf   Cooking Time: 2 Hour

Ingredients:

- 1-1/2 tablespoons vegetable oil
- 1 cup of water
- ½ teaspoon salt
- Two tablespoons honey
- ¾ cup whole-wheat flour
- ¾ cup rolled oats
- 1 1/2 teaspoons active dry yeast
- 1 1/2 cups bread flour
- ½ cup almonds, chopped
- ½ cup dates, chopped and pitted

Directions:
Put everything in your bread machine pan.   Select the primary cycle. Press the start button.   Take out the pan when done and set aside for 10 minutes.

Nutrition Info: Calories: 112 Cal;Carbohydrates: 17 g;Fat: 5g;Cholesterol: 0 mg;Protein: 3 g;Fibre: 3 g;Sugar: 7 g;Sodium: 98 mg;Potassium: 130 mg

341. Cream Cheese Bread

Servings: 1 Loaf   Cooking Time: 35 Minutes

Ingredients:
- 1/2 cup Water
- 1/2 cup Cream cheese, softened
- Two tablespoons melted butter
- 1 Beaten egg
- Four tablespoons Sugar
- One teaspoon salt
- 3 cups bread flour
- 1 1/2 teaspoons Active dry yeast

Directions:
Place the ingredients in the pan in order, as suggested by your bread machine.   After removing it from a machine, place it in a greased 9x5 loaf pan after the cycle. Cover and let rise until doubled.   Bake in a 350° oven for approximately 35 minutes.

Nutrition Info: Calories: 150 calories;Total Carbohydrate: 24 g ;Total Fat: 5 g ;Protein: 3 g

342. Hawaiian Sweet Bread

Servings: 1 Loaf   Cooking Time: 2 Hour

Ingredients:
- 3/4 cup pineapple juice
- One egg
- Two tablespoons vegetable oil
- 2 1/2 tablespoons honey
- 3/4 teaspoon salt
- 3 cups bread flour
- Two tablespoons dry milk
- Two teaspoons fast-rising yeast

Directions:
Place ingredients in bread machine container.   Select the white bread cycle.   Press the start button.   Take out the pan when done and set aside for 10 minutes.

Nutrition Info: Calories 169;Carbohydrates: 25g;Total Fat 5g;Cholesterol 25mg;Protein 4g;Fiber 1g;Sugar 5g;Sodium 165mg;Potassium 76mg

343. Chocolate Orange Bread

Servings: 14 Slices   Cooking Time: 10 Minutes Plus Fermenting Time

Ingredients:
- 1⅝ cups strong white bread flour
- 2 Tbsp cocoa
- 1 tsp ground mixed spice
- 1 egg, beaten
- ½ cup water
- ¼ cup orange juice
- 2 Tbsp butter
- 3 Tbsp light muscovado sugar
- 1 tsp salt
- 1½ tsp easy bake yeast
- ¾ cup mixed peel
- ¾ cup chocolate chips

Directions:
Preparing the Ingredients   Sift the flour, cocoa, and spices together in a bowl.   Add each ingredient to the bread machine in the order and at the temperature recommended by your bread machine manufacturer. Select the Bake cycle   Close the lid, select the sweet loaf, medium crust setting on your bread machine, and press start.   Add the mixed peel and chocolate chips 5 to 10 minutes before the last kneading cycle ends.   When the bread machine has finished baking, remove the bread and put it on a cooling rack.

344. Mexican Chocolate Bread

Servings: 1 Loaf   Cooking Time: 10 Minutes Plus Fermenting Time

Ingredients:
- ½ cup milk
- ½ cup orange juice
- 1 large egg plus 1 egg yolk
- 3 Tbsp unsalted butter cut into pieces
- 2½ cups bread flour
- ¼ cup light brown sugar
- 3 Tbsp unsweetened dutch-process cocoa powder
- 1 Tbsp gluten
- 1 tsp instant espresso powder
- ¾ tsp ground cinnamon
- ½ cup bittersweet chocolate chips
- 2½ tsp bread machine yeast

Directions:
Preparing the Ingredients.   Add each ingredient to the bread machine in the order and at the temperature recommended by your bread machine manufacturer. Select the Bake cycle   Close the lid, select the sweet loaf, low crust setting on your bread machine, and press start. When the bread machine has finished baking, remove the bread and put it on a cooling rack.

345. Chocolate Cherry Bread

Servings: 14 Slices   Cooking Time: 30 Minutes Plus Fermenting Time

Ingredients:
- 1 cup milk
- 1 egg

- 3 Tbsp water
- 4 tsp butter
- ½ tsp almond extract
- 4 cups bread flour
- 3 Tbsp sugar
- 1 tsp salt
- 1¼ tsp active dry yeast
- ½ cup dried cherries, snipped
- ½ cup semisweet chocolate pieces, chilled

Directions:
Preparing the Ingredients   Add each ingredient to the bread machine in the order and at the temperature recommended by your   bread machine manufacturer. Select the Bake cycle   Close the lid, select the sweet loaf, low crust setting on your bread machine, and press start. When the bread machine has finished baking, remove the bread and put it on a cooling rack.

346. Olive And Cheddar Loaf

Servings: 1 Loaf   Cooking Time: 45 Minutes

Ingredients:
- 1 cup water, room temperature
- Four teaspoons sugar
- ¾ teaspoon salt
- 1 and 1/ cups sharp cheddar cheese, shredded
- 3 cups bread flour
- Two teaspoons active dry yeast
- ¾ cup pimiento olives, drained and sliced

Directions:
Add the listed ingredients to your bread machine (except salami), following the manufactures instructions.   Set the bread machine's program to Basic/White Bread and the crust type to light. Press Start.   Let the bread machine work and wait until it beeps this your indication to add the remaining ingredients. At this point, add the salami.   Wait until the remaining bake cycle completes. Once the loaf is done, take the bucket out from the bread machine and let it rest for 5 minutes.   Gently shake the bucket and remove the loaf, transfer the loaf to a cooling rack and slice.   Serve and enjoy!

Nutrition Info: Calories: 124 calories; Total Carbohydrate: 19 g ; Total Fat: 4 g ; Protein: 5 g ; Sugar: 5 g

347. Coffee Cake Banana Bread

Servings: 14 Slices   Cooking Time: 10 Minutes Plus

Ingredients:
- 4 medium bananas, mushed
- 2 Tbsp brown sugar
- 1½ tsp vanilla extract
- ¾ tsp ground cinnamon
- ½ cup butter, softened
- 1 cup sugar
- 2 eggs
- 2 cups all-purpose flour
- 1 tsp baking soda
- ¼ tsp salt
- 2 Tbsp Greek yogurt

Directions:

Preparing the Ingredients.   Add each ingredient to the bread machine in the order and at the temperature recommended by your bread machine manufacturer. Select the Bake cycle   Close the lid, select the sweet loaf, low crust setting on your bread machine, and press start. When the bread machine has finished baking, remove the bread and put it on a cooling rack.

348. Strawberry Bread

Servings: 10   Cooking Time: 3 Hours And 25 Minutes
Ingredients:
- Lukewarm water – 1 ¾ cups
- Kosher salt – 2 ½ tsp.
- Bread machinc flour – 4 cups, sifted
- Bread machine yeast – 1 tsp.
- Fresh strawberries – 1 cup, chopped

Directions:
Place everything in the bread machine (except strawberries) according to the bread machine recommendations.   Select French bread and Medium crust.   Add the strawberries after the beep.   Remove the bread when done.   Cool, slice, and serve.
Nutrition Info:(Per Serving): Calories: 313; Total Fat: 0.9 g; Saturated Fat: 0.1 g; Carbohydrates: 65.7 g; Cholesterol: 0 mg; Fiber: 2.9 g; Calcium: 42 mg; Sodium: 973 mg; Protein: 9 g

349. Mozzarella And Salami Bread

Servings: 1 Loaf   Cooking Time: 10 Minutes Plus Fermenting Time
Ingredients:
- 12 slice bread (1½ pounds)
- 1 cup water plus 2 tablespoons, at 80°F to 90°F
- ½ cup (2 ounces) shredded mozzarella cheese
- 2 tablespoons sugar
- 1 teaspoon salt
- 1 teaspoon dried basil
- ¼ teaspoon garlic powder
- 3¼ cups white bread flour
- 1½ teaspoons bread machine or instant yeast
- ¾ cup finely diced hot German salami

Directions:
Preparing the Ingredients.   Place the ingredients, except the salami, in your bread machine as recommended by the manufacturer.   Program the machine for Basic/White bread, select light or medium crust, and press Start.   When the loaf is done, remove the bucket from the machine.   Select the Bake cycle Add the salami when your machine signals or 5 minutes before the second kneading cycle is finished.   Let the loaf cool for 5 minutes. Gently shake the bucket to remove the loaf, and turn it out onto a rack to cool.

350. Mexican Style Jalapeno Cheese Bread

Servings: 1 Loaf
Ingredients:
- 16 slice bread (2 pounds)
- 1 small jalapeno pepper, seeded and minced
- 1 cup lukewarm water

- 3 tablespoons nonfat dry milk powder
- 1½ tablespoons unsalted butter, melted
- 1½ tablespoons sugar
- 1½ teaspoons table salt
- ¼ cup finely shredded cheese (Mexican blend or Monterrey Jack)
- 3 cups white bread flour
- 2 teaspoons bread machine yeast
- 12 slice bread (1½ pounds)
- 1 small jalapeno pepper, seeded and minced
- ¾ cup lukewarm water
- 2 tablespoons nonfat dry milk powder
- 1 tablespoon unsalted butter, melted
- 1 tablespoon sugar
- 1 teaspoon salt
- 3 tablespoons finely shredded cheese (Mexican blend or Monterrey Jack)
- 2 cups white bread flour
- 1½ teaspoons bread machine yeast

Directions:
Choose the size of loaf you would like to make and measure your ingredients.   Add the ingredients to the bread pan in the order listed above.   Place the pan in the bread machine and close the lid.   Turn on the bread maker. Select the White/Basic setting, then the loaf size, and finally the crust color. Start the cycle. When the cycle is finished and the bread is baked, carefully remove the pan from the machine. Use a potholder as the handle will be very hot. Let rest for a few minutes.   Remove the bread from the pan and allow to cool on a wire rack for at least 10 minutes before slicing.
Nutrition Info:(Per Serving):Calories 220, fat 9.4 g, carbs 18.6 g, sodium 206 mg, protein 9 g

351. Sweet Banana Bread

Servings: 10   Cooking Time: 2 Hours
Ingredients:
- Warm milk – ½ cup.
- Vanilla extract – 1 tsp.
- Butter – 8 tbsps.
- Eggs – 2
- Salt – ½ tsp.
- All-purpose flour – 2 cups.
- Sugar – 1 cup.
- Bananas – 3, mashed
- Baking soda – 1 tsp.
- Baking powder – 2 tsps.

Directions:
Add all ingredients into the bread machine pan. Select quick bread setting then select light crust and press start. Once loaf is done, remove the loaf pan from the machine. Allow it to cool for 10 minutes. Slice and serve.

352. Cinnamon   Bread

Servings: 1 Loaf   Cooking Time: 10 Minutes Plus Fermenting Time
Ingredients:
- 12 slice bread (1½ pounds)
- ¾ cup lukewarm water
- 1 egg, at room temperature

- 3 tablespoons butter, melted and cooled
- 3 tablespoons sugar
- 1 tablespoon rum extract
- 1¼ teaspoons table salt
- 3 cups white bread flour
- 1 teaspoon ground cinnamon
- ¼ teaspoon ground nutmeg
- 1 teaspoon bread machine yeast

Directions:
Preparing the Ingredients. Choose the size of loaf of your preference and then measure the ingredients. Add all of the ingredients mentioned previously in the list. Close the lid after placing the pan in the bread machine. Select the Bake cycle Turn on the bread machine. Select the Basic/White setting, select the loaf size, and the crust color. Press start. When the cycle is finished, carefully remove the pan from the bread maker and let it rest. Remove the bread from the pan, put in a wire rack to Cool about 5 minutes. Slice

353. Blue Cheese Bread

Servings: 12 Slices   Cooking Time: 10 Minutes
Ingredients:
- 3/4 cup warm water
- 1 large egg
- 1 teaspoon salt
- 3 cups bread flour
- 1 cup blue cheese, crumbled
- 2 tablespoons nonfat dry milk
- 2 tablespoons sugar
- 1 teaspoon bread machine yeast

Directions:
Preparing the Ingredients   Add the ingredients to bread machine pan in the order listed above, (except yeast) ; be sure to add the cheese with the flour. Make a well in the flour; pour the yeast into the hole.   Select the Bake cycle   Select Basic bread cycle, medium crust color, and press Start.   When finished, transfer to a cooling rack for 10 minutes and serve warm.

354. Apple Cider Bread

Servings: 1 Loaf   Cooking Time: 10 Minutes Plus Fermenting Time
Ingredients:
- 8 slices bread (1 pound)
- ¼ cup milk, at 80°F to 90°F
- 2 tablespoons apple cider, at room temperature
- 2 tablespoons sugar
- 4 teaspoons melted butter, cooled
- 1 tablespoon honey
- ¼ teaspoon salt
- 2 cups white bread flour
- ¾ teaspoons bread machine or instant yeast
- ⅔ apple, peeled, cored, and finely diced

Directions:
Preparing the Ingredients.   Place the ingredients, except the apple, in your bread machine as recommended by the manufacturer.   Select the Bake cycle   Program the machine for Basic/White bread, select light or medium crust, and press Start.   Add the

apple when the machine signals or 5 minutes before the last kneading cycle is complete.   When the cycle is finished, carefully remove the pan from the bread maker and let it rest.   Remove the bread from the pan, put in a wire rack to Cool about 5 minutes. Slice

355. Beer Cheese Bread

Servings: 10   Cooking Time: 2 hours
Ingredients:
- Monterey Jack cheese – 4 oz., shredded
- American cheese – 4 oz., shredded
- Beer – 10 oz.
- Butter – 1 tbsp.
- Sugar – 1 tbsp.
- Bread flour – 3 cups.
- Active dry yeast – 1 packet
- Salt – 1 ½ tsps.

Directions:
Add all ingredients into the bread machine pan. Select basic setting then select light crust and start. Once loaf is done, remove the loaf pan from the machine. Allow it to cool for 10 minutes. Slice and serve.

356. Ginger Spiced Bread

Servings: 1 Loaf
Ingredients:
- 16 slice bread (2 pounds)
- 1⅓ cups lukewarm buttermilk
- 1 egg, at room temperature
- ⅓ cup dark molasses
- 4 teaspoons unsalted butter, melted
- ¼ cup sugar
- 2 teaspoons table salt
- 4¼ cups white bread flour
- 2 teaspoons ground ginger
- 1¼ teaspoons ground cinnamon
- ⅔ teaspoon ground nutmeg
- ⅓ teaspoon ground cloves
- 2¼ teaspoons bread machine yeast
- 12 slice bread (1½ pounds)
- 1 cup lukewarm buttermilk
- 1 egg, at room temperature
- ¼ cup dark molasses
- 1 tablespoon unsalted butter, melted
- 3 tablespoons sugar
- 1½ teaspoons table salt
- 3½ cups white bread flour
- 1 teaspoon ground cinnamon
- ½ teaspoon ground nutmeg
- ¼ teaspoon ground cloves
- 1½ teaspoons ground ginger
- 2 teaspoons bread machine yeast

Directions:
Choose the size of loaf you would like to make and measure your ingredients.   Add the ingredients to the bread pan in the order listed above.   Place the pan in the bread machine and close the lid.   Turn on the bread maker. Select the Sweet setting, then the loaf size, and finally the crust color. Start the cycle.   When the cycle is finished and the bread is baked, carefully remove

the pan from the machine. Use a potholder as the handle will be very hot. Let rest for a few minutes. Remove the bread from the pan and allow to cool on a wire rack for at least 10 minutes before slicing.

Nutrition Info:(Per Serving):Calories 187, fat 2.3 g, carbs 36.7 g, sodium 312 mg, protein 4.6 g

357. American Cheese Beer Bread

Servings: 1 Loaf
Ingredients:
- 16 slice bread (2 pounds)
- 1⅔ cups warm beer
- 1½ tablespoons sugar
- 2 teaspoons table salt
- 1½ tablespoons unsalted butter, melted
- ¾ cup American cheese, shredded
- ¾ cup Monterrey Jack cheese, shredded
- 4 cups white bread flour
- 2 teaspoons bread machine yeast
- 12 slice bread (1½ pounds)
- 1¼ cups warm beer
- 1 tablespoon sugar
- 1½ teaspoons table salt
- 1 tablespoon unsalted butter, melted
- ½ cup American cheese, shredded
- ½ cup Monterrey Jack cheese, shredded
- 3 cups white bread flour
- 1½ teaspoons bread machine yeast

Directions:
Choose the size of loaf you would like to make and measure your ingredients. Add the ingredients to the bread pan in the order listed above. Place the pan in the bread machine and close the lid. Turn on the bread maker. Select the White/Basic setting, then the loaf size, and finally the crust color. Start the cycle. When the cycle is finished and the bread is baked, carefully remove the pan from the machine. Use a potholder as the handle will be very hot. Let rest for a few minutes. Remove the bread from the pan and allow to cool on a wire rack for at least 10 minutes before slicing.

Nutrition Info:(Per Serving):Calories 173, fat 5.3 g, carbs 26.1 g, sodium 118 mg, protein 6.2 g

358. Ricotta Bread

Servings: 14 Slices   Cooking Time: 3 H. 15 Min.
Ingredients:
- 3 Tbsp skim milk
- ⅔ cup ricotta cheese
- 4 tsp unsalted butter, softened to room temperature
- 1 large egg
- 2 Tbsp granulated sugar
- ½ tsp salt
- 1½ cups bread flour, + more flour, as needed
- 1 tsp active dry yeast

Directions:
Add each ingredient to the bread machine in the order and at the temperature recommended by your bread machine manufacturer. Close the lid, select the basic bread, medium crust setting on your bread machine, and

press start. When the bread machine has finished baking, remove the bread and put it on a cooling rack.

359. Chocolate Chip Peanut Butter Banana Bread

Servings: 1 Loaf   Cooking Time: 10 Minutes Plus Fermenting Time
Ingredients:
- 12 to 16 slice bread (1½ to 2 pounds)
- 2 bananas, mashed
- 2 eggs, at room temperature
- ½ cup melted butter, cooled
- 2 tablespoons milk, at room temperature
- 1 teaspoon pure vanilla extract
- 2 cups all-purpose flour
- ½ cup sugar
- 1¼ teaspoons baking powder
- ½ teaspoon baking soda
- ½ teaspoon salt
- ½ cup peanut butter chips
- ½ cup semisweet chocolate chips

Directions:
Preparing the Ingredients. Stir together the bananas, eggs, butter, milk, and vanilla in the bread machine bucket and set it aside. In a medium bowl, toss together the flour, sugar, baking powder, baking soda, salt, peanut butter chips, and chocolate chips. Add the dry ingredients to the bucket. Select the Bake cycle Program the machine for Quick/Rapid bread, and press Start. When the loaf is done, stick a knife into it, and if it comes out clean, the loaf is done. If the loaf needs a few more minutes, check the control panel for a Bake Only button and extend the time by 10 minutes. When the loaf is done, remove the bucket from the machine. Let the loaf cool for 5 minutes. Gently shake the bucket to remove the loaf, and turn it out onto a rack to cool.

360. Apple Butter Bread

Servings: 1 Loaf   Cooking Time: 10 Minutes Plus Fermenting Time
Ingredients:
- 8 slices bread (1 pound)
- ⅔ cup milk, at 80°F to 90°F
- ⅓ cup apple butter, at room temperature
- 4 teaspoons melted butter, cooled
- 2 teaspoons honey
- ⅔ teaspoon salt
- ⅔ cup whole-wheat flour
- 1½ cups white bread flour
- 1 teaspoon bread machine or instant yeast

Directions:
Preparing the Ingredients. Choose the size of loaf of your preference and then measure the ingredients. Add all of the ingredients mentioned previously in the list. Close the lid after placing the pan in the bread machine. Select the Bake cycle   Turn on the bread machine. Select the Quick/Rapid setting, select the loaf size, and the crust color. Press start. When the cycle is finished,

carefully remove the pan from the bread maker and let it rest.   Remove the bread from the pan, put in a wire rack to Cool about 5 minutes. Slice

361. Dry Fruit Bread

Servings: 12   Cooking Time: 3 Hours And 25 Minutes
Ingredients:
- Water – 1 cup, plus 2 tbsp.
- Egg – 1
- Butter – 3 tbsp., softened
- Packed brown sugar – ¼ cup
- Salt – 1 ½ tsp.
- Ground nutmeg – ¼ tsp.
- Dash allspice
- Bread flour – 3 ¾ cups, plus 1 tbsp.
- Active dry yeast – 2 tsp.
- Dried fruit – 1 cup
- Chopped pecans – 1/3 cup

Directions:
Add everything (except fruit and pecans) in the bread machine according to the machine recommendations. Select Basic bread cycle.   Add fruit and pecans at the beep.   Remove the bread when done.   Cool, slice, and serve.
Nutrition Info:(Per Serving): Calories: 214; Total Fat: 6 g; Saturated Fat: 2 g; Carbohydrates: 36 g; Cholesterol: 25 mg; Fiber: 2 g; Calcium: 38 mg; Sodium: 330 mg; Protein: 6 g

362. Cinnamon Cranberry Bread

Servings: 10   Cooking Time: 3 Hours
Ingredients:
- Water – 1 ¼ cups.
- Butter – 2 tbsps.
- Sugar – 2 ½ tbsps.
- Bread flour – 3 ½ cups.
- Dry yeast – 2 ¼ tsps.
- Dried cranberries – 1 cup.
- Cinnamon – 1 ½ tsps.
- Salt – 1 tsp.

Directions:
Add all ingredients except for cranberries and cinnamon into the bread machine pan. Select basic setting then select light crust and press start. Add cranberries and cinnamon just before the final kneading cycle. Once loaf is done, remove the loaf pan from the machine. Allow it to cool for 10 minutes. Slice and serve.

363. Apple Bread

Servings: 12   Cooking Time: 3 Hours And 25 Minutes
Ingredients:
- Bread machine yeast - 2½ tsp.
- Bread machine flour -3½ cups, sifted
- Sea salt - ½ tsp.
- Sugar - 6 tbsp.
- Vanillin - 1 bag
- Olive oil - 6 tbsp.
- Eggs - 3
- Lukewarm water - 1 cup

- Apples - 1 cup, peeled and diced

Directions:
Add everything according to bread machine recommendations.   Select Basic and Dark crust. Remove the bread when done.   Cool, slice, and serve.
Nutrition Info:(Per Serving): Calories: 379; Total Fat: 12.5 g; Saturated Fat: 1.9 g; Carbohydrates: 59.1 g; Cholesterol: 61 mg; Fiber: 3.1 g; Calcium: 45 mg; Sodium: 173 mg; Protein: 8.4 g

364. Parmesan Tomato Basil Bread

Servings: 10   Cooking Time: 2 Hours
Ingredients:
- Sun-dried tomatoes – ¼ cup, chopped
- Yeast – 2 tsps.
- Bread flour – 2 cups.
- Parmesan cheese – 1/3 cup, grated
- Dried basil – 2 tsps.
- Sugar – 1 tsp.
- Olive oil – 2 tbsps.
- Milk – ¼ cup.
- Water – ½ cup.
- Salt – 1 tsp.

Directions:
Add all ingredients except for sun-dried tomatoes into the bread machine pan. Select basic setting then select medium crust and press start. Add sun-dried tomatoes just before the final kneading cycle. Once loaf is done, remove the loaf pan from the machine. Allow it to cool for 10 minutes. Slice and serve.

365. Pear Kuchen With Ginger Topping

Servings: 12 Servings   Cooking Time: 20 Minutes Plus Fermenting Time
Ingredients:
- Bread dough
- ½ cup milk
- 2 tablespoons butter, softened
- 1 egg
- 2 cups bread flour
- 2 tablespoons sugar
- 1 teaspoon salt
- 1¾ teaspoons bread machine or fast-acting dry yeast
- Topping
- 3 cups sliced peeled pears
- 1 cup sugar
- 2 tablespoons butter, softened
- 1 tablespoon chopped crystallized ginger
- ½ cup whipping cream
- 1 egg yolk

Directions:
Preparing the Ingredients.   Measure carefully, placing all bread dough ingredients in bread machine pan in the order recommended by the manufacturer.   Select the Bake cycle   Select Dough/Manual cycle. Do not use delay cycle.   Remove dough from pan, using lightly floured hands. Cover and let rest 10 minutes on lightly floured surface.   Grease 13×9-inch pan with shortening. Press dough evenly in bottom of pan.

Arrange pears on dough. In small bowl, mix 1 cup sugar, 2 tablespoons butter and the ginger. Reserve 2 tablespoons of the topping; sprinkle remaining topping over pears. Cover and let rise in warm place 30 to 45 minutes or until doubled in size. Dough is ready if indentation remains when touched. Heat oven to 375°F. Bake 20 minutes. Mix whipping cream and egg yolk; pour over hot kuchen. Bake 15 minutes longer or until golden brown. Sprinkle with reserved 2 tablespoons topping. Serve warm.

366. Sweet Pineapple Bread

Servings: 1 Loaf   Cooking Time: 10 Minutes Plus Fermenting Time
Ingredients:
- 16 slice bread (2 pounds)
- 6 tablespoons unsalted butter, melted
- 2 eggs, at room temperature
- ½ cup coconut milk, at room temperature
- ½ cup pineapple juice, at room temperature
- 1 cup sugar
- 1½ teaspoons coconut extract
- 2 cups all-purpose flour
- ¾ cup shredded sweetened coconut
- 1 teaspoon baking powder
- ½ teaspoon table salt

Directions:
Preparing the Ingredients.   Place the ingredients, except the apple, in your bread machine as recommended by the manufacturer.   Select the Bake cycle   Program the machine for Quick/Rapid bread, select light or medium crust, and press Start.   Add the apple when the machine signals or 5 minutes before the last kneading cycle is complete.   When the cycle is finished, carefully remove the pan from the bread maker and let it rest.   Remove the bread from the pan, put in a wire rack to Cool about 5 minutes. Slice

367. Oregano Cheese Bread

Servings: 1 Loaf   Cooking Time: 10 Minutes
Ingredients:
- 3 cups bread flour
- 1 cup water
- ½ cup freshly grated parmesan cheese
- 3 Tbsp sugar
- 1 Tbsp dried leaf oregano
- 1½ Tbsp olive oil
- 1 tsp salt
- 2 tsp active dry yeast

Directions:
Preparing the Ingredients   Add each ingredient to the bread machine in the order and at the temperature recommended by your bread machine manufacturer. Select the Bake cycle   Close the lid, select the basic bread, medium crust setting on your bread machine, and press start.   When the bread machine has finished baking, remove the bread and put it on a cooling rack.

368. Green Cheese Bread

Servings: 8   Cooking Time: 3 Hours And 25 Minutes
Ingredients:
- Lukewarm water - ¾ cup
- Sugar - 1 tbsp.
- Kosher salt - 1 tsp.
- Green cheese - 2 tbsp.
- Wheat bread flour - 1 cup
- Whole-grain flour - 9/10 cup, finely ground
- Bread machine yeast - 1 tsp.
- ground paprika - 1 tsp.

Directions:
Add everything (except the paprika) in the bread machine pan according to bread machine recommendations.   Select Basic cycle and Dark crust. Add the paprika after the beep.   Remove the bread when it is done.   Cool, slice, and serve.
Nutrition Info:(Per Serving): Calories: 118; Total Fat: 1 g; Saturated Fat: 0.4 g; Carbohydrates: 23.6 g; Cholesterol: 2 mg; Fiber: 2.3 g; Calcium: 35 mg; Sodium: 304 mg; Protein: 4.1 g

369. Triple Chocolate Bread

Servings: 1 Loaf   Cooking Time: 10 Minutes Plus Fermenting Time
Ingredients:
- 8 slices bread (1 pound)
- ⅔ cup milk, at 80°F to 90°F
- 1 egg, at room temperature
- 1½ tablespoons melted butter, cooled
- 1 teaspoon pure vanilla extract
- 2 tablespoons light brown sugar
- 1 tablespoon unsweetened cocoa powder
- ½ teaspoon salt
- 2 cups white bread flour
- 1 teaspoon bread machine or instant yeast
- ¼ cup semisweet chocolate chips
- ¼ cup white chocolate chips

Directions:
Preparing the Ingredients.   Place the ingredients, except the chocolate chips, in your bread machine as recommended by the manufacturer.   Select the Bake cycle   Program the machine for Basic/White bread, select light or medium crust, and press Start.   When the machine signals, add the chocolate chips, or put them in the nut/raisin hopper and the machine will add them automatically.   When the loaf is done, remove the bucket from the machine.   Let the loaf cool for 5 minutes.   Gently shake the bucket to remove the loaf, and turn it out onto a rack to cool.

370. Buttery Sweet Bread

Servings: 1 Loaf   Cooking Time: 1 Hour And 15 Minutes
Ingredients:
- 1/3 cup water
- ½ cup milk
- ¼ cup of sugar
- One beaten egg
- One teaspoon of salt

- ¼ cup margarine or ¼ cup butter
- Two teaspoons bread machine yeast
- 3 1/3 cups bread flour

Directions:

Put everything in your bread machine pan.   Select the white bread setting.   Take out the pan when done and set aside for 10 minutes.

Nutrition Info: Calories 168;Carbohydrates: 28g;Total Fat 5g;Cholesterol 0mg;Protein 4g;Fiber 1g;Sugars 3g;Sodium 292mg;Potassium 50mg

371. Rich Cheddar Bread

Servings: 1 Loaf   Cooking Time: 10 Minutes Plus Fermenting Time

Ingredients:
- 12 slice bread (1½ pounds)
- 1 cup milk, at 80°F to 90°F
- 2 tablespoons butter, melted and cooled
- 3 tablespoons sugar
- 1 teaspoon salt
- ½ cup (2 ounces) grated aged Cheddar cheese
- 3 cups white bread flour
- 2 teaspoons bread machine or instant yeast

Directions:

Preparing the Ingredients.   Choose the size of loaf of your preference and then measure the ingredients. Add all of the ingredients mentioned previously in the list. Close the lid after placing the pan in the bread machine. Select the Bake cycle   Turn on the bread machine. Select the Quick/Rapid setting, select the loaf size, and the crust color. Press start.   When the cycle is finished, carefully remove the pan from the bread maker and let it rest.   Remove the bread from the pan, put in a wire rack to Cool about 5 minutes. Slice

372. Swedish Coffee Bread

Servings: 14 Slices   Cooking Time: 10 Minutes

Ingredients:
- 1 cup milk
- ½ tsp salt
- 1 egg yolk
- 2 Tbsp softened butter
- 3 cups all-purpose flour
- ⅓ cup sugar
- 1 envelope active dry yeast
- 3 tsp ground cardamom
- 2 egg whites, slightly beaten

Directions:

Preparing the Ingredients   Add each ingredient to the bread machine in the order and at the temperature recommended by your bread machine manufacturer. Select the Bake cycle   Select the dough cycle and press start. Grease your baking sheet.   When the dough cycle has finished, divide the dough into three equal parts. Roll each part into a rope 12-14" long. Lay 3 ropes side by side, and then braid them together.   Tuck the ends underneath and put onto the sheet. Next, cover the bread, using kitchen towel, and let it rise until it has doubled in size. Brush your bread with beaten egg white and sprinkle with pearl sugar.   Bake until golden brown at 375°F in a preheated oven for 20-25 minutes. When baked, remove the bread and put it on a cooling rack.

373. Nectarine Cobbler Bread

Servings: 1 Loaf   Cooking Time: 10 Minutes Plus Fermenting Time /

Ingredients:
- 12 to 16 slice bread (1½ to 2 pounds)
- ½ cup (1 stick) butter, at room temperature
- 2 eggs, at room temperature
- 1 cup sugar
- ¼ cup milk, at room temperature
- 1 teaspoon pure vanilla extract
- 1 cup diced nectarines
- 1¾ cups all-purpose flour
- 1 teaspoon baking soda
- ½ teaspoon salt
- ½ teaspoon ground nutmeg
- ¼ teaspoon baking powder

Directions:

Preparing the Ingredients.   Place the butter, eggs, sugar, milk, vanilla, and nectarines in your bread machine.   Select the Bake cycle   Program the machine for Quick/Rapid bread and press Start. While the wet ingredients are mixing, stir together the flour, baking soda, salt, nutmeg, and baking powder in a small bowl.   After the first fast mixing is done and the machine signals, add the dry ingredients.   When the cycle is finished, carefully remove the pan from the bread maker and let it rest.   Remove the bread from the pan, put in a wire rack to Cool about 10 minutes. Slice

374. Jalapeño Corn Bread

Servings: 1 Loaf   Cooking Time: 10 Minutes

Ingredients:
- 12 to 16 slices bread (1½ to 2 pounds)
- 1 cup buttermilk, at 80°F to 90°F
- ¼ cup melted butter, cooled
- 2 eggs, at room temperature
- 1 jalapeño pepper, chopped
- 1⅓ cups all-purpose flour
- 1 cup cornmeal
- ½ cup (2 ounces) shredded Cheddar cheese
- ¼ cup sugar
- 1 tablespoon baking powder
- ½ teaspoon salt

Directions:

Preparing the Ingredients.   Choose the size of loaf of your preference and then measure the ingredients. Add all of the ingredients mentioned previously in the list. Close the lid after placing the pan in the bread machine. Select the Bake cycle   Turn on the bread machine. Select the Quick/Rapid setting, select the loaf size, and the crust color. Press start.   When the cycle is finished, carefully remove the pan from the bread maker and let it rest.   Remove the bread from the pan, put in a wire rack to Cool about 5 minutes. Slice

375. Cinnamon Rum Bread

Servings: 1 Loaf
Ingredients:
- 16 slice bread (2 pounds)
- 1⅛ cups lukewarm water
- 1 egg, at room temperature
- ¼ cup butter, melted and cooled
- ¼ cup sugar
- 4 teaspoons rum extract
- 1⅔ teaspoons table salt
- 4 cups white bread flour
- 1⅓ teaspoons ground cinnamon
- ¼ teaspoon ground nutmeg
- 1⅓ teaspoons bread machine yeast
- 12 slice bread (1½ pounds)
- ¾ cup lukewarm water
- 1 egg, at room temperature
- 3 tablespoons butter, melted and cooled
- 3 tablespoons sugar
- 1 tablespoon rum extract
- 1¼ teaspoons table salt
- 3 cups white bread flour
- 1 teaspoon ground cinnamon
- ¼ teaspoon ground nutmeg
- 1 teaspoon bread machine yeast

Directions:
Choose the size of loaf you would like to make and measure your ingredients. Add the ingredients to the bread pan in the order listed above. Place the pan in the bread machine and close the lid. Turn on the bread maker. Select the Sweet setting, then the loaf size, and finally the crust color. Start the cycle. When the cycle is finished and the bread is baked, carefully remove the pan from the machine. Use a potholder as the handle will be very hot. Let rest for a few minutes. Remove the bread from the pan and allow to cool on a wire rack for at least 10 minutes before slicing.

Nutrition Info:(Per Serving):Calories 156, fat 3.7 g, carbs 26.3 g, sodium 248 mg, protein 4.3 g

376. Wine And Cheese Bread

Servings: 1 Loaf   Cooking Time: 10 Minutes Plus Fermenting Time
Ingredients:
- 3/4 cup white wine
- 1/2 cup white cheddar or gruyere cheese, shredded
- 1 1/2 tablespoons butter
- 1/2 teaspoon salt
- 3/4 teaspoon sugar
- 2 1/4 cups bread flour
- 1 1/2 teaspoons active dry yeast

Directions:
Preparing the Ingredients   Add liquid ingredients to the bread maker pan.Add dry ingredients, except yeast, to the bread pan.   Use your fingers to form a well-like hole in the flour where you will pour the yeast; yeast must never come into contact with a liquid when you are adding the ingredients. Carefully pour the yeast into the well.   Select the Bake cycle   Select Basic bread

setting, light crust color, and press Start. Allow to cool on a wire rack before serving.

377. Milk Sweet Bread

Servings: 1 Loaf
Ingredients:
- 16 slice bread (2 pounds)
- 1⅓ cups lukewarm milk
- 1 egg, at room temperature
- 2⅔ tablespoons butter, softened
- ⅔ cup sugar
- 1⅓ teaspoons table salt
- 4 cups white bread flour
- 2¼ teaspoons bread machine yeast
- 12 slice bread (1½ pounds)
- 1 cup lukewarm milk
- 1 egg, at room temperature
- 2 tablespoons butter, softened
- ½ cup sugar
- 1 teaspoon table salt
- 3 cups white bread flour
- 2¼ teaspoons bread machine yeast

Directions:
Choose the size of loaf you would like to make and measure your ingredients. Add the ingredients to the bread pan in the order listed above. Place the pan in the bread machine and close the lid. Turn on the bread maker. Select the Sweet setting, then the loaf size, and finally the crust color. Start the cycle. When the cycle is finished and the bread is baked, carefully remove the pan from the machine. Use a potholder as the handle will be very hot. Let rest for a few minutes. Remove the bread from the pan and allow to cool on a wire rack for at least 10 minutes before slicing.

Nutrition Info:(Per Serving):Calories 178, fat 3.2 g, carbs 32.6 g, sodium 227 mg, protein 4.8 g

378. Honey Goat Cheese Bread

Servings: 1 Loaf   Cooking Time: 10 Minutes Plus Fermenting Time
Ingredients:
- 12 slice bread (1½ pounds)
- 1 cup lukewarm milk
- 1½ tablespoons honey
- 1 teaspoon table salt
- 1 teaspoon freshly cracked black pepper
- ¼ cup goat cheese, shredded or crumbled
- 3 cups white bread flour
- 1½ teaspoons bread machine yeast

Directions:
Preparing the Ingredients.   Choose the size of loaf of your preference and then measure the ingredients. Add all of the ingredients mentioned previously in the list. Close the lid after placing the pan in the bread machine. Select the Bake cycle   Turn on the bread machine. Select the Quick/Rapid setting, select the loaf size, and the crust color. Press start.   When the cycle is finished, carefully remove the pan from the bread maker and let it rest.   Remove the bread from the pan, put in a wire rack to Cool about 5 minutes. Slice

379. Spinach And Feta Bread

Servings: 14 Slices   Cooking Time: 10 Minutes

Ingredients:
- 1 cup water
- 2 tsp butter
- 3 cups flour
- 1 tsp sugar
- 2 tsp instant minced onion
- 1 tsp salt
- 1¼ tsp instant yeast
- 1 cup crumbled feta
- 1 cup chopped fresh spinach leaves

Directions:
Preparing the Ingredients   Add each ingredient except the cheese and spinach to the bread machine in the order and at the temperature recommended by your bread machine manufacturer.   Select the Bake cycle Close the lid, select the basic bread, medium crust setting on your bread machine, and press start.   When only 10 minutes are left in the last kneading cycle add the spinach and cheese.   When the bread machine has finished baking, remove the bread and put it on a cooling rack.

380. Cheddar And Bacon Bread

Servings: 14 Slices   Cooking Time: 10 Minutes Plus Fermenting Time

Ingredients:
- 1⅓ cups water
- 2 Tbsp vegetable oil
- 1¼ tsp salt
- 2 Tbsp plus 1½ tsp sugar
- 4 cups bread flour
- 3 Tbsp nonfat dry milk
- 2 tsp dry active yeast
- 2 cups cheddar
- 8 slices crumbled bacon

Directions:
Preparing the Ingredients   Add each ingredient to the bread machine except the cheese and bacon in the order and at the temperature recommended by your bread machine manufacturer.   Select the Bake cycle   Close the lid, select the basic bread, medium crust setting on your bread machine, and press start.   Add the cheddar cheese and bacon 30 to 40 minutes into the cycle. When the bread machine has finished baking, remove the bread and put it on a cooling rack.

381. Delicious Italian Cheese Bread

Servings: 10   Cooking Time: 2 Hours

Ingredients:
- Active dry yeast – 2 tsps.
- Brown sugar – 2 tbsps.
- Parmesan cheese – 2 tbsps., grated
- Ground black pepper – 1 tsp.
- Italian seasoning – 2 tsps.
- Pepper jack cheese – 1/2 cup., shredded
- Bread flour – 3 cups.
- Warm water – 1 ¼ cups

- Salt – 1 ½ tsps.

Directions:
Add all ingredients into the bread machine pan. Select basic setting then select light/medium crust and start. Once loaf is done, remove the loaf pan from the machine. Allow it to cool for 10 minutes. Slice and serve.

382. Chocolate Oatmeal Banana Bread

Servings: 1 Loaf   Cooking Time: 10 Minutes Plus Fermenting Time

Ingredients:
- 12 to 16 slice bread (1½ to 2 pounds)
- 3 bananas, mashed
- 2 eggs, at room temperature
- ¾ cup packed light brown sugar
- ½ cup (1 stick) butter, at room temperature
- ½ cup sour cream, at room temperature
- ¼ cup sugar
- 1½ teaspoons pure vanilla extract
- 1 cup all-purpose flour
- ½ cup quick oats
- 2 tablespoons unsweetened cocoa powder
- 1 teaspoon baking soda

Directions:
Preparing the Ingredients.   Place the banana, eggs, brown sugar, butter, sour cream, sugar, and vanilla in your bread machine.   Program the machine for Quick/Rapid bread and press Start.   While the wet ingredients are mixing, stir together the flour, oats, cocoa powder, and baking soda in a small bowl.   Select the Bake cycle   After the first fast mixing is done and the machine signals, add the dry ingredients.   When the loaf is done, remove the bucket from the machine.   Let the loaf cool for 5 minutes.   Gently shake the bucket to remove the loaf, and turn it out onto a rack to cool.

383. Almond Chocolate Chip Bread

Servings: 14 Slices   Cooking Time: 10 Minutes Plus Fermenting Time

Ingredients:
- 1 cup plus 2 Tbsp water
- 2 Tbsp softened butter
- ½ tsp vanilla
- 3 cups Gold Medal Better for Bread flour
- ¾ cup semisweet chocolate chips
- 3 Tbsp sugar
- 1 Tbsp dry milk
- ¾ tsp salt
- 1½ tsp quick active dry yeast
- ⅓ cup sliced almonds

Directions:
Preparing the Ingredients   Add each ingredient except the almonds to the bread machine in the order and at the temperature recommended by your bread machine manufacturer.   Select the Bake cycle   Close the lid, select the sweet loaf, low crust setting on your bread machine, and press start.   Add almonds 10 minutes before last kneading cycle ends. When the bread machine has finished baking, remove the bread and put it on a cooling rack.

384. Pumpkin Coconut Bread

Servings: 1 Loaf   Cooking Time: 10 Minutes Plus Fermenting Time

Ingredients:
- 12 to 16 slice bread (1½ to 2 pounds)
- 1 cup pure canned pumpkin
- ½ cup (1 stick) butter, at room temperature
- 1½ teaspoons pure vanilla extract
- 1 cup sugar
- ½ cup dark brown sugar
- 2 cups all-purpose flour
- ¾ cup sweetened shredded coconut
- 1½ teaspoons ground cinnamon
- 1 teaspoon baking soda
- 1 teaspoon baking powder
- ½ teaspoon ground nutmeg
- ½ teaspoon ground ginger
- ⅛ teaspoon ground allspice

Directions:
Preparing the Ingredients.   Place the pumpkin, butter, vanilla, sugar, and dark brown sugar in your bread machine.   Select the Bake cycle   Program the machine for Quick/Rapid bread and press Start.   After the first fast mixing is done, add the flour, coconut, cinnamon, baking soda, baking powder, nutmeg, ginger, and allspice.   When the cycle is finished, carefully remove the pan from the bread maker and let it rest. Remove the bread from the pan, put in a wire rack to Cool about 5 minutes. Slice.

385. Romano Oregano Bread

Servings: 1 Loaf

Ingredients:
- 16 slice bread (2 pounds)
- 1⅓ cups lukewarm water
- ¼ cup sugar
- 2 tablespoons olive oil
- 1⅓ teaspoons table salt
- 1⅓ tablespoons dried leaf oregano
- ⅔ cup cheese (Romano or Parmesan), freshly grated
- 4 cups white bread flour
- 2½–3 teaspoons bread machine yeast
- 12 slice bread (1½ pounds)
- 1 cup lukewarm water
- 3 tablespoons sugar
- 1½ tablespoons olive oil
- 1 teaspoon table salt
- 1 tablespoon dried leaf oregano
- ½ cup cheese (Romano or Parmesan), freshly grated
- 3 cups white bread flour
- 2 teaspoons bread machine yeast

Directions:
Choose the size of loaf you would like to make and measure your ingredients.   Add the ingredients to the bread pan in the order listed above.   Place the pan in the bread machine and close the lid.   Turn on the bread maker. Select the White/Basic setting, then the

loaf size, and finally the crust color. Start the cycle. When the cycle is finished and the bread is baked, carefully remove the pan from the machine. Use a potholder as the handle will be very hot. Let rest for a few minutes.   Remove the bread from the pan and allow to cool down on a wire rack for at least 10 minutes or more before slicing.

Nutrition Info:(Per Serving):Calories 207, fat 6.2 g, carbs 27 g, sodium 267 mg, protein 9.3 g

386. Easy Donuts

Servings: 12   Cooking Time: 1 Hour

Ingredients:
- 2/3 cups milk, room temperature
- 1/4 cup water, room temperature
- ½ cup of warm water
- 1/4 cup softened butter
- One egg slightly has beaten
- 1/4 cup granulated sugar
- 1 tsp salt
- 3 cups bread machine flour
- 2 1/2 tsp bread machine yeast
- oil for deep frying
- 1/4 cup confectioners' sugar

Directions:
Place the milk, water, butter, egg sugar, salt, flour, and yeast in a pan.   Select dough setting and push start. Press the start button.   When the process is complete, remove dough from the pan and transfer it to a lightly floured surface.   Using a rolling pin lightly dusted with flour, roll dough to ½ inch thickness.   Cut with a floured dusted donut cutter or circle cookie cutter. Transfer donuts to a baking sheet that has been covered with wax paper. Place another layer of paper on top, then cover with a clean tea towel. Let rise 30-40 minutes. Heat vegetable oil to 375⁰ (190⁰C⁰) in a deep-fryer or large, heavy pot.   Fry donuts 2-3 at a time until golden brown on both sides for about 3 minutes.   Drain on a paper towel.   Sprinkle with confectioners' sugar.

Nutrition Info: Calories 180;Carbohydrates: 30g;Total Fat 5g;Cholesterol 25mg;Protein 4g;Fiber 2g;Sugar 7g;Sodium 240mg;Potassium 64mg

387. Onion And Cheese Bread

Servings: 12   Cooking Time: 3 Hours And 25 Minutes

Ingredients:
- Lukewarm water - ¾ cup
- Wheat bread flour - 3 2/3 cups
- Cottage cheese - ¾ cup
- Butter - 2 tbsp., softened
- White sugar - 2 tbsp.
- Sea salt - 1½ tsp.
- Sesame seeds - 1½ tbsp.
- Dried onions - 2 tbsp.
- Bread machine yeast - 1¼ tsp.

Directions:
Place everything in the bread pan according to bread machine recommendations.   Select Basic and Medium crust.   Remove the bread when done.   Cool, slice, and serve.

Nutrition Info:(Per Serving): Calories: 277; Total Fat: 4.7 g; Saturated Fat: 2.3 g; Carbohydrates: 48.4 g; Cholesterol: 9 mg; Fiber: 1.9 g; Calcium: 41 mg; Sodium: 547 mg; Protein: 9.4 g

388. Italian Cheese Bread

Servings: 14 Slices   Cooking Time: 10 Minutes
Ingredients:
- 1¼ cups water
- 3 cups bread flour
- ½ shredded pepper jack cheese
- 2 tsp Italian seasoning
- 2 Tbsp brown sugar
- 1½ tsp salt
- 2 tsp active dry yeast

Directions:
Preparing the Ingredients.   Add each ingredient to the bread machine in the order and at the temperature recommended by your bread machine manufacturer. Select the Bake cycle   Close the lid, select the basic bread, medium crust setting on your bread machine, and press start.   When the bread machine has finished baking, remove the bread and put it on a cooling rack.

389. Cinnamon Sugar Bread

Servings: 1 Loaf   Cooking Time: 1 Hour
Ingredients:
- One pack active dry yeast
- ½ cup of sugar
- 3 cups bread flour
- 1/4 cup cocoa powder
- One large egg
- 1/4 cup butter
- ½ teaspoon vanilla extract
- 1 cup milk

Directions:
Put everything in the pan of your bread machine. Select the quick bread or equivalent setting.   Take out the pan when done and set aside for 10 minutes.
Nutrition Info: Calories 184;Carbohydrates: 31g;Total Fat 5g;Cholesterol 13mg;Protein 5g;Fiber 2g;Sugar 8g;Sodium 214mg;Potassium 92mg

390. Apple Honey Bread

Servings: 1 Loaf   Cooking Time: 10 Minutes Plus Fermenting Time
Ingredients:
- 12 slice bread (1½ pounds)
- 5 tablespoons lukewarm milk
- 3 tablespoons apple cider, at room temperature
- 3 tablespoons sugar
- 2 tablespoons unsalted butter, melted
- 1½ tablespoons honey
- ¼ teaspoon table salt
- 3 cups white bread flour
- 1¼ teaspoons bread machine yeast
- 1 apple, peeled, cored, and finely diced

Directions:

Preparing the Ingredients.   Choose the size of loaf of your preference and then measure the ingredients. Add all of the ingredients mentioned previously in the list, except for the apples. Close the lid after placing the pan in the bread machine.   Select the Bake cycle   Turn on the bread maker. Select the White/Basic or Fruit/Nut (if your machine has this setting) setting, then the loaf size, and finally the crust color. Start the cycle.   When the machine signals to add ingredients, add the apples. When the cycle is finished, carefully remove the pan from the bread maker and let it rest. Remove the bread from the pan, put in a wire rack to Cool about 5 minutes. Slice

391. Italian Herb Cheese Bread

Servings: 10   Cooking Time: 3 Hours
Ingredients:
- Yeast – 1 ½ tsps.
- Italian herb seasoning – 1 tbsp.
- Brown sugar – 2 tbsps.
- Cheddar cheese – 1 cup., shredded
- Bread flour – 3 cups.
- Butter – 4 tbsps.
- Warm milk – 1 ¼ cups.
- Salt – 2 tsps.

Directions:
Add milk into the bread pan. Add remaining ingredients except for yeast to the bread pan. Make a small hole into the flour with your finger and add yeast to the hole. Make sure yeast will not be mixed with any liquids. Select basic setting then select light crust and start. Once loaf is done, remove the loaf pan from the machine. Allow it to cool for 10 minutes. Slice and serve.

392. Simple Cottage Cheese Bread

Servings: 1 Loaf   Cooking Time: 10 Minutes   Plus Fermenting Time
Ingredients:
- 12 slice bread (1½ pounds)
- ½ cup water, at 80°F to 90°F
- ¾ cup cottage cheese, at room temperature
- 1 egg, at room temperature
- 2 tablespoons butter, melted and cooled
- 1 tablespoon sugar
- 1 teaspoon salt
- ¼ teaspoon baking soda
- 3 cups white bread flour
- 2 teaspoons bread machine or instant yeast

Directions:
Preparing the Ingredients.   Choose the size of loaf of your preference and then measure the ingredients. Add all of the ingredients mentioned previously in the list. Close the lid after placing the pan in the bread machine. Select the Bake cycle   Turn on the bread machine. Select the White/Basic setting, select the loaf size, and the crust color. Press start.   When the cycle is finished, carefully remove the pan from the bread maker and let it rest.   Remove the bread from the pan, put in a wire rack to Cool about 5 minutes. Slice

393. Black Bread

Servings: 1 Loaf   Cooking Time: 10 Minutes Plus Fermenting Time

Ingredients:
- 12 slice bread (1½ pounds)
- ¾ cup water, at 80°F to 90°F
- ⅓ cup brewed coffee, at 80°F to 90°F
- 1½ tablespoons balsamic vinegar
- 1½ tablespoons olive oil
- 1½ tablespoons dark molasses
- ¾ tablespoon light brown sugar
- ¾ teaspoon salt
- 1½ teaspoons caraway seeds
- 3 tablespoons unsweetened cocoa powder
- ¾ cup dark rye flour
- 1¾ cups white bread flour
- 1½ teaspoons bread machine or instant yeast

Directions:
Preparing the Ingredients.   Place the ingredients in your bread machine as recommended by the manufacturer.   Select the Bake cycle   Program the machine for Whole-Wheat/Whole-Grain bread, select light or medium crust, and press Start.   When the loaf is done, remove the bucket from the machine. Let the loaf cool for 5 minutes. Gently shake the bucket to remove the loaf, and turn it out onto a rack to cool.

394. Jalapeno Cheese Bread

Servings: 14 Slices   Cooking Time: 3 H.

Ingredients:
- 3 cups bread flour
- 1½ tsp active dry yeast
- 1 cup water
- 2 Tbsp sugar
- 1 tsp salt
- ½ cup shredded cheddar cheese
- ¼ cup diced jalapeno peppers

Directions:
Add each ingredient to the bread machine in the order and at the temperature recommended by your bread machine manufacturer.   Close the lid, select the basic bread, medium crust setting on your bread machine, and press start.   When the bread machine has finished baking, remove the bread and put it on a cooling rack.

395. Cranberry-cornmeal Bread

Servings: 1 Loaf   Cooking Time: 10 Minutes Plus Fermenting Time

Ingredients:
- 12 slice bread (1½ pounds)
- 1 cup plus 1 tablespoon water
- 3 tablespoons molasses or honey
- 2 tablespoons butter, softened
- 3 cups bread flour
- ⅓ cup cornmeal
- 1½ teaspoons salt
- 2 teaspoons bread machine yeast
- ½ cup sweetened dried cranberries

Directions:

Preparing the Ingredients.   Choose the size of loaf of your preference and then measure the ingredients. Add all of the ingredients mentioned previously in the list except cranberries   Close the lid after placing the pan in the bread machine.   Add cranberries at the Raisin/Nut signal or 5 to 10 minutes before last kneading cycle ends.   Select the Bake cycle   Program the machine for White/Basic bread and press Start.   After the first fast mixing is done, add the flour, coconut, cinnamon, baking soda, baking powder, nutmeg, ginger, and allspice. When the cycle is finished, carefully remove the pan from the bread maker and let it rest.   Remove the bread from the pan, put in a wire rack to Cool about 5 minutes. Slice.

396. Olive Cheese Bread

Servings: 8 Pcs   Cooking Time: 15 Minutes

Ingredients:
- 2/3 cup milk, set at 80°F to 90°F
- One tablespoon melted butter cooled
- 2/3 Teaspoon minced garlic
- One tablespoon sugar
- 2/3 teaspoon salt
- 2 cups white bread flour
- ½ cup (2 ounces) shredded Swiss cheese
- ¾ teaspoon bread machine or instant yeast
- ¼ cup chopped black olives

Directions:
Place the ingredients in your device as recommended on it.   Make a program on the machine for basic white Bread, select Light or medium crust, and press Start. When the loaf is finished, remove the bucket from the machine.   Let the loaf cool for a minute.   Gently shake the bucket and remove the loaf and turn it out onto a rack to cool.

Nutrition Info: Calories: 175 calories; Total Carbohydrate: 27 g ; Total Fat: 5g ; Protein: 6 g ; Sodium: 260 mg

397. Peach Bread

Servings: 10   Cooking Time: 3 Hours And 48 Minutes

Ingredients:
- Wholemeal flour – 4 cups
- Bread machine yeast – 2 tsp.
- Lukewarm water – 1 ¼ cups
- Flaxseed oil – 1 ½ tsp.
- Brown sugar – 1 ½ tsp.
- Kosher salt – 1 ½ tsp.
- Peaches – 2, peeled and diced

Directions:
Add everything in the bread machine (except the peaches) according to bread machine recommendations. Select Whole-Grain and Medium crust.   Add the peaches after the beep.   Remove the bread when done. Cool, slice, and serve.

Nutrition Info: (Per Serving): Calories: 246; Total Fat: 4 g; Saturated Fat: 0.3 g; Carbohydrates: 44.3 g; Cholesterol: 0 mg; Fiber: 6.4 g; Calcium: 50 mg; Sodium: 440 mg; Protein: 8.2 g

398. Hot Cross Buns

Servings: 16 Bouns   Cooking Time: 10 Minutes Plus Fermenting Time

Ingredients:
- Dough
- 2 eggs plus enough water to equal 1⅓ cups
- ½ cup butter, softened
- 4 cups bread flour
- ¾ teaspoon ground cinnamon
- ¼ teaspoon ground nutmeg
- 1½ teaspoons salt
- 2 tablespoons granulated sugar
- 1½ teaspoons bread machine or fast-acting dry yeast
- ½ cup raisins
- ½ cup golden raisins
- 1 egg
- 2 tablespoons cold water
- Icing
- 1 cup powdered sugar
- 1 tablespoon milk or water
- ½ teaspoon vanilla

Directions:
Preparing the Ingredients.   Measure carefully, placing all dough ingredients except raisins, 1 egg and the cold water in bread machine pan in the order recommended by the manufacturer. Add raisins at the Raisin/Nut signal.   Select the Bake cycle   Select Dough/Manual cycle. Do not use delay cycle. Remove dough from pan, using lightly floured hands. Cover and let rest 10 minutes on lightly floured surface. Grease cookie sheet or 2 (9-inch) round pans. Divide dough in half. Divide each half into 8 equal pieces. Shape each piece into a smooth ball. Place balls about 2 inches apart on cookie sheet or 1 inch apart in pans. Using scissors, snip a cross shape in top of each ball. Cover and let rise in warm place about 40 minutes or until doubled in size.   Heat oven to 375°F. Beat egg and cold water slightly; brush on buns. Bake 18 to 20 minutes or until golden brown. Remove from cookie sheet to cooling rack. Cool slightly.   In small bowl, mix all icing ingredients until smooth and spreadable. Make a cross on top of each bun with icing.

399. Blue Cheese Onion Bread

Servings: 1 Loaf   Cooking Time: 10 Minutes Plus Fermenting Time

Ingredients:
- 12 slice bread (1½ pounds)
- 1¼ cup water, at 80°F to 90°F
- 1 egg, at room temperature
- 1 tablespoon melted butter, cooled
- ¼ cup powdered skim milk
- 1 tablespoon sugar
- ¾ teaspoon salt
- ½ cup (2 ounces) crumbled blue cheese
- 1 tablespoon dried onion flakes
- 3 cups white bread flour
- ¼ cup instant mashed potato flakes
- 1 teaspoon bread machine or active dry yeast

Directions:

Preparing the Ingredients.   Choose the size of loaf of your preference and then measure the ingredients. Add all of the ingredients mentioned previously in the list. Close the lid after placing the pan in the bread machine. Select the Bake cycle   Turn on the bread machine. Select the Quick/Rapid setting, select the loaf size, and the crust color. Press start.   When the cycle is finished, carefully remove the pan from the bread maker and let it rest.   Remove the bread from the pan, put in a wire rack to Cool about 10 minutes. Slice

400. Cheddar Cheese Basil Bread

Servings: 1 Loaf   Cooking Time: 10 Minutes

Ingredients:
- 12 slice bread (1½ pounds)
- 1 cup milk, at 80°F to 90°F
- 1 tablespoon melted butter, cooled
- 1 tablespoon sugar
- 1 teaspoon dried basil
- ¾ cup (3 ounces) shredded sharp Cheddar cheese
- ¾ teaspoon salt
- 3 cups white bread flour
- 1½ teaspoons bread machine or active dry yeast

Directions:
Preparing the Ingredients.   Choose the size of loaf of your preference and then measure the ingredients. Add all of the ingredients mentioned previously in the list. Close the lid after placing the pan in the bread machine. Select the Bake cycle   Turn on the bread machine. Select the White/Basic setting, select the loaf size, and the crust color. Press start.   When the cycle is finished, carefully remove the pan from the bread maker and let it rest.   Remove the bread from the pan, put in a wire rack to Cool about 5 minutes. Slice

401. Olive Loaf

Servings: 1 Loaf   Cooking Time: 10 Minutes Plus Fermenting Time

Ingredients:
- 1 cup plus 2 tablespoons water
- 1 tablespoon olive oil
- 3 cups bread flour
- 2 tablespoons instant nonfat dry milk
- 1 tablespoon sugar
- 1 1/4 teaspoons salt
- 1/4 teaspoon garlic powder
- 2 teaspoons active dry yeast
- 2/3 cup grated parmesan cheese
- 1 cup pitted Greek olives, sliced and drained

Directions:
Preparing the Ingredients   Add ingredients, except yeast, olives and cheese, to bread maker in order listed above.   Make a well in the flour; pour the yeast into the hole.   Select the Bake cycle   Select Basic cycle, light crust color, and press Start; do not use delay cycle. Just before the final kneading, add the olives and cheese.   Remove and allow to cool on a wire rack for 15 minutes before serving.

402. Chocolate Sour Cream Bread

Servings: 1 Loaf   Cooking Time: 20 Minutes Plus Fermenting Time

Ingredients:
- 12 slice bread (1½ pounds)
- 1 cup sour cream
- 2 eggs, at room temperature
- 1 cup sugar
- ½ cup (1 stick) butter, at room temperature
- ¼ cup plain Greek yogurt
- 1¾ cups all-purpose flour
- ½ cup unsweetened cocoa powder
- ½ teaspoon baking powder
- ½ teaspoon salt
- 1 cup milk chocolate chips

Directions:
Preparing the Ingredients.   In a small bowl, whisk together the sour cream, eggs, sugar, butter, and yogurt until just combined.   Transfer the wet ingredients to the bread machine bucket, and then add the flour, cocoa powder, baking powder, salt, and chocolate chips. Program the machine for Quick/Rapid bread, and press Start. When the loaf is done, stick a knife into it, and if it comes out clean, the loaf is done.   Select the Bake cycle If the loaf needs a few more minutes, check the control panel for a Bake Only button and extend the time by 10 minutes.   When the loaf is done, remove the bucket from the machine. Let the loaf cool for 5 minutes. Gently shake the bucket to remove the loaf, and turn it out onto a rack to cool.

403. Everyday Fruit Bread

Servings: 15   Cooking Time: 3 Hours And 25 Minutes

Ingredients:
- Egg – 1
- Water – 1 cup, plus 2 tbsp.
- Ground cardamom – ½ tsp.
- Salt – 1 tsp.
- Sugar – 1 ½ tbsp.
- Butter – ¼ cup
- Bread flour – 3 cups
- Bread machine yeast – 1 tsp.
- Raisins – 1/3 cup
- Mixed candied fruit – 1/3 cup

Directions:
Place all ingredients (except fruit and raisins) in the bread machine according to machine recommendation. Select Basic White or Fruit and Nut setting.   Add the fruit and raisins after the beep.   When finished, remove the bread.   Cool, slice, and serve.

Nutrition Info:(Per Serving): Calories: 144; Total Fat: 3.6 g; Saturated Fat: 2.1 g; Carbohydrates: 24.6 g; Cholesterol: 19 mg; Fiber: 1 g; Calcium: 9 mg; Sodium: 183 mg; Protein: 3.2 g

404. Cashew Butter/peanut Butter Bread

Servings: 1 Loaf   Cooking Time: 10 Minutes Plus Fermenting Time

Ingredients:
- 12 slice bread (1½ pounds)
- 1 cup peanut butter or cashew butter
- 1 cup lukewarm milk
- ½ cup packed light brown sugar
- ¼ cup sugar
- ¼ cup butter, at room temperature
- 1 egg, at room temperature
- 2 teaspoons pure vanilla extract
- 2 cups all-purpose flour
- 1 tablespoon baking powder
- ½ teaspoon table salt

Directions:
Preparing the Ingredients.   Choose the size of loaf of your preference and then measure the ingredients. Add all of the ingredients mentioned previously in the list. Close the lid after placing the pan in the bread machine. Select the Bake cycle   Turn on the bread machine. Select the Quick/Rapid setting, select the loaf size, and the crust color. Press start.   When the cycle is finished, carefully remove the pan from the bread maker and let it rest.   Remove the bread from the pan, put in a wire rack to Cool about 5 minutes. Slice

405. Crusty Honey Bread

Servings: 1 Loaf   Cooking Time: 10 Minutes Plus Fermenting Time

Ingredients:
- 12 slice bread (1½ pounds)
- 1 cup minus 1 tablespoon water, at 80°F to 90°F
- 1½ tablespoons honey
- 1⅛ tablespoons melted butter, cooled
- ¾ teaspoon salt
- 2⅔ cups white bread flour
- 1½ teaspoons bread machine or instant yeast

Directions:
Preparing the Ingredients.   Choose the size of loaf of your preference and then measure the ingredients. Add all of the ingredients mentioned previously in the list. Close the lid after placing the pan in the bread machine. Select the Bake cycle   Turn on the bread machine. Select the Basic/White setting, select the loaf size, and the crust color. Press start.   When the cycle is finished, carefully remove the pan from the bread maker and let it rest.   Remove the bread from the pan, put in a wire rack to Cool about 5 minutes. Slice

406. Basil Cheese Bread

Servings: 1 Loaf   Cooking Time: 10 Minutes Plus Fermenting Time

Ingredients:
- 12 slice bread (1½ pounds)
- 1 cup lukewarm milk
- 1 tablespoon unsalted butter, melted
- 1 tablespoon sugar
- 1 teaspoon dried basil
- ¾ teaspoon table salt
- ¾ cup sharp Cheddar cheese, shredded
- 3 cups white bread flour
- 1½ teaspoons bread machine yeast

Directions:

Preparing the Ingredients. Choose the size of loaf of your preference and then measure the ingredients. Add all of the ingredients mentioned previously in the list. Close the lid after placing the pan in the bread machine. Select the Bake cycle Turn on the bread machine. Select the Quick/Rapid setting, select the loaf size, and the crust color. Press start. When the cycle is finished, carefully remove the pan from the bread maker and let it rest. Remove the bread from the pan, put in a wire rack to Cool about 5 minutes. Slice

407. Saffron And Tomato Bread

Servings: 10   Cooking Time: 3 Hours And 25 Minutes
Ingredients:
- Bread machine yeast - 1 tsp.
- Wheat bread flour - 2½ cups
- Panifarin - 1 tbsp.
- Salt - 1½ tsp.
- White sugar - 1½ tbsp.
- Olive oil - 2 tbsp.
- Tomatoes - 2 tbsp. dried and chopped
- Tomato paste - 1 tbsp.
- Firm cheese - ½ cup (cubes)
- Feta cheese - ½ cup
- Saffron/safflower - 1 pinch
- Serum - 1½ cups

Directions:
Add everything in the bread machine pan according to bread machine recommendations. Select Basic and Medium crest. Remove the bread when done. Cool, slice, and serve.
Nutrition Info:(Per Serving): Calories: 260; Total Fat: 9.2 g; Saturated Fat: 4 g; Carbohydrates: 35.5 g; Cholesterol: 20 mg; Fiber: 1.3 g; Calcium: 27 mg; Sodium: 611 mg; Protein: 8.9 g

408. Tomato Cheese Bread

Servings: 8   Cooking Time: 3 Hours And 25 Minutes
Ingredients:
- Bread machine yeast - 1 tsp.
- Wheat bread flour - 2 ½ cups
- Sea salt - 1 ½ tsp.
- Sugar - 1 tbsp.
- Extra-virgin olive oil - 1 tbsp.
- Tomatoes - 5 tbsp. dried and filled with oil, chopped
- Parmesan cheese - ½ cup, grated
- Whole milk - 1 cup lukewarm

Directions:
Place all the ingredients (except tomatoes) in the pan according to bread machine recommendations. Select Basic cycle and Medium crust. Add the tomatoes after the beep. Remove the bread when done. Cool, slice, and serve.
Nutrition Info:(Per Serving): Calories: 209; Total Fat: 5.1 g; Saturated Fat: 2.2 g; Carbohydrates: 33.4 g; Cholesterol: 10 mg; Fiber: 1.2 g; Calcium: 42 mg; Sodium: 498 mg; Protein: 7 g

409. Fruit Bread

Servings: 12   Cooking Time: 3 Hours And 27 Minutes
Ingredients:
- Nondairy milk – 1 ¼ cups, warm
- Olive oil – 2 ½ tbsp.
- Granulated sugar – ¼ cup
- Salt – 1 ¼ tsp.
- White bread flour – 3 cups
- Ground nutmeg – ¾ tsp.
- Cinnamon – ½ tsp.
- Bread machine yeast – 1 ¼ tsp.
- Dried fruit – ½ cup

Directions:
Add everything (except the dried fruits) in the bread machine according to machine recommendations. Select Sweetbread setting and press Start. Add the dried fruit after the beep. Remove the bread when done. Cool, slice, and serve.
Nutrition Info:(Per Serving): Calories: 184; Total Fat: 3.7 g; Saturated Fat: 0.6 g; Carbohydrates: 34.2 g; Cholesterol: 0 mg; Fiber: 1.8 g; Calcium: 44 mg; Sodium: 260 mg; Protein: 4.3 g

410. Mixed Herb Cheese Bread

Servings: 1 Loaf
Ingredients:
- 16 slice bread (2 pounds)
- 1⅓ cups lukewarm water
- 2 tablespoons olive oil
- 1 teaspoon table salt
- 1 tablespoon sugar
- 2 cloves garlic, crushed
- 3 tablespoons mixed fresh herbs (basil, chives, oregano, rosemary, etc.)
- ¼ cup Parmesan cheese, grated
- 4 cups white bread flour
- 2¼ teaspoons bread machine yeast
- 12 slice bread (1½ pounds)
- 1 cup lukewarm water
- 1½ tablespoons olive oil
- ¾ teaspoon table salt
- ¾ tablespoon sugar
- 2 cloves garlic, crushed
- 2 tablespoons mixed fresh herbs (basil, chives, oregano, rosemary, etc.)
- 3 tablespoons Parmesan cheese, grated
- 3 cups white bread flour
- 1⅔ teaspoons bread machine yeast

Directions:
Choose the size of loaf you would like to make and measure your ingredients. Add the ingredients to the bread pan in the order listed above. Place the pan in the bread machine and close the lid. Turn on the bread maker. Select the White/Basic setting, then the loaf size, and finally the crust color. Start the cycle. When the cycle is finished and the bread is baked, carefully remove the pan from the machine. Use a potholder as the handle will be very hot. Let rest for a few minutes. Remove the bread from the pan and allow to cool on a wire rack for at least 10 minutes before slicing.

Nutrition Info:(Per Serving):Calories 147, fat 3.2 g, carbs 25.3 g, sodium 37 mg, protein 5.1 g

411. Swiss Olive Bread

Servings: 1 Loaf
Ingredients:
- 16 slice bread (2 pounds)
- 1⅓ cups lukewarm milk
- 2 tablespoons unsalted butter, melted
- 1⅓ teaspoons minced garlic
- 2 tablespoons sugar
- 1⅓ teaspoons table salt
- 1 cup Swiss cheese, shredded
- 4 cups white bread flour
- 1½ teaspoons bread machine yeast
- ½ cup chopped black olives
- 12 slice bread (1½ pounds)
- 1 cup lukewarm milk
- 1½ tablespoons unsalted butter, melted
- 1 teaspoon minced garlic
- 1½ tablespoons sugar
- 1 teaspoon table salt
- ¾ cup Swiss cheese, shredded
- 3 cups white bread flour
- 1 teaspoon bread machine yeast
- ⅓ cup chopped black olives

Directions:
Choose the size of loaf you would like to make and measure your ingredients.   Add all of the ingredients except for the olives to the bread pan in the order listed above.   Place the pan in the bread machine and close the lid.   Turn on the bread maker. Select the White/Basic or Fruit/Nut (if your machine has this setting), then the loaf size, and finally the crust color. Start the cycle.   When the machine signals to add ingredients, add the olives. (Some machines have a fruit/nut hopper where you can add the olives when you start the machine. The machine will automatically add them to the dough during the baking process.)   When the cycle is finished and the bread is baked, carefully remove the pan from the machine. Use a potholder as the handle will be very hot. Let rest for a few minutes. Remove the bread from the pan and allow to cool on a wire rack for at least 10 minutes before slicing.
Nutrition Info:(Per Serving):Calories 147, fat 4.8 g, carbs 26.7 g, sodium 263 mg, protein 5.8 g

412. Apricot–cream Cheese Ring

Servings: 10 Servings   Cooking Time: 10 Minutes
Ingredients:
- ⅓ cup water
- 2 tablespoons butter, softened
- 1 egg
- 2 cups bread flour
- 2 tablespoons sugar
- ½ teaspoon salt
- 1¾ teaspoons bread machine or fast-acting dry yeast
- filling
- 1 package (3 oz) cream cheese, softened

- 1½ tablespoons bread flour
- ¼ cup apricot preserves
- 1 egg, beaten
- 2 tablespoons sliced almonds

Directions:
Preparing the Ingredients.   Measure carefully, placing all bread dough ingredients in bread machine pan in the order recommended by the manufacturer.   Select Dough/Manual cycle. Do not use delay cycle.   Remove dough from pan, using lightly floured hands. Cover and let rest 10 minutes on lightly floured surface. In small bowl, mix cream cheese and 1½ tablespoons flour.   4 Grease 9-inch round pan with shortening. Roll dough into 15-inch round.   Place in pan, letting side of dough hang over edge of pan. Spread cream cheese mixture over dough in pan; spoon apricot preserves onto cream cheese mixture.   Select the Bake cycle   Make cuts along edge of dough at 1-inch intervals to about ½ inch above cream cheese mixture. Twist pairs of dough strips and fold over cream cheese mixture.   Cover and let rise in warm place 40 to 50 minutes or until almost double.   5 Heat oven to 375°F. Brush beaten egg over dough. Sprinkle with almonds.   Bake 30 to 35 minutes or until golden brown. Cool at least 30 minutes before cutting.

413. Coconut Ginger Bread

Servings: 1 Loaf   Cooking Time: 1 Hour
Ingredients:
- 1 cup + 2 tbsp Half & Half
- One ¼ cup toasted shredded coconut
- Two large eggs
- ¼ cup oil
- 1 tsp coconut extract
- 1 tsp lemon extract
- 3/4 cup sugar
- 1 tbsp grated lemon peel
- 2 cups all-purpose flour
- 2 tbsp finely chopped candied ginger
- 1 tbsp baking powder
- ½ tsp salt
- One ¼ cup toasted shredded coconut

Directions:
Put everything in your bread machine pan.   Select the quick bread mode.   Press the start button.   Allow bread to cool on the wire rack until ready to serve (at least 20 minutes).
Nutrition Info: Calories 210;Carbohydrates: 45g;Total Fat 3g;Cholesterol 3mg;Protein 5g;Fiber 2g;Sugar 15g;Sodium 185mg;Potassium 61mg

414. Caramel Apple And Pecan Bread

Servings: 1 Loaf   Cooking Time: 10 Minutes Plus Fermenting Time
Ingredients:
- 12 slice bread (1½ pounds)
- 1 cup water
- 2 tablespoons butter, softened
- 3 cups bread flour
- ¼ cup packed brown sugar
- ¾ teaspoon ground cinnamon

- 1 teaspoon salt
- 2 teaspoons bread machine or fast-acting dry yeast
- ½ cup chopped unpeeled apple
- ⅓ cup coarsely chopped pecans, toasted

Directions:

Preparing the Ingredients. Choose the size of loaf of your preference and then measure the ingredients. Add all of the ingredients mentioned previously in the list except apple and pecans in bread maker. Add apple and pecans at the Raisin/Nut signal or 5 to 10 minutes before last kneading cycle ends. Select the Bake cycle Program the machine for Basic/White bread and press Start. When the cycle is finished, carefully remove the pan from the bread maker and let it rest. Remove the bread from the pan, put in a wire rack to Cool about 5 minutes. Slice

415. Cheesebuttermilk Bread

Servings: 10   Cooking Time: 2 Hours

Ingredients:
- Buttermilk – 1 1/8 cups
- Active dry yeast – 1 ½ tsps.
- Cheddar cheese – ¾ cup., shredded
- Sugar – 1 ½ tsps.
- Bread flour – 3 cups.
- Buttermilk – 1 1/8 cups.
- Salt – 1 1/2 tsps.

Directions:

Add all ingredients to the bread machine pan according to the bread machine manufacturer instructions. Select basic bread setting then select light/medium crust and start. Once loaf is done, remove the loaf pan from the machine. Allow it to cool for 10 minutes. Slice and serve.

416. Choco Chip Bread

Servings: 10   Cooking Time: 2 Hours

Ingredients:
- Yeast – 1 ½ tsps.
- Bread flour – 3 cups.
- Brown sugar – 2 tbsps.
- Sugar – 2 tbsps.
- Salt – 1 tsp.
- Ground cinnamon – 1 tsp.
- Butter – 4 tbsps., softened
- Egg – 1, slightly beaten
- Warm milk – 1 cup.
- Water – ¼ cup.
- Chocolate chips – 1 cup.

Directions:

Add all ingredients except for chocolate chips into the bread machine pan. Select basic setting then select light crust and press start. Add chocolate chips just before the final kneading cycle. Once loaf is done, remove the loaf pan from the machine. Allow it to cool for 10 minutes. Slice and serve.

417. Prosciutto Parmesan Breadsticks

Servings: 12   Cooking Time: 10 Minutes

Ingredients:
- 1 1/3 cups warm water
- 1 tablespoon butter
- 1 1/2 tablespoons sugar
- 1 1/2 teaspoons salt
- 4 cups bread flour
- 2 teaspoons yeast
- For the topping:
- 1/2 pound prosciutto, sliced very thin
- 1/2 cup of grated parmesan cheese
- 1 egg yolk
- 1 tablespoon of water

Directions:

Preparing the Ingredients   Place the first set of dough ingredients (except yeast) in the bread pan in the order indicated. Do not add any of the topping ingredients yet. Make a well in the center of the dry ingredients and add the yeast. Select the Bake cycle   Select the Dough cycle on the bread machine. When finished, drop the dough onto a lightly-floured surface. Roll the dough out flat to about 1/4-inch thick, or about half a centimeter. Cover with plastic wrap and let rise for 20 to 30 minutes. Sprinkle dough evenly with parmesan and carefully lay the prosciutto slices on the surface of the dough to cover as much of it as possible. Preheat an oven to 400°F. Cut the dough into 12 long strips, about one inch wide. Twist each end in opposite directions, twisting the toppings into the bread stick. Place the breadsticks onto a lightly greased baking sheet. Whisk the egg yolk and water together in a small mixing bowl and lightly baste each breadstick. Bake for 8 to 10 minutes or until golden brown. Remove from oven and serve warm.

418. Citrus Bread

Servings: 10   Cooking Time: 3 Hours And 25 Minutes

Ingredients:
- 1 whole egg
- Butter - 3 tbsp., melted
- White sugar - 1/3 cup
- Vanilla sugar - 1 tbsp.
- Tangerine juice - ½ cup
- Whole milk - 2/3 cup
- Kosher salt - 1 tsp.
- Bread machine flour - 4 cups
- Bread machine yeast - 1 tbsp.
- Candied oranges - ¼ cup
- Candied lemon - ¼ cup
- Lemon zest -2 tsp., finely grated
- Almonds - ¼ cup, chopped

Directions:

Add everything in the bread machine (except fruits, zest, and almonds) according to bread machine recommendations. Select Basic/Sweetbread and Medium crust. Add zest, fruits, and chopped almonds after the beep. Remove the bread when done. Cool, slice, and serve.

Nutrition Info:(Per Serving): Calories: 404; Total Fat: 9.1 g; Saturated Fat: 3.5 g; Carbohydrates: 71.5 g; Cholesterol: 34 mg; Fiber: 2.9 g; Calcium: 72 mg; Sodium: 345 mg; Protein: 9.8 g

419. Cheddar Cheese Bread

Servings: 20   Cooking Time: 3 Hours And 25 Minutes
Ingredients:
- Water – ¾ cup
- Egg – 1
- Salt – 1 tsp.
- Bread flour – 3 cups
- Shredded sharp cheddar cheese – 1 cup
- Nonfat dry milk – 2 tbsp.
- Sugar – 2 tbsp.
- Bread machine yeast – 1 tsp.

Directions:
Add everything according to bread machine recommendations.   Select Basic/White bread and Medium crust.   Remove the bread when done.   Cool, slice, and serve.

Nutrition Info:(Per Serving): Calories: 101; Total Fat: 2.3 g; Saturated Fat: 1.3 g; Carbohydrates: 15.8 g; Cholesterol: 15 mg; Fiber: 0.6 g; Calcium: 48 mg; Sodium: 157 mg; Protein: 3.8 g

420. Mozzarella-herb Bread

Servings: 1 Loaf   Cooking Time: 10 Minutes Plus Fermenting Time
Ingredients:
- 12 slice bread (1½ pounds)
- 1¼ cups milk, at 80°F to 90°F
- 1 tablespoon butter, melted and cooled
- 2 tablespoons sugar
- 1 teaspoon salt
- 2 teaspoons dried basil
- 1 teaspoon dried oregano
- 1½ cups (6 ounces) shredded mozzarella cheese
- 3 cups white bread flour
- 2¼ teaspoons bread machine or instant yeast

Directions:
Preparing the Ingredients.   Choose the size of loaf of your preference and then measure the ingredients. Add all of the ingredients mentioned previously in the list. Close the lid after placing the pan in the bread machine. Select the Bake cycle   Turn on the bread machine. Select the Quick/Rapid setting, select the loaf size, and the crust color. Press start.   When the cycle is finished, carefully remove the pan from the bread maker and let it rest.   Remove the bread from the pan, put in a wire rack to Cool about 5 minutes. Slice

421. Zesty Cheddar Bread

Servings: 1 Loaf   Cooking Time: 10 Minutes
Ingredients:
- 12 slice bread (1½ pounds)
- 1 cup buttermilk
- ⅓ cup butter, melted
- 1 tablespoon sugar
- 2 tablespoons finely chopped chipotle chiles in adobo sauce (from 7-oz can) 2 eggs
- 2 cups all-purpose flour
- 1 cup shredded Cheddar cheese (4 oz)
- 2 teaspoons baking powder

- 1 teaspoon baking soda
- ½ teaspoon salt

Directions:
Preparing the Ingredients.   Choose the size of loaf of your preference and then measure the ingredients. Add all of the ingredients mentioned previously in the list. Close the lid after placing the pan in the bread machine. Select the Bake cycle   Turn on the bread machine. Select the White/Basic setting, select the loaf size, and the crust color. Press start.   When the cycle is finished, carefully remove the pan from the bread maker and let it rest.   Remove the bread from the pan, put in a wire rack to Cool about 5 minutes. Serve warm

422. Walnut Cocoa Bread

Servings: 14 Servings   Cooking Time: 20 Minutes Plus Fermenting Time
Ingredients:
- ⅔ cup milk
- ⅓ cup water
- 5 Tbsp butter, softened
- ⅓ cup packed brown sugar
- 5 Tbsp baking cocoa
- 1 tsp salt
- 3 cups bread flour
- 2¼ tsp active dry yeast
- ⅔ cup chopped walnuts, toasted

Directions:
Preparing the Ingredients   Add each ingredient except the walnuts to the bread machine in the order and at the temperature recommended by your bread machine manufacturer.   Select the Bake cycle   Close the lid, select the sweet loaf, low crust setting on your bread machine, and press start.   Just before the final kneading, add the walnuts.   When the bread machine has finished baking, remove the bread and put it on a cooling rack.

423. Parmesan Cheese Bread

Servings: 8   Cooking Time: 3 Hours And 25 Minutes
Ingredients:
- Wheat bread flour - 2½ cups
- Fresh bread machine yeast - 1½ tsp.
- Whole milk - ½ cup, lukewarm
- Butter - 1 tbsp., melted
- Sugar - 2 tbsp.
- Kosher salt - ½ tsp.
- Whole eggs – 2
- Fresh/dried rosemary -2 tsp., ground
- Parmesan - 3 tbsp. (divided - 2 tbsp. for dough and 1 tbsp. for sprinkling)
- Garlic - 2 cloves, crushed

Directions:
Place all the dry and liquid ingredients (except for parmesan, yeast, milk, rosemary, and garlic) in the bread pan according to bread machine recommendations. Dissolve the yeast in the warm milk and add.   Add the garlic, parmesan, and rosemary after the beep. Choose Basic cycle and Light crust.   Remove the bread when done.   Cool, slice, and serve.

424. Coconut Delight Bread

Servings: 1 Loaf   Cooking Time: 10 Minutes Plus Fermenting Time

Ingredients:
- 16 slice bread (2 pounds)
- 1⅓ cups lukewarm milk
- 1 egg, at room temperature
- 2 tablespoons unsalted butter, melted
- 2⅔ teaspoons pure coconut extract
- 3⅓ tablespoons sugar
- 1 teaspoon table salt
- ⅔ cup sweetened shredded coconut
- 4 cups white bread flour
- 2 teaspoons bread machine yeast

Directions:
Preparing the Ingredients.   Choose the size of loaf of your preference and then measure the ingredients. Add all of the ingredients mentioned previously in the list. Close the lid after placing the pan in the bread machine. Select the Bake cycle   Turn on the bread machine. Select the Sweet setting, select the loaf size, and the crust color. Press start.   When the cycle is finished, carefully remove the pan from the bread maker and let it rest. Remove the bread from the pan, put in a wire rack to Cool about 5 minutes. Slice

425. Savory Cheddar Cheese Bread

Servings: 16   Cooking Time: 3 Hours And 25 Minutes

Ingredients:
- Lukewarm milk – 1 cup
- All-purpose flour – 3 cups
- Salt - 1 ¼ tsp.
- Sugar – 1 tbsp.
- Grated cheddar cheese – 1 cup
- Cheese powder – ¼ cup
- Instant yeast – 1 ½ tsp.
- Tabasco sauce – ½ tsp.

Directions:
Add everything in the bread machine according to bread machine recommendations.   Select Basic cycle and Light crust.   Remove the bread when finished.   Cool, slice, and serve.

426. Honey And Milk White Bread

Servings: 1 Pound Loaf   Cooking Time: 3 Hours

Ingredients:
- Lukewarm whole milk :½ cup
- Unsalted butter :¾ tbsp
- Honey :¾ tbsp
- White all-purpose Flour :1 ½ cups
- Salt :1 pinch
- Bread machine yeast :2/4 tsp

Directions:
Add the ingredients into the bread machine as per the order of the ingredients listed above or follow your bread machine's instruction manual.   Select the white bread function and the light crust function.   When ready, turn the bread out onto a drying rack and allow it to cool, then serve.

Nutrition Info:(Per Serving):Calories: 102.5 kcal / Total fat: 1.9 g / Saturated fat: 0.7 g / Cholesterol: 2.4 mg / Total carbohydrates: 18.3 g / Dietary fiber: 0.7 g / Sodium: 202.8 mg / Protein: 2.9 g

427. Rye Bread With Caraway

Servings: 1 Pound Loaf   Cooking Time: 4 Hours

Ingredients:
- Lukewarm water :¾ cup
- Unsalted butter, diced :1 tbsp
- Molasses :1 tbsp
- Rye flour :½ cup
- Plain bread flour :1 cup
- Whole wheat flour :½ cup
- Milk powder :1 tbsp
- Salt :¾ tsp
- Brown sugar :2 tbsp
- Caraway seeds :1 tbsp
- Instant dry yeast :1 ¼ tsp

Directions:
Add the ingredients into the bread machine as per the order of the ingredients listed above or follow your bread machine's instruction manual.   Select the whole wheat setting and medium crust function.   When ready, turn the bread out onto a drying rack and allow it to cool, then serve.

Nutrition Info:(Per Serving):Calories: 93 kcal / Total fat: 2.3 g / Saturated fat: 1.3 g / Cholesterol: 5 mg / Total carbohydrates: 16.5 g / Dietary fiber: 2.3 g / Sodium: 218 mg / Protein: 2.4 g

428. French Baguettes

Servings: 2 Loaves   Cooking Time: 15 Minutes

Ingredients:
- One ¼ cups warm water
- 3 ½ cups bread flour
- One teaspoon salt
- One package active dry yeast

Directions:
Place ingredients in the bread machine. Select the dough cycle. Hit the start button.   When the dough cycle is finished, remove it with floured hands and cut in half on a well-floured.   Take each half of dough and roll it to make a loaf about 12 inches long in the shape of French bread.   Place on a greased baking sheet and cover with a towel.   Let rise until doubled, about 1 hour.   Preheat oven to 450 F (220 ° C).   Bake until golden brown, turning the pan around once halfway during baking.   Transfer the loaves to a rack.

Nutrition Info: Calories 201;Carbohydrates: 42 g;Total Fat 0.6 g;Cholesterol 0 mg;Protein 6 g;Fiber 1.7 g;Sugar 0.1 g;Sodium 293 mg

429. Low-carb Apple Bread

Servings: 1 Loaf   Cooking Time: 1 Hour And 30 Minutes

Ingredients:
- Two apples, peeled and chopped
- 2 cups almond flour
- ½ cup golden flaxseed, milled
- ½ cup no-calorie sweetener of your choice
- Two teaspoons cinnamon
- ¾ teaspoon baking soda
- ¾ teaspoon salt
- ½ teaspoon nutmeg
- Four eggs, lightly beaten
- ¼ cup of water
- ¼ cup heavy cream
- Four tablespoons coconut oil
- Two teaspoons vanilla extract
- 1 ½ teaspoon apple cider vinegar

Directions:
Place all ingredients in the pan according to the order specified above.   Set the bread machine to "Cake" or "Quick" mode.   Let the cycles finish.   Remove the bread pan from the machine, but keep the bread in the pan for another 10 minutes.   Slice the bread only when it has cooled down.

Nutrition Info: Calories: 242;Carbohydrates: 11g;Fat: 20g;Protein: 7g

430. Sauerkraut Bread

Servings: 1 Loaf (22 Slices)   Cooking Time: 1 Hour And 30 Minutes

Ingredients:
- 1 cup lukewarm water (80 degrees F)
- ¼ cup cabbage brine
- ½ cup finely chopped cabbage
- Two tablespoons sunflower oil
- Two teaspoons white sugar
- 1½ teaspoons salt
- 2 1/3 cups rye flour
- 2 1/3 cups wheat flour
- Two teaspoons dry kvass
- Two teaspoons active dry yeast

Directions:

Prepare all of the ingredients for your bread and measuring means (a cup, a spoon, kitchen scales). Finely chop the sauerkraut. Carefully measure the ingredients into the pan. Place all of the ingredients into a bucket in the right order, follow your manual bread machine. Close the cover. Select the program of your bread machine to BASIC and choose the crust colour to DARK. Press START. Wait until the program completes. When done, take the bucket out and let it cool for 5-10 minutes. Shake the loaf from the pan and let cool for 30 minutes on a cooling rack. Slice, serve and enjoy the taste of fragrant homemade bread.

Nutrition Info: Calories 297;Total Fat 4.9g;Saturated Fat 0.5g;Cholesterol 0g;Sodium 442mg;Total Carbohydrate 55.5g;Dietary Fiber 9.7g;Total Sugars 1.6g;Protein 9.5g

431. Healthy Low Carb Bread

Servings: 8 Slices   Cooking Time: 35 Minutes
Ingredients:
- 2/3 cup coconut flour
- 2/3 cup coconut oil (softened not melted)
- Nine eggs
- 2 tsp. Cream of tartar
- ¾ tsp. xanthan gum
- 1 tsp. Baking soda
- ¼ tsp. salt

Directions:
Preheat the oven to 350F. Grease a loaf pan with 1 to 2 tsp. Melted coconut oil and place it in the freezer to harden. Add eggs into a bowl and mix for 2 minutes with a hand mixer. Add coconut oil into the eggs and mix. Add dry ingredients to a second bowl and whisk until mixed. Put the dry ingredients into the egg mixture and mix on low speed with a hand mixer until dough is formed and the mixture is incorporated. Add the dough into the prepared loaf pan, transfer into the preheated oven, and bake for 35 minutes. Take out the bread pan from the oven. Cool, slice, and serve.

Nutrition Info: Calories: 229;Fat: 25.5g Carb: 6.5g;Protein: 8.5g

432. Keto Focaccia Bread

Servings: 1 Loaf   Cooking Time: 23-30 Minutes
Ingredients:
- 1 cup almond flour
- 1/3 cup coconut flour
- 1/3 cup protein powder, unflavored and unsweetened
- Two tablespoons rosemary, chopped
- One tablespoon baking powder
- ¾ teaspoon salt
- ½ teaspoon garlic powder
- Two eggs, whole
- Two egg whites
- ½ cup extra-virgin olive oil
- ½ cup of water

Directions:

Place the wet ingredients first in the bread pan, followed by the dry ingredients. Set the bread machine to "Manual" or "Dough" mode. Once the cycles are completed, put the dough on a surface with a light dusting of flour. Shape the dough into a ball. Flatten the dough on a greased baking sheet until it becomes a 10-inch circle. Cover the dough, and allow it to rise for 15 minutes. Preheat the oven to 375F. Bake for 25 to 30 minutes.

Nutrition Info: Calories: 174 Cal;Carbohydrates: 5 g;Fat: 15g

433. Cream Hazelnut Bread

Servings: 1 Loaf   Cooking Time: 1 Hour
Ingredients:
- 3½ cups (450 g) wheat bread machine flour
- 1¾ cups (230 g) cornflour
- 5 ounces (150 ml) cream
- 2 tbsp. vegetable oil
- 2 tsp. bread machine yeast
- 1 tbsp. sugar
- ½ cup hazelnuts, ground
- 2 tsp. sea salt

Directions:
Place all the dry and liquid ingredients in the pan and follow the instructions for your bread machine. Pay particular attention to measuring the ingredients. Use a cup, measuring spoon, and kitchen scales to do so. Set the baking program to BASIC also set the crust type to MEDIUM. If the dough is too wet, adjust the recipe's flour and liquid quantity. After the dough finishes mixing moisten the merchandise's surface with water and sprinkle with hazelnut. When the program has ended, take the pan out of the bread machine and cool for five minutes. Shake the loaf out of the pan. If necessary, use a spatula. Wrap the bread with a kitchen towel and set it aside for an hour. Otherwise, you'll calm on a wire rack.

Nutrition Info: Calories: 405 Cal;Fat: 11.8 g;Cholesterol: 13 g;Sodium: 607 mg;Carbohydrates: 66.3 g;Fiber: 4 g

434. Multigrain Sandwich Loaf

Servings: 1 Pound Loaf   Cooking Time: 3 Hours
Ingredients:
- Milk, warmed :½ cup
- Unsalted butter :2 tbsp
- Plain bread flour :1 ½ cups
- Multigrain cereal :½ cup
- Granulated brown sugar :¼ cup
- Salt :¾ tsp
- Bread machine yeast :¾ tsp

Directions:
Add the ingredients into the bread machine as per the order of the ingredients listed above or follow your bread machine's instruction manual. Select the basic setting and medium crust function. When ready, turn the bread out onto a drying rack and allow it to cool, then serve.

Nutrition Info:(Per Serving):Calories: 194 kcal / Total fat: 4.8 g / Saturated fat: 2.7 g / Cholesterol: 12 mg / Total carbohydrates: 33.1 g / Dietary fiber: 1.4 g / Sodium: 335 mg / Protein: 4.6 g

435. Spiced Jalapeno Cheese Bread

Servings: 1 Pound Loaf   Cooking Time: 3 Hours
Ingredients:
- Lukewarm water :½ cup
- Milk powder :2 tbsp
- Unsalted butter :2 tbsp
- Plain bread flour :1 ½ cup
- Cheddar cheese :½ cup
- Jalapeno pepper, finely diced :½
- Granulated brown sugar :1 tbsp
- Salt :1 tsp
- Bread machine yeast :¾ tsp

Directions:
Combine the water and instant milk powder first, then add it to your bread machine.   Add the remaining ingredients into the bread machine as per the order of the ingredients listed above or follow your bread machine's instruction manual.   Select the basic setting and soft crust function.   When ready, turn the bread out onto a drying rack and allow it to cool, then serve.
Nutrition Info:(Per Serving):Calories: 135 kcal / Total fat: 4.9 g / Saturated fat: 3 g / Cholesterol: 14 mg / Total carbohydrates: 18.1 g / Dietary fiber: 0.7 g / Sodium: 327 mg / Protein: 4.6 g

436. Dinner Rolls

Servings: 15 Rolls   Cooking Time: 2 Hours And 35 Minutes
Ingredients:
- 1 egg
- 1 cup water
- 3 ¼ cups plain bread flour
- ¼ cup sugar
- 1 tsp salt
- 3 tsp active dry yeast
- 2 tbsp unsalted butter, softened

Directions:
Add the ingredients into the bread machine as per the order of the ingredients listed above or follow your bread machine's instruction manual. Do not add the softened butter in.   Select the dough setting.   Transfer the dough onto a floured surface and allow to rest for 10 minutes. Then split the dough evenly into 15 balls.   On a greased baking tray, place the dough balls 2" apart. Allow the rolls to rest in a warm area for 30 minutes or until they have doubled in size.   Preheat your oven to 375 °F and bake the rolls for 15 minutes or until they have turned a honeyed color.   Brush the tops of the rolls with the softened butter, then serve.
Nutrition Info:(Per Serving):Calories: 135 kcal / Total fat: 2 g / Saturated fat: 0 g / Cholesterol: 15 mg / Total carbohydrates: 26 g / Dietary fiber: 1 g / Sodium: 170 mg / Protein: 4 g

437. Portugese Sweet Bread

Servings: 1 Loaf   Cooking Time: 3 Hours
Ingredients:
- 1 cup milk
- 1 egg
- 2 tablespoons margarine
- ⅓ cup white sugar
- ¾ teaspoon salt
- 3 cups bread flour
- 2 ½ teaspoons active dry yeast

Directions:
Add ingredients in order suggested by your manufacturer.   Select "sweet bread" setting.
Nutrition Info: Calories 56 ;Protein 1.5g;Carbohydrates 6.9g;Fat: 2.6g

438. Mediterranean Bread

Servings: 8   Cooking Time: 3 Hours And 25 Minutes
Ingredients:
- Water – 1 cup
- Crumbled feta cheese – 1/3 cup
- Garlic cloves – 3, minced
- Salt – 1 ¼ tsp.
- Honey – 1 tsp.
- Olive oil – 1 tbsp.
- Bread flour – 3 ¼ cups
- Kalamata olive – ½ cup, sliced
- Dried oregano – 2 tsp.
- Bread machine yeast – ¾ tsp.

Directions:
Add everything in the bread machine according to bread machine recommendations.   Select Basic cycle and press Start.   Remove the bread when done.   Cool, slice, and serve.
Nutrition Info:(Per Serving): Calories: 237; Total Fat: 4.5 g; Saturated Fat: 1.4 g; Carbohydrates: 42.4 g; Cholesterol: 5.6 mg; Fiber: 1.9 g; Calcium: 22 mg; Sodium: 497.3 mg; Protein: 6.5 g

439. Seeded Whole Wheat Bread

Servings: 1 Pound Loaf   Cooking Time: 3 Hours
Ingredients:
- Lukewarm water :⅔ cups
- Milk powder :3 tbsp
- Honey :1 tbsp
- Unsalted butter, softened :1 tbsp
- Plain bread flour :1 cup
- Whole wheat flour :1 cup
- Poppy seeds :2 tbsp
- Sesame seeds :2 tbsp
- Sunflower seeds :2 tbsp
- Salt :¾ tsp
- Instant dry yeast :2 tsp

Directions:
Add the ingredients into the bread machine as per the order of the ingredients listed above or follow your bread machine's instruction manual.   Select the basic setting and medium crust function.   When ready, turn the

bread out onto a drying rack and allow it to cool, then serve.

Nutrition Info:(Per Serving):Calories: 84 kcal / Total fat: 2 g / Saturated fat: 1 g / Cholesterol: 2 mg / Total carbohydrates: 14 g / Dietary fiber: 1 g Sodium: 133 mg / Protein: 3 g

440. Fluffy Paleo Bread

Servings: 15 Slices   Cooking Time: 40 Minutes
Ingredients:
- One ¼ cup almond flour
- Five eggs
- 1 tsp. lemon juice
- 1/3 cup avocado oil
- One dash black pepper
- ½ tsp. sea salt
- 3 to 4 tbsp. tapioca flour
- 1 to 2 tsp. Poppyseed
- ¼ cup ground flaxseed
- ½ tsp. baking soda
- Top with:
- Poppy seeds
- Pumpkin seeds

Directions:
Preheat the oven to 350F.   Line a baking pan with parchment paper and set aside.   In a bowl, add eggs, avocado oil, and lemon juice and whisk until combined. In another bowl, add tapioca flour, almond flour, baking soda, flaxseed, black pepper, and poppy seed. Mix. Add the lemon juice mixture into the flour mixture and mix well.   Add the batter into the prepared loaf pan and top with extra pumpkin seeds and poppy seeds. Cover loaf pan and transfer into the prepared oven, and bake for 20 minutes. Remove cover and bake until an inserted knife comes out clean after about 15 to 20 minutes.   Remove from oven and cool.   Slice and serve.

Nutrition Info: Calories: 149 Cal;Fat: 12.9 g;Carbohydrates: 4.4 g

441. Whole Wheat Bread

Servings: 1 Pound Loaf   Cooking Time: 3 Hours
Ingredients:
- Lukewarm whole milk :½ cup
- Unsalted butter, diced :2 tbsp
- Whole wheat flour :1 cup
- Plain bread flour :1 cup
- Brown sugar :2 ½ tbsp
- Salt :¾ tsp
- Bread machine yeast :¾ tsp

Directions:
Add the ingredients into the bread machine as per the order of the ingredients listed above or follow your bread machine's instruction manual.   Select the whole wheat setting and medium crust function.   When ready, turn the bread out onto a drying rack and allow it to cool, then serve.

Nutrition Info:(Per Serving):Calories: 131.6 kcal / Total fat: 3.2 g / Saturated fat: 1.8 g / Cholesterol: 8 mg

/ Total carbohydrates: 22.9 g / Dietary fiber: 2.1 g / Sodium: 139.3 mg / Protein: 3.9 g

442. Cinnamon Babaka

Servings: 1 Loaf   Cooking Time: 45 Minutes
Ingredients:
- For the Dough
- ¾ c milk, warmed to 80-90F
- 2 ¼ tsp (1 packet) active dry yeast
- 4 Tbsp unsalted butter
- 3 Tbsp sugar
- 2 egg yolks (reserve the whites, separately, see below)
- 1 tsp pure vanilla extract
- 2 eggs (whole)
- 3 ½ - 4 c unbleached all-purpose flour
- 1 tsp salt
- For the Filling
- 1 c brown sugar
- 1 Tbsp cinnamon
- ¼ tsp salt
- 2 Tbsp unsalted butter melted and cooled
- 1 egg white (see above)
- For the Egg Wash
- 1 egg white (see above), lightly beaten

Directions:
FOR THE DOUGH: In a small bowl, mix the warmed milk and yeast. Let this mixture to rest aside for 5-10 minutes, until the yeast starts to foam.   Meanwhile, cream the butter and sugar together with an electric hand mixer in a medium bowl. Add, one at a time, the egg yolks, while beating them. Set this mixture aside too. Give the yeast mixture a stir, then add it to the bowl of your bread machine. Add the egg and butter mixture to the milk.   Pour the salt and 3 cups of flour..   Start your bread machine on its Dough Cycle. Watch your dough as it begins to knead. Once it looks like the ingredients are completely mixed, add more flour, a ¼ cup at a time, letting the machine knead between each addition, until the dough comes together and pulls away from the sides of the bowl.   When it happens, close your bread machine and let the machine run through its Dough Cycle. When the cycle is done, wait for the bread to become double its size.   FOR THE FILLING: Now make the filling by whisking all of the filling ingredients together in a medium bowl, until it becomes smooth and then let it set aside.   PUTTING IT ALL TOGETHER   Grease a 9x5 loaf pan and line it with greased parchment paper.   Tip the dough out of its rising bowl onto a well-floured surface.   Punch the dough down and roll it out into a roughly 18x15 inch rectangle.   Spread filling evenly over dough, leaving a 1 inch border on the long sides.   Roll the dough, starting from one of the long sides.   Cut the roll in half, lengthwise, turning it into two strands.   Twist the two strands together, trying to keep the cut (exposed filling) side on top, as much as possible.   Finally, shape your twisted dough into a figure 8, again keeping the cut sides up as much as possible. Place this twisted figure 8 into the greased and lined loaf pan.   Cover the dough in the pan loosely with plastic wrap and let rise for 30 minutes.

After 30 minutes, preheat your oven to 350F. When the dough has risen slightly and looks puffy, remove the plastic wrap and brush the top of the dough with the beaten egg white egg wash. Bake the bread at 350F for 45-55 minutes, until the top crust is deeply golden and the loaf sounds hollow when tapped. (The internal temperature of the loaf should read around 180F when the bread is done). (It may be helpful to place a piece of aluminum foil or an aluminum foil lined baking sheet on the rack under the bread to catch any filling that my bubble out of the loaf.) Once the loaf is done, cool the bread in the pan for 10 minutes, before gently removing the bread from the pan to continue to cool for 10-20 minutes before slicing. The babka will stay fresh stored in airtight container at room temperature for up to 3 days, then move the bread to the refrigerator.

Nutrition Info: Calories 219 ;Protein 6.6g;Carbohydrates 32g;Fat: 10.5g

443. Peanut Butter Cookies

Servings: 12 Pcs   Cooking Time: 12 Minutes

Ingredients:
- 1 cup Peanut Butter(sugar-free)
- ½ cup Erythritol
- 1 Whole Egg

Directions:
Mix all ingredients into a bowl until it is combined. Scoop the dough into a baking sheet lined with parchment. Press slightly to flatten. Bake for 12 minutes.

Nutrition Info: Kcal per serve: 136;Fat: 12 g;Protein: 5 g;Carbs: 2g.

444. Hot Dog Buns

Servings: 10 Pcs   Cooking Time: 50 Minutes

Ingredients:
- One ¼ cups almond flour
- 5 tbsp. psyllium husk powder
- 1 tsp. sea salt
- 2 tsp. baking powder
- One ¼ cups boiling water
- 2 tsp. lemon juice
- Three egg whites

Directions:
Preheat the oven to 350F   In a bowl, put all dry ingredients and mix well.   Add boiling water, lemon juice, and egg whites into the dry mixture and whisk until combined.   Mould the dough into ten portions and roll into buns.   Transfer into the preheated oven and cook for 40 to 50 minutes on the lower oven rack.   Check for doneness and remove it.   Top with desired toppings and hot dogs and serve.

Nutrition Info: Calories: 104;Fat: 8g;Carb: 1g;Protein: 4g

445. Sour Cream Chieve Bread

Servings: 1 Loaf   Cooking Time: 3 Hours

Ingredients:
- 2/3 cup whole milk (70° to 80°)
- 1/4 cup water (70° to 80°)
- 1/4 cup sour cream
- 2 tablespoons butter
- 1-1/2 teaspoons sugar
- 1-1/2 teaspoons salt
- 3 cups bread flour
- 1/8 teaspoon baking soda
- 1/4 cup minced chives
- 2-1/4 teaspoons active dry yeast

Directions:
Place all the ingredients in the bread machine pan, in the order suggested by the manufacturer.   Select basic bread setting.   Choose crust coolor and loaf size if available.   Bake according to bread machine directions   Check the dough after 5 minutes of mixing and add 1 or 2 tablespoons of water or flour if needed.

Nutrition Info: Calories 105;Fat 2g;Saturated fat 2g;Cholesterol 8mg;Sodium 253mg;Carbohydrate 18g;Protein 4g

446. Pepper Bread

Servings: 1 Loaf (8 Slices)   Cooking Time: 1 Hour And 10 Minutes

Ingredients:
- ¾ cup + 1 tablespoon lukewarm milk
- Three tablespoons ground red pepper
- Four teaspoons fresh red pepper, chopped and roasted
- Two tablespoons butter, melted
- Two tablespoons brown sugar
- 2/3 teaspoon salt
- 2 cups wheat flour
- One teaspoon active dry yeast

Directions:
Prepare all of the ingredients for your bread and measuring means (a cup, a spoon, kitchen scales). Carefully measure the ingredients into the pan.   Place all of the ingredients into a bucket in the right order. Follow your manual for the bread machine.   Close the cover.   Select the program of your bread machine to BASIC and choose the crust colour to MEDIUM. Press START.   Wait until the program completes. When done, take the bucket out and let it cool for 5-10 minutes.   Shake the loaf from the pan and let cool for 30 minutes on a cooling rack.   Slice, serve and enjoy the taste of fragrant homemade bread.

Nutrition Info: Calories: 189;Fat: 4.5 g;Cholesterol: 10 g;Sodium: 34 mg;Carbohydrates: 33 g Fiber 2.3 g;Sugar: 6.8 g;Protein: 5.1 g

447. Ethiopian Milk And Honey Bread

Servings: 1 Loaf   Cooking Time: 1 Hour And 15 Minutes

Ingredients:
- Three tablespoons honey
- 1 cup + 1 tablespoon milk
- 3 cups bread flour
- Three tablespoons melted butter
- Two teaspoons active dry yeast
- 1 ½ teaspoons salt

Directions:

Add everything to the pan of your bread   Select the white bread or basic setting and the medium crust setting.   Hit the start button.   Take out your hot loaf once it is done.   Keep on your wire rack for cooling. Slice your bread once it is cold and serve.
Nutrition Info: Calories 129;Carbohydrates: 20 g;Total Fat 3.8 g;Cholesterol 0 mg;Protein 2.4 g;Fiber 0.6 g;Sugars 3.3 g;Sodium 78 mg

448. Challah

Servings: 12   Cooking Time: 1 Hour 40 Minutes
Ingredients:
- 1/2 cup warm water
- 1 package active dry yeast
- 1 tablespoon sugar
- 3 tablespoons butter, softened
- 1/2 teaspoon kosher salt
- 2 to 2 1/2 cups kosher all-purpose flour
- 2 eggs
- 1 egg yolk
- 1 teaspoon water

Directions:
Add sugar and salt to bread maker pan.   Add butter, eggs, then water.   Add flour and yeast.   Select Dough cycle and press Start.   Transfer dough to a large mixing bowl sprayed with non-stick cooking spray. Spray dough with non-stick cooking spray and cover. Let rise in a warm place until doubled in size; about 45 minutes.   Punch dough down. Remove dough to lightly floured surface; pat dough and shape into a 10-by-6-inch rectangle.   Divide into 3 equal strips with a pizza cutter. Braid strips and place into a 9-by-5-inch loaf pan sprayed with non-stick cooking spray. Cover and let rise in warm place for about 30 to 45 minutes.   Beat egg yolk with 1 teaspoon water and baste loaf.   Bake at 375°F for 25 to 30 minutes, or until golden.   Let cool on a rack for 5 minutes before removing from loaf pan and serve.
Nutrition Info: Calories: 64, Sodium: 129 mg, Dietary Fiber: 0.3 g, Fat: 4 g, Carbs: 5.2 g, Protein: 1.9 g.

449. Nut Bread

Servings: 1 Pound Loaf   Cooking Time: 3 Hours
Ingredients:
- Lukewarm water :⅔ cup
- Vegetable oil :½ tbsp
- Lemon juice :½ tsp
- Salt :1 tsp
- Molasses :⅙ cup

- Quick oatmeal :⅓ cup
- Whole wheat flour :½ cup
- Plain bread flour :1 ⅓ cup
- Walnuts :1 ½ cups
- Instant dry yeast :1 ½ tsp

Directions:
Add the ingredients into the bread machine as per the order of the ingredients listed above or follow your bread machine's instruction manual.   Select the basic setting

and soft crust function.   When ready, turn the bread out onto a drying rack and allow it to cool, then serve.
Nutrition Info:(Per Serving):Calories: 163 kcal / Total fat: 6.3 g / Saturated fat: 0.5 g / Cholesterol: 0 mg / Total carbohydrates: 22.8 g / Dietary fiber: 2.3 g / Sodium: 198 mg / Protein: 5.3 g

450. Low-carb Zucchini Loaf

Servings: 1 Loaf   Cooking Time: 1 Hour And 30 Minutes
Ingredients:
- Two ¼ cup almond flour
- 1 ½ cup zucchini, grated
- ¾ cup no-calorie sweetener of your choice
- ½ cup walnuts, chopped
- ½ cup pecans, chopped
- Two tablespoons coconut flour
- Three teaspoons baking powder
- One teaspoon ground cinnamon
- ¼ teaspoon nutmeg
- ¼ teaspoon ginger, grated
- Five eggs, beaten
- ½ cup of coconut oil
- Two teaspoons vanilla extract

Directions:
First, put the wet ingredients into the pan, followed by all dry ingredients.   Press the "Quick" or "Cake" mode of your bread machine.   Allow the machine to complete all the cycles.   Take out the pan from the machine, but keep the loaf in the pan for another 10 minutes. Remove the loaf from the pan to let it cool down faster. Slice and serve.
Nutrition Info: Calories: 217;Carbohydrates: 5g;Fat: 15g;Protein: 5g

451. Syrian Bread

Servings: 8 Pcs   Cooking Time: 20 Minutes
Ingredients:
- Two tablespoons vegetable oil
- 1 cup of water
- 1 ½ teaspoons salt
- ½ teaspoon white sugar
- 1 ½ teaspoon active dry yeast
- 3 cups all-purpose flour

Directions:
Put everything in your bread machine pan.   Select the dough cycle. Hit the start button.   Preheat your oven to 475 degrees F.   Turn to dough on a lightly floured surface once done.   Divide it into eight equal pieces. Form them into rounds.   Take a damp cloth and cover the rounds with it.   Now roll the dough into flat thin circles. They should have a diameter of around 8 inches. Cook in your preheated baking sheets until they are golden brown and puffed.
Nutrition Info: Calories 204;Carbohydrates: 36g;Total Fat 5g;Cholesterol 0mg;Protein 5g;Fiber 1g;Sugar 0g;Sodium 438mg;Potassium 66mg

452. Whole Wheat And Honey Bread

Servings: 1 Pound Loaf   Cooking Time: 3 Hours

Ingredients:
- Lukewarm water :1 ⅛ cups
- Honey :3 tbsp
- Vegetable oil :2 tbsp
- Plain bread flour :1 ½ cups
- Whole wheat flour :1 ½ cups
- Salt :⅓ tsp
- Instant dry yeast :1 ½ tsp

Directions:
Add the ingredients into the bread machine as per the order of the ingredients listed above or follow your bread machine's instruction manual.   Select the whole wheat setting and medium crust function.   When ready, turn the bread out onto a drying rack and allow it to cool, then serve.

Nutrition Info:(Per Serving):Calories: 180 kcal / Total fat: 3.5 g / Saturated fat: 0 g / Cholesterol: 0 mg / Total carbohydrates: 33.4 g / Dietary fiber: 2.8 g / Sodium: 79 mg / Protein: 5.2 g

453. Thin Crust Pizza Dough

Servings: 1 Pizza   Cooking Time: 1 Hour And 30 Minutes

Ingredients:
- Warm water – ¾ cup, 100°F to 110°F
- All-purpose flour – 2 cups
- Salt – ½ tsp.
- White sugar – ¼ tsp.
- Active dry yeast – 1 tsp.
- Olive oil 2 tsp.

Directions:
Add everything in the bread machine according to bread machine recommendations.   Select dough setting and start.   Transfer the dough to a well-floured work surface when done.   Roll the dough out into a thin crust and bake.

Nutrition Info:(Per Serving): Calories: 126.2; Total Fat: 1.5 g; Saturated Fat: 0.2 g; Carbohydrates: 24.2 g; Cholesterol: 0 mg; Fiber: 0.9 g; Calcium: 5.8 mg; Sodium: 146.9 mg; Protein: 3.4 g

454. Pita Bread With Black Cumin

Servings: 8 Pcs   Cooking Time: 15 Minutes

Ingredients:
- 2 cups almond flour, sifted
- ½ cup of water
- 2 Tbsp. olive oil
- Salt, to taste
- 1 tsp. black cumin

Directions:
Preheat the oven to 400F.   Combine the flour with salt. Add the water and olive oil.   Knead the dough and let stand about 15 minutes.   Shape the dough into eight balls.   Line a baking sheet with parchment paper and flatten the balls into eight thin rounds.   Sprinkle black cumin.   Bake for 15 minutes, serve.

Nutrition Info: Calories: 73;Fat: 6.9g;Carbohydrates: 1.6g;Protein: 1.6g

455. Spicy Bread

Servings: 6 Pcs   Cooking Time: 40 Minutes

Ingredients:
- ½ cup coconut flour
- Six eggs
- Three large jalapenos, sliced
- 4 ounces' turkey bacon, sliced
- ½ cup ghee
- ¼ tsp. baking soda
- ¼ tsp. salt
- ¼ cup of water

Directions:
Preheat the oven to 400F.   Cut bacon and jalapenos on a baking tray and roast for 10 minutes.   Flip and bake for five more minutes.   Remove seeds from the jalapenos.   Place jalapenos and bacon slices in a food processor and blend until smooth.   In a bowl, add ghee, eggs, and ¼-cup water. Mix well.   Then add some coconut flour, baking soda, and salt. Stir to mix.   Add bacon and jalapeno mix.   Grease the loaf pan with ghee.   Pour batter into the loaf pan.   Bake for 40 minutes.   Enjoy.

Nutrition Info: Calories: 240;Fat: 20g

456. Almond Banana Pancakes

Servings: 4 Pcs   Cooking Time: 10 Minutes

Ingredients:
- 1 Ripe Banana, mashed
- 4 Eggs
- 1/2 cup Almond Flour
- 2 tbsp Erythritol
- 1 tsp Baking Powder
- 1 tsp Ground Cinnamon

Directions:
Whisk together almond flour, baking powder, and cinnamon in a bowl.   In a separate bowl, mix mashed banana, eggs, and erythritol.   Gradually fold in the dry ingredients until becoming a wet mixture.   Preheat a skillet and coat with non-stick spray.   Spoon in the batter and cook for 1-2 minutes per side.

Nutrition Info: Kcal per serve: 235;Fat: 17 g. (64%);Protein: 11 g. (21%);Carbs: 10 g. (16%)

457. Breakfast Bread

Servings: 16 Slices   Cooking Time: 40 Minutes

Ingredients:
- ½ tsp. Xanthan gum
- ½ tsp. salt
- 2 Tbsp. coconut oil
- ½ cup butter, melted
- 1 tsp. baking powder
- 2 cups of almond flour
- Seven eggs

Directions:
Preheat the oven to 355F.   Beat eggs in a bowl on high for 2 minutes.   Add coconut oil and butter to the eggs and continue to beat.   Line a pan with baking paper and then pour the beaten eggs.   Pour in the rest of the

ingredients and mix until it becomes thick.   Bake until a toothpick comes out dry. It takes 40 to 45 minutes.
Nutrition Info: Calories: 234 ;Fat: 23g ;Carb: 1g;Protein: 7g ;

458. Sweet Ho Yin

Servings: 15   Cooking Time: 1 Hour And 20 Minutes
Ingredients:
- Lukewarm water – 1 ¼ cups
- White bread flour – 3 cups
- Brown sugar – ¼ cup
- Salt – 1 ½ tsp.
- Butter – 1 tbsp.
- Chinese five-spice powder – 1 ½ tsp.
- Cashews – 1/3 cup, chopped
- Orange extract – 1 ½ tsp.
- Active dry yeast – 2 tsp.

Directions:
Combine everything in the bread machine according to bread machine recommendations.   Use the Regular or Rapid bake cycle.   Remove the bread when done. Cool, slice, and serve.
Nutrition Info:(Per Serving): Calories: 128; Total Fat: 2.5 g; Saturated Fat: 0.8 g; Carbohydrates: 22.7 g; Cholesterol: 2 mg; Fiber: 1 g; Calcium: 8 mg; Sodium: 241 mg; Protein: 3.3 g

459. Sweet Pizza Dough

Servings: 1 Pizza   Cooking Time: 1 Hour And 30 Minutes
Ingredients:
- Dried granulated yeast – 2 tsp.
- Bread flour – 3 cups
- Salt – 1 tsp.
- Sugar – 2 tbsp.
- Oil – 2 tbsp.
- Water – 1 cup, and more if needed
- Water – 2 tbsp.

Directions:
Place everything in the bread machine according to bread machine recommendations.   Select Dough cycle and press Start.   When finished, remove the dough and place it in a greased bowl. Roll the dough around so it is coated with oil.   Cover and allow to rise for ½ hour in a warm place. Knead the dough.   Shake and bake.
Nutrition Info:(Per Serving): Calories: 1727.2; Total Fat: 31.3 g; Saturated Fat: 4.4 g; Carbohydrates: 314.7 g; Cholesterol: 0 mg; Fiber: 12.3 g; Calcium: 144 mg; Sodium: 2,345.8 mg; Protein: 42 g

460. No Salt Added White Bread

Servings: 1 Pound Loaf   Cooking Time: 3 Hours
Ingredients:
- Lukewarm water :½ cup
- Sugar :¾ tsp
- Instant dry yeast :¾ tsp
- White all-purpose flour :2 ⅛ cups
- Extra-virgin olive oil :½ tbsp
- Egg white :½

Directions:
In a mixing bowl, combine the sugar and water. Stir until the sugar has dissolved then add in the yeast.   Add the flour, water mixture, and oil into the bread maker. Select the French loaf setting and medium crust function. Five minutes into the cycle, add in the egg white and allow the bread cycle to continue.   When ready, turn the bread out onto a drying rack and allow it to cool, then serve.
Nutrition Info:(Per Serving):Calories: 275.3 kcal / Total fat: 3 g / Saturated fat: 0.4 g / Cholesterol: 0 mg / Total carbohydrates: 52.9 g / Dietary fiber: 2 g / Sodium: 12.2 mg / Protein: 7.9 g

461. Portuguese Corn Bread

Servings: 8   Cooking Time: 2 Hours
Ingredients:
- 1 cup yellow cornmeal
- 1 1/4 cups cold water, divided
- 1 1/2 teaspoons active dry yeast
- 1 1/2 cups bread flour
- 2 teaspoons sugar
- 3/4 teaspoon salt
- 1 tablespoon olive oil

Directions:
Stir cornmeal into 3/4 cup of the cold water until lumps disappear.   Add cornmeal mixture and oil to bread maker pan.   Add remaining dry ingredients, except yeast, to pan.   Make a well in the center of the dry ingredients and add the yeast.   Choose Sweet bread cycle, light crust color and press Start.   Transfer to plate and serve warm.
Nutrition Info: Calories: 108, Sodium: 152 mg, Dietary Fiber: 1.3 g, Fat: 1.7 g, Carbs: 20.6 g, Protein: 2.6 g

462. Bread Machine Pizza Dough

Servings: 1 Pizza Dough   Cooking Time: 1 Hour And 30 Minutes
Ingredients:
- Water – 1 ½ cups
- Oil – 1 ½ tbsp.
- Bread flour – 3 ¾ cups
- Sugar – 1 tbsp. plus 1 tsp.
- Salt – 1 ½ tsp.
- Active dry yeast – 1 ½ tsp.

Directions:
Add everything in the bread machine according to bread machine recommendations.   Select the Dough cycle. Remove the dough when done.   Roll it out and bake.
Nutrition Info:(Per Serving): Calories: 40; Total Fat: 2 g; Saturated Fat: 0 g; Carbohydrates: 5 g; Cholesterol: 0 mg; Fiber: 1 g; Calcium: 14 mg; Sodium: 307 mg; Protein: 1 g

463. Italian Bread

Servings: 2 Loaves   Cooking Time: 1 Hour And 10 Minutes
Ingredients:

- One tablespoon of light brown sugar
- 4 cups all-purpose flour, unbleached
- 1 ½ teaspoon of salt
- One 1/3 cups + 1 tablespoon warm water
- One package active dry yeast
- 1 ½ teaspoon of olive oil
- One egg
- Two tablespoons cornmeal

Directions:
Place flour, brown sugar, 1/3 cup warm water, salt, olive oil, and yeast in your bread machine. Select the dough cycle. Hit the start button.   Deflate your dough. Turn it on a floured surface.   Form two loaves from the dough. Keep them on your cutting board. The seam side should be down. Sprinkle some cornmeal on your board. Place a damp cloth on your loaves to cover them.   Wait for 40 minutes. The volume should double.   In the meantime, preheat your oven to 190 °C.   Beat 1 tablespoon of water and an egg in a bowl.   Brush this mixture on your loaves.   Make an extended cut at the center of your loaves with a knife.   Shake your cutting board gently, making sure that the loaves do not stick. Now slide your loaves on a baking sheet.   Bake in your oven for about 35 minutes.

Nutrition Info: Calories 105;Carbohydrates: 20.6 g;Total Fat 0.9 g;Cholesterol 9 mg;Protein 3.1 g;Fiber 1 g;Sugar 1g;Sodium 179 mg;Potassium 39 mg

464. Sweet Challa

Servings: 1 Loaf   Cooking Time: 45 Minutes
Ingredients:
- 1 ½ cup cream cheese
- 1 cup protein powder, unflavored and unsweetened
- 2/3 cup protein powder, vanilla flavour and unsweetened
- 1/3 cup no-calorie sweetener of your choice
- ¼ cup dried cranberries
- ¼ cup butter
- ¼ cup almond flour
- 2 ½ teaspoons baking powder
- One teaspoon xanthan gum
- ½ teaspoon salt
- 1/3 teaspoon salt
- Four eggs, beaten
- ¼ cup heavy cream
- ¼ cup oil

Directions:
Set aside two tablespoons of the beaten eggs for later use. Put the wet ingredients first, then the dry ingredients into the bread pan.   Press the "Manual" or "Dough" setting on the bread machine.   Once completed, transfer the dough to a surface that has been lightly dusted with almond flour.   Remove the air bubbles by punching the dough.   Divide the dough into 3.   Roll each piece until it becomes 16 inches long.   Braid the three pieces together on a lightly greased baking sheet. Allow the dough to rise for about 30 minutes while preheating the oven to 400F.   Brush the dough on the top with the reserved eggs from earlier.   Bake for 45 minutes, or until it is golden brown.

Nutrition Info: Calories: 158;Carbohydrates: 2g;Fat: 13g;Protein: 9g

465. Raisin Bread

Servings: 1 Pound Loaf   Cooking Time: 3 Hours
Ingredients:
- Lukewarm water :⅙ cup
- Unsalted butter, diced :1 ¼ tbsp
- Plain bread flour :2 cups
- Orange zest :1 pinch
- Ground cinnamon :1 ⅓ tsp
- Ground clove :1 pinch
- Ground nutmeg :1 pinch
- Salt :1 pinch
- Sugar :1 ¼ tbsp
- Active dry yeast :1 ½ tsp
- Raisins :½ cup

Directions:
Add the ingredients into the bread machine as per the order of the ingredients listed above or follow your bread machine's instruction manual. Do not add the raisins in yet.   Select the nut or raisin setting and medium crust function.   When the machine signals you to add the raisins, do so.   When ready, turn the bread out onto a drying rack and allow it to cool, then serve.

Nutrition Info:(Per Serving):Calories: 78 kcal / Total fat: 1 g / Saturated fat: 1 g / Cholesterol: 3m g / Total carbohydrates: 16 g / Dietary fiber: 1 g / Sodium: 106 mg / Protein: 2 g

466. Portuguese Sweet Bread

Servings: 1 Loaf   Cooking Time: 1 Hour And 5 Minutes
Ingredients:
- One egg beaten
- 1 cup milk
- 1/3 cup sugar
- Two tablespoons margarine
- 3 cups bread flour
- ¾ teaspoon salt
- 2 ½ teaspoons active dry yeast

Directions:
Place everything into your bread machine.   Select the sweet bread setting. Hit the start button.   Transfer the loaves to a rack for cooling once done.

Nutrition Info: Calories 139;Carbohydrates: 24 g;Total Fat 8.3 g;Cholesterol 14 mg;Protein 3 g;Fiber 0g;Sugar 4 g;Sodium 147 mg

467. German Pumpernickel Bread

Servings: 1 Loaf   Cooking Time: 1 Hour And 10 Minutes
Ingredients:
- 1 1/2 tablespoon vegetable oil
- 1 1/8 cups warm water
- Three tablespoons cocoa
- 1/3 cup molasses
- 1 ½ teaspoons salt
- One tablespoon caraway seeds
- 1 cup rye flour
- 1 ½ cups of bread flour

- 1 ½ tablespoon wheat gluten
- 1 cup whole wheat flour
- 2 ½ teaspoons bread machine yeast

Directions:

Put everything in your bread machine. Select the primary cycle. Hit the start button. Transfer bread to a rack for cooling once done.

Nutrition Info: Calories 119;Carbohydrates: 22.4 g;Total Fat 2.3 g;Cholesterol 0mg;Protein 3 g;Sodium 295 mg

468. German Rye Bread

Servings: 20   Cooking Time: 3 Hour And 48 Minutes

Ingredients:
- Buttermilk – 1 ½ cups
- Whole wheat flour – 2 ½ cups
- Rye flour – ½ cup
- Bread flour – ½ cup
- Buckwheat flour – ¼ cup
- Wheat germ – ¼ cup
- Salt - 1 tsp.
- Flax seeds – ¼ cup
- Soft butter – 1 tbsp.
- Molasses – 3 tbsp.
- Active dry yeast – 3 tsp.

Directions:

Add everything according to the bread machine recommendations. Select Whole Grain and Dark crust. Remove the bread when done. Cool, slice, and serve.

Nutrition Info:(Per Serving): Calories: 151; Total Fat: 4 g; Saturated Fat: 2.3 g; Carbohydrates: 23.8 g; Cholesterol: 10 mg; Fiber: 2.4 g; Calcium: 93 mg; Sodium: 193 mg; Protein: 5.6 g

469. Briosches

Servings: 1 Loaf   Cooking Time: 1 Hour And 20 Minutes

Ingredients:
- 1/4 cup milk
- 2 tablespoons water
- 1 tablespoon extra virgin olive oil
- 3 tablespoons honey
- 2 whole eggs
- 1 egg yolk
- 2 cups all-purpose flour
- 3/4 teaspoon Himalayan salt
- 1 3/4 teaspoons active dry yeast
- 7 tablespoons butter

Directions:

Add the first six ingredients into the pail of your bread machine. Mix the flour and the salt in a bowl; then add it to the wet ingredients. Make a small well in the flour, then add the yeast. Choose the "sweet" setting in your bread machine and choose se "light crust" option. Start the machine. After around 30 seconds, drop the 7 tablespoons of butter, one by one. It is important to give time to each tablespoon of butter to get incorporated with the flour mixture. Let the bread bake. When done, leave the bread in the machine for about 15 to 20 minutes with the lid open. Remove the bread from the pail and enjoy!

Nutrition Info: Calories 219 ;Protein 6.6g;Carbohydrates 32g;Fat: 10.5g

470. Mexican Sweet Bread

Servings: 12   Cooking Time: 3 Hours

Ingredients:
- 1 cup whole milk
- 1/4 cup butter
- 1 egg
- 1/4 cup sugar
- 1 teaspoon salt
- 3 cups bread flour
- 1 1/2 teaspoons yeast

Directions:

Add wet ingredients to bread maker pan. Add dry ingredients, except yeast. Make a well in the center of the dry ingredients and add the yeast. Set to Sweet Bread cycle, light crust color, and press Start. Remove to a cooling rack for 15 minutes before serving.

Nutrition Info: Calories: 182, Sodium: 235 mg, Dietary Fiber: 1 g, Fat: 5.2 g, Carbs: 29.2 g, Protein: 4.6 g

471. Paleo And Dairy-free Bread

Servings: 1 Pound Loaf   Cooking Time: 3 Hours

Ingredients:
- Flax meal :¼ cup
- Chia seeds :2 tbsp
- Coconut oil, melted :⅛ cup
- Egg :1 ½
- Almond milk :¼ cup
- Honey :½ tbsp
- Almond flour :1 cup
- Tapioca flour :⅔ cup
- Coconut flour :⅛ cup
- Salt :½ tsp
- Cream of tartar :1 tsp
- Bread machine yeast :1 tsp

Directions:

In a mixing bowl, combine one tablespoon of flax meal with the chia seeds. Stir in the water and set aside. In a separate mixing bowl, pour in the melted coconut oil, eggs, almond milk, and honey. Whisk together. Followed by whisking in the flax meal and chia seed mixture. Pour this into the bread machine. In a mixing bowl, combine the almond, tapioca, and coconut flour. Add the remainder of the flax meal and salt. Add in the cream of tartar and baking soda. Pour the dry ingredients on top of the wet ingredients. Finish by adding the yeast. Select the whole wheat setting and medium crust function. When ready, turn the bread out onto a drying rack and allow it to cool, then serve.

Nutrition Info:(Per Serving):Calories: 142 kcal / Total fat: 6.3 g / Saturated fat: 1.8g / Cholesterol: 34.9 mg / Total carbohydrates: 15.5 g / Dietary fiber: 4.4 g / Sodium: 236.8 mg / Protein: 4.1 g

472. Greek Bread

Servings: 18   Cooking Time: 3 Hours And 25 Minutes

Ingredients:
- Milk – 1 cup
- Crumbled feta cheese – ½ cup
- Chopped pitted kalamata olives – 1/3 cup
- Water – 2 tbsp.
- Oil – 2 tsp.
- Bread flour – 3 cups
- Sugar – 1 tbsp.
- Dried rosemary – 1 tsp., crushed
- Salt – ½ tsp.
- Active dry yeast – 1 tsp.

Directions:
Add everything in the bread machine according to bread machine recommendations.   Select Basic White bread cycle.   Remove the bread when done.   Cool, slice, and serve.

Nutrition Info:(Per Serving): Calories: 110; Total Fat: 2 g; Saturated Fat: 0.5 g; Carbohydrates: 18 g; Cholesterol: 4 mg; Fiber: 1 g; Calcium: 38 mg; Sodium: 118 mg; Protein: 4 g

473. Coffee Cake

Servings: 8   Cooking Time: 1 Hour And 30 Minutes

Ingredients:
- • Yolk of one egg
- • ¾ cup whole milk
- • 1 tbsp unsalted butter, melted
- • 2 ¼ cups plain bread flour
- • ¼ cup sugar
- • 1 tsp salt
- • 2 tsp active dry yeast
- for glaze topping:
- • ¼ cup pecan nuts
- • ¼ cup walnuts
- • 1 tsp ground cinnamon
- • ½ cup sugar
- • 2 tbsp unsalted butter, melted

Directions:
Add the ingredients into the bread machine as per the order of the ingredients listed above or follow your bread machine's instruction manual.   Select the dough setting.   Prepare a 8 x 8" baking pan by greasing it. When the dough cycle is finished, transfer the cake dough into the greased baking pan.   For the topping, glaze the two tablespoons of melted butter over the top. In a small mixing bowl, combine the nuts, sugar, and cinnamon and sprinkle over the top of the cake dough. Cover the cake dough with a cloth and allow to rest in a warm area for 30 minutes.   Preheat your oven to 375 °F and bake the cake for 20 minutes or until it has turned a golden color.   When ready, turn the bread out onto a drying rack and allow it to cool, then serve.

Nutrition Info:(Per Serving):Calories: 313.1 kcal / Total fat: 11.1 g / Saturated fat: 4 g / Cholesterol: 35.9 mg / Total carbohydrates: 48.5 g / Dietary fiber: 2 g / Sodium: 344.1 mg / Protein: 5.9 g

474. Peanut Butter And Jelly Bread

Servings: 1 Loaf   Cooking Time: 1 Hour And 10 Minutes

Ingredients:
- 1 1/2 tablespoons vegetable oil
- 1 cup of water
- ½ cup blackberry jelly
- ½ cup peanut butter
- One teaspoon salt
- One tablespoon white sugar
- 2 cups of bread flour
- 1 cup whole-wheat flour
- 1 1/2 teaspoons active dry yeast

Directions:
Put everything in your bread machine pan.   Select the basic setting.   Press the start button.   Take out the pan when done and set aside for 10 minutes.

Nutrition Info: Calories: 153 Cal;Carbohydrates: 20 g;Fat: 9g;Cholesterol: 0mg;Protein: 4g;Fiber: 2g ;Sugar: 11g;Sodium: 244mg;Potassium: 120mg

475. European Black Bread

Servings: 1 Loaf   Cooking Time: 1 Hour And 5 Minutes

Ingredients:
- ¾ teaspoon cider vinegar
- 1 cup of water
- ½ cup rye flour
- 1 ½ cups flour
- One tablespoon margarine
- ¼ cup of oat bran
- One teaspoon salt
- 1 ½ tablespoons sugar
- One teaspoon dried onion flakes
- One teaspoon caraway seed
- One teaspoon yeast
- Two tablespoons unsweetened cocoa

Directions:
Put everything in your bread machine.   Now select the basic setting.   Hit the start button.   Transfer bread to a rack for cooling once done.

Nutrition Info: Calories 114;Carbohydrates: 22 g;Total Fat 1.7 g;Cholesterol 0mg;Protein 3 g;Sugar 2 g;Sodium 247 mg

476. Garlic And Herb Bread

Servings: 1 Pound Loaf   Cooking Time: 2 Hours

Ingredients:
- Unsalted butter, diced :1 tbsp
- Lukewarm 1% milk :1 cup
- White all-purpose flour :3 cups
- Italian seasoning :1 ½ tsp
- Garlic powder :3 tsp
- Sugar :1 tbsp
- Salt :1 ½ tsp
- Instant dry yeast :2 tsp

Directions:
Add the ingredients into the bread machine as per the order of the ingredients listed above or follow your bread machine's instruction manual.   Select the basic setting and medium crust function.   When ready, turn the

bread out onto a drying rack and allow it to cool, then serve.

Nutrition Info:(Per Serving):Calories: 203.8 kcal / Total fat: 2.2 g / Saturated fat: 1.2 g / Cholesterol: 5.4 mg / Total carbohydrates: 39 g / Dietary fiber: 1.5 g / Sodium: 451.4 mg / Protein: 6.2 g

477. Butter Bread

Servings: 1 Pound Loaf   Cooking Time: 3 Hours And 35 Minutes

Ingredients:
- Egg :1
- Lukewarm whole milk :1 ¼ cup
- Unsalted butter, diced :½ cup
- Plain bread flour :2 cups
- Salt :1 pinch
- Sugar :1 pinch
- Instant dry yeast :2 tsp

Directions:
Add the ingredients into the bread machine as per the order of the ingredients listed above or follow your bread machine's instruction manual.   Select the French setting and medium crust function.   When ready, turn the bread out onto a drying rack and allow it to cool, then serve.

Nutrition Info:(Per Serving):Calories: 262.2 kcal / Total fat: 13.5 g / Saturated fat: 8.2 g / Cholesterol: 58.6 mg / Total carbohydrates 29.8 g / Dietary fiber: 1.3 g / Sodium: 45.3 mg / Protein: 5.9 g

478. Za'atar Bread

Servings: 12 - 14   Cooking Time: 3 Hours

Ingredients:
- 1/3 cup za'atar seasoning
- 2 tablespoons onion powder
- 1 cup warm water
- 2 tablespoons agave nectar
- 1/4 cup applesauce
- 3 cups bread flour
- 1 teaspoon salt
- 2 1/4 teaspoons rapid rise yeast

Directions:
Mix dry ingredients together in a bowl, except for yeast. Add wet ingredients to bread pan first; top with dry ingredients.   Make a well in the center of the dry ingredients and add the yeast.   Press Basic bread cycle, choose medium crust color, and press Start.   Remove from bread pan and allow to cool before serving.

Nutrition Info: Calories: 125, Sodium: 196 mg, Dietary Fiber: 2 g, Fat: 1.2 g, Carbs: 24.6 g, Protein: 4.1 g

479. Pizza Dough Recipe

Servings: 6 Servings   Cooking Time: 1 Hour And 30 Minutes

Ingredients:
- • 2 cups plain bread flour
- • 1 tbsp unsalted butter, softened
- • 1 tbsp sugar
- • 1 tsp instant dry yeast

- • 1 tsp salt
- • ½ cup lukewarm water

Directions:
Add the ingredients into the bread machine as per the order of the ingredients listed above or follow your bread machine's instruction manual.   Select the dough setting and press start.   Ten minutes into the bread machine's cycle, check on the dough to ensure that the ingredients have mixed evenly and that the dough is not too wet or dry.   Preheat your oven to 400 °F.   When ready, turn the dough out onto a floured surface and knead into a pizza or pan dish shape.   Top with your desired toppings and bake for 20 to 25 minutes.

Nutrition Info:(Per Serving):Calories: 536 kcal / Total fat: 7 g / Saturated fat: 4 g / Cholesterol: 15 mg / Total carbohydrates: 102 g / Dietary fiber: 4 g / Sodium: 1221 mg / Protein: 14 g

480. Bacon And Cheese Bread

Servings: 1 Pound Loaf   Cooking Time: 3 Hours

Ingredients:
- Egg, lightly beaten :½
- Lukewarm water :½ cup
- Unsalted butter, diced :½ tbsp
- Shredded cheddar cheese :½ cup
- Bacon bits :2 tbsp
- Plain bread flour :2 cups
- Salt :½ tsp
- Sugar :1 tbsp
- Active dry yeast :1 tsp

Directions:
Add the ingredients into the bread machine as per the order of the ingredients listed above or follow your bread machine's instruction manual.   Select the basic cycle and light crust function.   When ready, turn the bread out onto a drying rack and allow it to cool, then serve.

Nutrition Info:(Per Serving):Calories: 171.3 kcal / Total fat: 4.6 g / Saturated fat: 2.5 g / Cholesterol: 26.9 mg / Total carbohydrates: 25.8 g / Dietary fiber: 1 g / Sodium: 283.1 mg / Protein: 6.2 g

481. Coconut Bran Bread

Servings: 1 Loaf   Cooking Time: 1 Hour And 30 Minutes

Ingredients:
- 3¾ cups (480 g) wheat bread machine / white flour
- 1¾ cups (200 g) bran meal
- 1¼ cups (300 ml) cream
- 1/3 cup (70 ml) coconut milk
- 2 Tbsp. liquid honey
- 2 Tbsp. vegetable oil
- 2 tsp. salt

Directions:
Place all the dry and liquid ingredients in the pan and follow the instructions for your bread   Pay particular attention to measuring the ingredients. Use a cup, measuring spoon, and kitchen scales to do so.   Set the baking program to BASIC also set the crust type to MEDIUM.   If the dough is too wet, adjust the bread machine and cool for five minutes.   Wrap the bread

with a kitchen towel and set it aside for an hour. Otherwise, you'll calm on a wire rack.

Nutrition Info: Calories 348;Total Fat 8.6g;Saturated Fat 4.2g;Cholesterol 7g;Carbohydrate 59.4g;Dietary Fiber 3.2g;Total Sugars 6.7g;Protein 8.1g

482. Italian Parmesan Bread

Servings: 1 Pound Loaf   Cooking Time: 3 Hours

Ingredients:
- Lukewarm water :¾ cups
- White all-purpose flour :2 cups
- Shredded parmesan cheese :⅛ cup
- Salt :¾ tsp
- Italian mixed herbs :½ tsp
- Garlic powder :½ tsp
- Instant dry yeast :1 ¼ tsp

Directions:
Add the ingredients into the bread machine as per the order of the ingredients listed above or follow your bread machine's instruction manual.   Select the basic setting and medium crust function.   When ready, turn the bread out onto a drying rack and allow it to cool, then serve.

Nutrition Info:(Per Serving):Calories: 103.1 kcal / Total fat: 0.4 g / Saturated fat: 0.1 g / Cholesterol: 0.2 mg / Total carbohydrates: 21.3 g / Dietary fiber: 0.8 g / Sodium: 14.1 g / Protein: 3 g

483. Matcha Coconut Cookies

Servings: 12 Pcs   Cooking Time: 12 Minutes

Ingredients:
- 1/3 cup Almond Flour
- 1/3 cup Coconut Flour
- 2 tbsp Matcha Powder
- ½ cup Swerve Granular Sweetener
- ½ tsp Baking Powder
- ½ cup Coconut Oil
- 1 Whole Egg

Directions:
Put Whisk together almond flour, coconut flour, sweetener, matcha, and baking powder in a bowl.   Add in the egg and coconut oil. Mix until well combined. Scoop the dough into a baking sheet lined with parchment. Press slightly to flatten.   Bake for 12 minutes.

Nutrition Info: Kcal per serve: 112;Fat: 12 g. (91%);Protein: 2 g. (5%);Carbs: 1 g. (4%)

484. Mexican Sweetbread

Servings: 12   Cooking Time: 3 Hours And 25 Minutes

Ingredients:
- Milk – 1 cup
- Butter – ¼ cup
- Egg – 1
- Sugar – ¼ cup
- Salt – 1 tsp.
- Bread flour – 3 cups
- Yeast – 1 ½ tsp.

Directions:

Place all ingredients in the bread machine according to bread machine recommendations.   Select Basic or Sweet cycle. Press Start.   Remove the bread when done.   Cool, slice, and serve.

Nutrition Info:(Per Serving): Calories: 184.3; Total Fat: 5.3 g; Saturated Fat: 1.3 g; Carbohydrates: 29.2 g; Cholesterol: 20.5 mg; Fiber: 0.9 g; Calcium: 38 mg; Sodium: 254.8 mg; Protein: 4.7 g

485. Walnut Bread

Servings: 1 Loaf (20 Slices)   Cooking Time: 2 Hours

Ingredients:
- 4 cups (500 g) wheat flour, sifted
- ½ cup (130 ml) lukewarm water (80 degrees F)
- ½ cup (120 ml) lukewarm milk (80 degrees F)
- Two whole eggs
- ½ cup walnuts, fried and chopped
- One tablespoon walnut oil
- One tablespoon brown sugar
- One teaspoon salt
- One teaspoon active dry yeast

Directions:
Prepare all of the ingredients for your bread and measuring means (a cup, a spoon, kitchen scales). Carefully measure the ingredients into the pan.   Place all of the ingredients into the bread bucket in the right order. Follow your manual bread machine.   Close the cover.   Select your bread machine's program to FRENCH BREAD and choose the crust colour to MEDIUM.   Press START.   Wait until the program completes.   When done, take the bucket out and let it cool for 5-10 minutes.   Shake the loaf from the pan and let cool for 30 minutes on a cooling rack.   Slice, serve and enjoy the taste of fragrant homemade bread.

Nutrition Info: Calories 257;Total Fat 6.7g;Saturated Fat 1g;Cholesterol 34g;Sodium 252mg;Total Carbohydrate 40.8g;Total Sugars 2g;Protein 8.3g

486. Brazilian Cornbread

Servings: 12   Cooking Time: 3 Hours And 25 Minutes

Ingredients:
- Milk – 1 cup
- Water – ¼ cup
- Egg – 1
- Margarine – 3 tbsp.
- Sugar – 6 tbsp.
- Salt 1 ½ tsp.
- Yellow corn flour – 1 ½ cups
- Bread flour – 2 ½ cups
- Anise seed – 1 tsp.
- Active dry yeast – 2 ½ tsp.

Directions:
Add everything in the bread machine according to bread machine recommendations.   Select White bread and press Start.   Remove bread when done.   Cool, slice, and serve.

Nutrition Info:(Per Serving): Calories: 219.5; Total Fat: 4.9 g; Saturated Fat: 1.2 g; Carbohydrates: 38.8 g; Cholesterol: 20.5 mg; Fiber: 2.9 g; Calcium: 57 mg; Sodium: 341.5 mg; Protein: 5.3 g

487. Italian Herb Pizza Dough

Servings: 1 Crust   Cooking Time: 1 Hour And 30 Minutes

Ingredients:
- Warm water – 1 cup
- Olive oil – 3 tbsp.
- White sugar – 3 tbsp.
- Sea salt – 1 tsp.
- All-purpose flour – 3 cups
- Minced garlic – 1 tsp.
- Dried oregano – ¼ tsp.
- Dried basil – ¼ tsp.
- Ground black pepper – ¼ tsp.
- Dried cilantro – ¼ tsp.
- Paprika – ¼ tsp.
- Active dry yeast – 2 ¼ tsp.

Directions:
Add everything in the bread machine according to bread machine recommendations. Select the Dough cycle and press Start. Remove when done. Allow the dough to rise 30 minutes before using.

Nutrition Info:(Per Serving): Calories: 476; Total Fat: 11.2 g; Saturated Fat: 1.6 g; Carbohydrates: 82.3 g; Cholesterol: 0 mg; Fiber: 3.2 g; Calcium: 23.5 mg; Sodium: 445.3 mg; Protein: 10.7 g

488. Apple Cake

Servings: 10   Cooking Time: 3 Hours

Ingredients:
- • ⅔ cup water
- • 3 tbsp unsalted butter, softened
- • 2 cups plain bread flour
- • 3 tbsp granulated sugar
- • 1 tsp salt
- • 1 ½ tsp active dry yeast
- • 1 can apple pie filling

Directions:
Add the ingredients into the bread machine as per the order of the ingredients listed above or follow your bread machine's instruction manual. Do not add the pie filling. Select the dough setting. Remove the dough and place it onto a floured surface. Cover with a cotton cloth for 15 minutes. Roll the dough out into an even rectangular shape 13" x 8". Transfer this onto a greased baking tray. Fill the dough with the apple filling, running lengthwise. On each 13-inch side, make cuts from filling to edge of dough at 1-inch intervals, using a sharp knife. Fold ends of the dough up over the filling. Fold strips diagonally over filling, overlapping in the center and alternating sides. Cover again with the cloth and allow to rest for 30 minutes or until the dough has doubled in size. Preheat your oven to 375 °F and bake the cake for 40 minutes or until it has reached a beautiful golden color. When ready, turn the apple cake out onto a drying rack and allow it to cool. When cooled, dust with powdered sugar and serve.

Nutrition Info:(Per Serving):Calories: 480 kcal / Total fat: 10 g / Saturated fat: 5 g / Cholesterol: 25 mg / Total carbohydrates: 92 g / Dietary fiber: 3 g / Sodium: 710 mg / Protein: 8 g

489. Russian Black Bread

Servings: 1   Cooking Time: 3 Hours

Ingredients:
- 1 1/4 cups dark rye flour
- 2 1/2 cups unbleached flour
- 1 teaspoon instant coffee
- 2 tablespoons unsweetened cocoa powder
- 1 tablespoon whole caraway seeds
- 1/2 teaspoon dried minced onion
- 1/2 teaspoon fennel seeds
- 1 teaspoon sea salt
- 2 teaspoons active dry yeast
- 1 1/3 cups water, at room temperature
- 1 teaspoon sugar
- 1 1/2 tablespoons dark molasses
- 1 1/2 tablespoons apple cider vinegar
- 3 tablespoons vegetable oil

Directions:
Mix dry ingredients together in a bowl, except for yeast. Add wet ingredients to bread pan first; top with dry ingredients. Make a well in the center of the dry ingredients and add the yeast. Select Basic bread cycle, medium crust color, and press Start. Let cool for 15 minutes before slicing.

Nutrition Info: Calories: 169, Sodium: 147 mg, Dietary Fiber: 3.9 g, Fat: 3.9 g, Carbs: 29.8 g, Protein: 4.6 g

490. Sausage Bread

Servings: 10   Cooking Time: 3 Hours And 25 Minutes

Ingredients:
- Bread machine yeast – 1 tsp.
- Wheat bread machine flour – 3 ½ cups
- Kosher salt – 1 tsp.
- Sugar – 1 tbsp.
- Olive oil – 1 ½ tbsp.
- Smoked sausage – 2 tbsp., chopped into small cubes
- Grated cheddar cheese – 2 tbsp., grated
- Garlic – 1 tbsp., crushed
- Lukewarm water – 1 cup

Directions:
Add everything (except the sausage) in the bread machine according to bread machine recommendations. Select Basic cycle and Medium crust. Add the sausage after the beep. Remove the bread when done. Cool, slice and serve.

Nutrition Info:(Per Serving): Calories: 260; Total Fat: 5.6 g; Saturated Fat: 1.4 g; Carbohydrates: 43.8 g; Cholesterol: 8 mg; Fiber: 1.6 g; Calcium: 55 mg; Sodium: 355 mg; Protein: 7.7 g

491. French Ham Bread

Servings: 10   Cooking Time: 3 Hours And 27 Minutes

Ingredients:
- Wheat bread flour – 3 1/3 cups
- Ham – 1 cup, chopped
- Milk powder – ½ cup
- Sugar – 1 ½ tbsp.
- Fresh yeast – 1 tsp.
- Kosher salt – 1 tsp.
- Parmesan cheese – 2 tbsp., grated

- Lukewarm water – 1 1/3 cups
- Oil – 2 tbsp.

Directions:
Add everything (except for the ham) in the bread machine according to bread machine recommendations. Select French bread and Medium crust. Add ham after the beep. Remove the bread when done. Cool, slice, and serve.

Nutrition Info:(Per Serving): Calories: 287; Total Fat: 5.5 g; Saturated Fat: 1.1 g; Carbohydrates: 47.2 g; Cholesterol: 11 mg; Fiber: 1.7 g; Calcium: 65 mg; Sodium: 557 mg; Protein: 11.4 g

492. Country-styled White Bread

Servings: 1 Pound Loaf   Cooking Time: 2 Hours And 5 Minutes

Ingredients:
- Lukewarm water :1 ½ cups
- Extra-virgin olive oil :1 ½ tbsp
- Plain bread flour :1 cup
- White all-purpose Flour :2 ½ cups
- Baking soda :¼ tsp
- Sugar :1 ½ tsp
- Salt :1 pinch
- Bread machine yeast :2 ½ tsp

Directions:
Add the ingredients into the bread machine as per the order of the ingredients listed above or follow your bread machine's instruction manual. Select the rapid setting and the medium crust function. When ready, turn the bread out onto a drying rack and allow it to cool, then serve.

Nutrition Info:(Per Serving):Calories: 122 kcal / Total fat: 5 g / Saturated fat: 1 g / Cholesterol: 0 mg / Total carbohydrates: 17 g / Dietary fiber: 2 g Sodium: 394 mg / Protein: 2 g

493. Low-carb Bagel

Servings: 12 Pcs   Cooking Time: 25 Minutes

Ingredients:
- 1 cup protein powder, unflavored
- 1/3 cup coconut flour
- 1 tsp. baking powder
- ½ tsp. sea salt
- ¼ cup ground flaxseed
- 1/3 cup sour cream
- 12 eggs
- Seasoning topping:
- 1 tsp. dried parsley
- 1 tsp. dried oregano
- 1 tsp. Dried minced onion
- ½ tsp. Garlic powder
- ½ tsp. Dried basil
- ½ tsp. sea salt

Directions:
Preheat the oven to 350F. In a mixer, blend sour cream and eggs until well combined. Whisk together the flaxseed, salt, baking powder, protein powder, and coconut flour in a bowl. Mix the dry ingredients until it becomes wet ingredients. Make sure it is well blended. Whisk the topping seasoning together in a small bowl. Set aside. Grease 2 donut pans that can contain six donuts each. Sprinkle pan with about 1 tsp. Topping

seasoning and evenly pour batter into each. Sprinkle the top of each bagel evenly with the rest of the seasoning mixture. Bake in the oven for 25 minutes, or until golden brown.

Nutrition Info: Calories: 134;Fat: 6.8g;Carb: 4.2g;Protein: 12.1g

494. Zesty Poppy Seed Bread

Servings: 1 Loaf   Cooking Time: 1 Hour And 30 Minutes

Ingredients:
- 9.5 ounces almond flour
- Two lemons, zest only
- ½ cup no-calorie sweetener of your choice
- Three tablespoons butter
- Two tablespoons poppy seeds
- ½ teaspoon baking powder
- Six eggs
- Two tablespoons lemon juice
- Two tablespoons water

Directions:
Put the wet ingredients, followed by the dry ingredients, into the bread pan. Select the "Quick" or "Cake" mode of your bread machine. Allow the cycles to be completed. Remove the bread pan from the machine but keep the bread in the container for another 10 minutes. Take out the bread from the bread pan, and let it cool down completely before slicing.

Nutrition Info: Calories: 70;Carbohydrates: 6g;Fat: 17g;Protein: 9g

495. No Sugar-added Pizza Dough

Servings: 2 Pizzas   Cooking Time: 1 Hour And 30 Minutes

Ingredients:
- Warm water – 1 cup, 105°F to 115°F
- Oil – 2 tbsp.
- Salt – 1 tsp.
- Unbleached all-purpose flour – 3 cups
- Active dry yeast – 1 tbsp.

Directions:
Add everything in the bread machine according to bread machine recommendations. Select the Dough setting and press Start. Transfer the dough on a lightly floured work surface when done. Knead and divide in half. Make 2 balls and cover with a clean towel. Allow to rise in a warm place for 40 minutes. Bake.

Nutrition Info:(Per Serving): Calories: 820; Total Fat: 16.1 g; Saturated Fat: 2.3 g; Carbohydrates: 145.4 g; Cholesterol: 0 mg; Fiber: 6.3 g; Calcium: 36 mg; Sodium: 1,173 mg; Protein: 21.7 g

496. Russian Rye Bread

Servings: 12   Cooking Time: 3 Hours

Ingredients:
- 1 1/4 cups warm water
- 1 3/4 cups rye flour
- 1 3/4 cups whole wheat flour
- 2 tablespoons malt (or beer kit mixture)
- 1 tablespoon molasses
- 2 tablespoons white vinegar
- 1 teaspoon salt
- 1/2 tablespoon coriander seeds

- 1/2 tablespoon caraway seeds
- 2 teaspoons active dry yeast

Directions:
Mix dry ingredients together in a bowl, except for yeast. Add wet ingredients to bread pan first; top with dry ingredients. Make a well in the center of the dry ingredients and add the yeast. Press Basic bread cycle, choose medium crust color, and press Start. Remove from bread pan and allow to cool on a wire rack before serving.

Nutrition Info: Calories: 141, Sodium: 196 mg, Dietary Fiber: 5.1 g, Fat: 0.8 g, Carbs: 29.7 g, Protein: 5 g

497. Low-carb Keto Bread

Servings: 1 Pound Loaf   Cooking Time: 3 Hours
Ingredients:
- Oat fiber :¼ cup
- Flaxseed meal :⅓ cup
- Wheat gluten :½ cup
- Salt :½ tsp
- Xylitol :⅛ cup
- Xanthan gum :¼ tsp
- Lukewarm water :½ cup
- Egg :1
- Honey :½ tsp
- Unsalted butter, softened :1 tbsp
- Active dry yeast :½ tbsp

Directions:
In a mixing bowl, combine the oat fiber, meal, gluten, salt, xylitol, and xanthan gum. Add the water, egg, honey, and butter into the bread machine, followed by the oat fiber mixture and yeast. Select the basic setting and soft crust function. When ready, turn the bread out onto a drying rack and allow it to cool, then serve.

Nutrition Info: (Per Serving): Calories: 122 kcal / Total fat: 5.4 g / Saturated fat: 1.4 g / Cholesterol: 72 mg / Total carbohydrates: 6.5 g / Dietary fiber: 2.4 g / Sodium: 158 mg / Protein: 13.3 g

498. Sweet Dinner Rolls

Servings: 1 Loaf   Cooking Time: 30 Minutes
Ingredients:
- 2 ½ cups almond flour
- 1 cup coconut flour
- ½ cup butter
- ¼ cup no-calorie sweetener of your choice
- ¾ teaspoons salt
- Two eggs
- 1 cup milk

Directions:
Add the wet ingredients into the bread pan, and then the dry ingredients. Use the "Manual" or "Dough" mode of the bread machine. Once done, put the dough in a lightly oiled bowl. Preheat the oven to 375F. Divide and shape the dough into 16 pieces. Cover and just let the dough rise for 30 minutes. Bake until golden brown. Cooldown and serve.

Nutrition Info: Calories: 125; Carbohydrates: 4g; Fat: 9g; Protein: 8g

499. Greek Easter Bread

Servings: 12   Cooking Time: 3 Hours
Ingredients:
- 2/3 cup fresh butter
- 1 cup milk
- 1 cup sugar
- 1 teaspoon mastic
- 1/2 teaspoon salt
- 1 package active dry yeast
- 3 eggs
- 5 cups strong yellow flour
- 1 egg, for brushing blended with 1 teaspoon water

Directions:
Heat milk and butter until melted in a saucepan; do not boil. Add to bread maker pan. Add sugar and mastic to a food processor and blend; add to bread maker pan. Add remaining ingredients. Set Dough cycle and press Start; leave dough to rise one hour after cycle. Shape into 2 loaves, cover, and leave to rise for 50 more minutes. Baste with egg wash. Bake at 320°F for 30 to 40 minutes or until golden brown. Transfer to cooling rack for 15 minutes before serving.

Nutrition Info: Calories: 554, Sodium: 182 mg, Dietary Fiber: 2.8 g, Fat: 12.9 g, Carbs: 97.6 g, Protein: 13.4 g

500. Ciabatta

Servings: 1 Pound Loaf   Cooking Time: 30 Minutes
Ingredients:
- Lukewarm water :¾ cup
- Extra-virgin olive oil :½ tbsp
- White all-purpose flour :1 ½ cups
- Salt :¾ tsp
- Sugar :½ tsp
- Bread machine yeast :¾ tsp

Directions:
Add the ingredients into the bread machine as per the order of the ingredients listed above or follow your bread machine's instruction manual. Select the dough cycle. When the dough is ready, place it onto a floured surface. Cover the dough with a ceramic or glass dish and allow it to rest for ten minutes. Shape the dough an oval shape. Split into two oval shapes when doubling up on the recipe. Place onto a greased baking tray, cover with a cloth and allow to rest for a further 30 minutes or until it has doubled in size. Allow the dough to rest in a dry, warm area of your kitchen. Preheat your oven to 425 °F. Using the bottom end of a wooden spoon make small indents on the top of each loaf. Drive the spoon down into the dough until it touches the baking tray. Then place into the oven and bake for 30 minutes. Sprinkle water lightly over the top of the loaves every 10 minutes while baking. When ready, turn the bread out onto a drying rack and allow it to cool, then serve.

Nutrition Info: (Per Serving): Calories: 190 kcal / Total fat: 2.2 g / Saturated fat: 0.3 g / Cholesterol: 0 mg / Total carbohydrates: 36.6 g / Dietary fiber: 1.4 g / Sodium: 441 mg / Protein: 5.1 g

CPSIA information can be obtained
at www.ICGtesting.com
Printed in the USA
LVHW050714180121
676772LV00008B/224

9 781801 248624